YES YOU CAN! ¡SI! SE PUEDE

YES YOU CAN!
¡SI! SE PUEDE

Every Latino's Guide
to Building Family Wealth

CHARLES GONZALEZ

WITH
JIM REICHERT AND PETER CALDWELL

Yes You Can!/¡Sí! Se Puede

Copyright ©1998 by Charles Gonzalez, Jim Reichert, and Peter Caldwell

ISBN 1-886284-26-1

Library of Congress Catalog Card Number: 98-72600

First Edition

ABCDEFGHIJK

Published by

Chandler House Press

335 Chandler Street
Worcester, MA 01602
USA

President: Lawrence J. Abramoff

Publisher/Editor-in-Chief: Richard J. Staron

Vice President of Sales: Irene S. Bergman

Editorial/Production Manager: Jennifer J. Goguen

Copy Editor: Robert Campbell

Book Design: Bookmakers

Cover Design: Marshall Henrichs

Chandler House Press books are available at special discounts for bulk purchases. For more information about how to arrange such purchases, please contact Irene Bergman at Chandler House Press, 335 Chandler Street, Worcester, MA 01602, or call (800) 642-6657, or fax (508) 756-9425, or find us on the World Wide Web at www.tatnuck.com.

Chandler House Press books are distributed to the trade by

National Book Network, Inc.
4720 Boston Way
Lanham, MD 20706
(800) 462-6420

For Loretta, Stacy, Janet, Adam, and Sydney

About the Authors

Charles Gonzalez, a second-generation Cuban émigré, is a manager with National Retirement Planning Associates, a financial services firm. He structures financial plans for businesses and individuals throughout the metropolitan New York area and specializes in helping his clients make intelligent decisions about their money to maximize wealth. A growing area of his practice is structuring financial plans for Latino professionals and business owners, an area that gives him direct experience with the aspirations, goals, and obstacles faced by Latinos. He worked for several years as an advocate for Latino economic empowerment through his activities as President of the Westchester Hispanic Chamber of Commerce. In this role he helped both established and new businesses identify areas of opportunity, develop business plans, obtain financing, and assist with marketing efforts.

Mr. Gonzalez is also active in the New York State Federation of Hispanic Chambers of Commerce, which represents the interests of Latino entrepreneurs and professionals statewide, and the United States Hispanic Chamber of Commerce. He holds an M.B.A. from George Washington University and a B.A. from SUNY, and he is life insurance and securities licensed. He lives in Pawling, New York, with his wife Loretta and dog Floyd. He can be reached at **Chagonz@yahoo.com**.

Peter Caldwell and **Jim Reichert** are partners in **The Business BookWorks**, a firm that writes and publishes business, creative nonfiction business, and self-help books. Their efforts produced *You WILL Be Satisfied,* published by HarperCollins, which recounted Bob Tasca's entrepreneurial success achieved through unique principles for achieving customer satisfaction.

Mr. Caldwell teaches Economics and Business, does academic research into economic history, and has published several articles in his field. His entrepreneurial pursuits have included several business start-ups, including one in the high-technology area of industrial controllers. He holds a Ph.D. in Economics from Connecticut, an M.A. from Tufts, and an M.B.A. and a B.A. from Dartmouth. He and his wife Janet live in Quincy, Massachusetts, with their cat Georgette.

Mr. Reichert, prior to taking up writing, held key marketing and sales positions with companies ranging in size from the Fortune 20 to start-ups. He has been a congressional aide and campaign manager, and he has been involved in business start-ups in the health-care and consumer products industries. He holds an M.G.A. from Pennsylvania, an M.A. from Washington (St. Louis), and a B.A. from Miami (Ohio). He lives in Mt. Kisco, New York, with his wife Stacy, daughter Sydney, and dogs Chelsea and Edgar.

Mr. Reichert and Mr. Caldwell are always willing to explore new book projects. They can be reached at **busbookworks@worldnet .att.net** or **jimreichert@juno.com**.

A Message to My Readers

On a Book That Never Got Written, and the One That Did

When my publisher, Dick Staron, first spoke to me about doing a personal financial planning book for Latinos, I grew excited about this chance to help my own people. Immediately, my mind began to conceive of a book that would be a personal finance guide, an introduction to basic financial planning tools and concepts—with a bit of a Latino "spin" to it. I was sure I knew exactly what this book would be—until I began researching, conducting interviews, and running focus groups with Latino professionals and business owners. Do you know what happened? The book that I first imagined never got written. You are reading a different book! Here is why.

As I thought about our relationship to money and wealth, things appeared that surprised me. Latinos seemed unaware of our own history of becoming wealthy in this country, a history now obscured by

hundreds of years of political and economic decline; we appeared unfo-
cused upon our own need to make wealth creation today an important
goal for tomorrow. Some of my own Latino clients appeared uncomfortable with the ideas of goal setting, long-range planning, and investing
in the stock market to maximize long-term returns. As I dug deeper
into my research work, I discovered how few Latinos have benefited
from the greatest expansion in stock market values in American history.
This should not be. Latinos once created a great engine for making new
wealth in America. We do not have to start from scratch; we have this
legacy—our history of hard work, diligence, and success—to build on.

The more I thought about it, the word "uncomfortable" seemed
right. Latinos do not actively resist these new ways of becoming wealthy
in America. When I realized that we need to learn more in order to
become wealthier, I decided to write a different book. A reality-check
kind of book. We need a wake-up call. We have been very successful in
the past; we can be so again. Many of us have not joined the great new
American wealth creation process; but we need to do this, for our families' sake.

So the book that actually got written looks like this: Part I has the
title *Cerro Rico Transformed: The New HispanicAmerica*. It will give you
a great attitude tune-up in just five short chapters! Learn about Latino
wealth creation past and present, about wealth itself, about a new
architecture for building future Latino wealth, about the historical
foundations of our wealth, and finally about the financial elevators of
life that can take us all to undreamed-of new heights.

Part II is *The Seven Building Blocks: Creating Latino Family Wealth*.
The seven chapters here will meet you where you live financially,
right now! These chapters will take you step by step along the way to

financial independence, the point where you will have enough money for every good thing that you want, and enough money and time to give something back to your community.

Part III, *Life Cycle Strategies for Developing Latino Wealth,* will meet you at one of the three most important times in your life: young and just starting out, more mature and wondering how you can ever afford college for the children, and a little older and worrying about living well during retirement. Each of these chapters will be just right for you—or for someone you know who you can pass the book along to.

The appendix to this book includes many useful resources and tools for you to use while doing your own personal financial planning with the help of this book. You will find a useful guide to other financial and investment resources that will give you more detailed help along your wealth creation journey.

If you will use a few of the basic ideas contained in this book, you will reap a large future rate of return on your own wealth, and a nearly infinite return on the book's cost. Use this book daily, and it may change your life, along with your spouse's and your children's. Use it when you have questions about financial decisions, or when you need a new perspective on your money and your wealth. Don't let it sit on a shelf and gather dust—and neither will your investments.

Let me tell you that I am so sure *¡Sí!, Se Puede* will help you achieve financial success that I am offering you a money-back guarantee: Read the book. Complete all the exercises, and adhere to my advice. Then if you don't feel you have received back more than the cost of the book in savings and financial knowledge, keep the book but send me copies of your exercises along with your original sales receipt, and I'll give you your money back. The reality here is simple: If you just apply one of any number of tools in this book, you will be thrilled. Finally, I want to know about your successes, too. E-mail me at **Chagonz @yahoo.com**, or visit **www.sisepuede.com**. *¡Sí!, se puede!*

Charles Gonzalez
Pawling, New York
June 1998

Contents

Acknowledgments

Writing a book is a complex, often convoluted task, and *¡Sí! Se Puede* would not have been possible without the help of several people. Quienes son los siguientes:

Our wives, Loretta, Stacy and Janet are owed our deepest appreciation. Without their support, patience and love, this project may have collapsed early. A special thanks is due Loretta, who has shared and supported my decade-long exploration of the Latino experience and work in support of Latino economic empowerment. Sin su apoyo, no podría hacerlo.

Dick Staron, Publisher & Editor-In-Chief, and Larry Abramoff, C.E.O., at Chandler House Press both had the vision and passion to take on this unique project, when the rest of the industry took cover. Irene Bergman, Jennifer Goguen, and Todd Poudrier were all key members of the Chandler House team, and each handled their assigned roles admirably and professionally.

Olga Luz Tirada, of Luz Tirada Communications deserves special thanks for her added expertise and her own special Latina energy and passion. Contigo, tendremos éxito.

Susan Glinert, at Bookmakers, brought a critical eye, unbelievable patience, and an amazing ability to turn around work at warp speed.

Thanks to my son, Adam, whose recent post-college experience and courage inspired Chapter 13.

We are all a product of nuestra família; and no one has had a greater influence on this project than my mother, Lupe. Gracias por todo.

Ilse Velez and Rosa Calderon awakened my consciousness to the dramatic changes in the Latino community, and inspire me with their passion and energy on behalf of young Latinos. Gracias por lo que han hecho, y todo lo que continúan a hacer.

We would be remiss if we didn't recognize Ed McCoyd and Victoria Hynes at the Authors Guild, Wendy Keller, at Forthwrite Literary Agency, and Wendy Bloom, at the Mount Kisco Public Library.

Many financial professionals, government officials and individuals shared their knowledge and experience with us. What they have taught is reflected throughout the book, and we are grateful for their help.

Charles Gonzalez

Jim Reichert

Peter Caldwell

Introduction

Why do you need a Latinos' *guide to family wealth creation?* Lots of personal finance books are in the market, a few of them quite good. (I'll recommend some in the course of this book.) Why not just buy one of *them*? After all, there is no such thing as a *Latino* mutual fund.

The answer is both simple, and complex. The simple part recognizes that personal financial planning is a *means*, not an *end*. First, we need to know more about what goals we can achieve as Latinos. Then, we can look at how we will reach our goals. I will tell you about *how* we will capitalize upon our opportunities through personal financial planning later in this book, but first I have to tell you about *what* we, as a people, need to do. This is a book about unique *opportunities for achieving great success for our families*. As Latinos, we need to see the future before us; we also need to see what keeps us from reaching it. Then, and only then, will we have the motivation to reach for the future. This is a wake up call for Latinos. *¡Sí!, se puede.*

Our needs differ from those of other people—because of our unique history. This is the complex part of the answer. To be Latino is to share in a remarkably complex story. The Latino experience in the United States shows incredible diversity; we are both one people and many peoples. Sadly, sometimes we experience conflicts that derive from our complex history. Yet we all share the same language; we all share in a common story; we all share a cultural heritage. We also all share a worldview that has been shaped by our past and that has allowed us to survive and even prosper under difficult circumstances. Much of our worldview we treasure as an invaluable inheritance: the love of family and Church, the value of hard work and honesty. We still hold to these things even when surrounded by a culture that frequently devalues them.

Our worldview also contains elements that once helped us but may now hold us back: We are likely to view time differently than people in the dominant culture; we also have a different relationship to money, and different feelings about wealth. Our view of time has tended to be short term—because for centuries as Latinos we knew that the future had little likelihood of becoming better than the present, and a good chance of becoming worse. We have lived as a strictly moral people in order to avoid the worst harms that would otherwise befall us. Now our future fills with opportunity; we need to let the future into our worldview and eagerly grasp it—without sacrificing our uprightness.

Did You Know?/¿Sabía Usted?

- The average older American household has over $100,000 in accumulated wealth—and that amount is growing every year.

- The older Latino household typically has less than $20,000 in accumulated wealth—and little time left to add to it.

- Very sadly, fully one-third of all older Latino households have no accumulated wealth at all! They have only their children and the government to keep them alive.

- Many middle-aged Latino families really struggle—to provide for parents and children, all at the same time.

- Wouldn't you like things to be different for you?

Source: *Barron's,* July 31, 1995.

LET'S DO A FINANCIAL ACUMEN TEST

The world of retirement planning has gotten turned upside down. It used to be that the company that we worked for, as a good paternalist, provided us with a company-paid pension—a guaranteed income at retirement with no questions asked, and no choices allowed. Now the trend is toward plans paid for and managed by the individual employees—so-called 401(k) plans. Or Keogh plans for self-employed people. Each of us can now decide how much to contribute to our own plan, and how to invest the contributions we choose to make. These plans offer none of the guarantees that the traditional company pension plans provided. They also offer potentially greater rewards. Your retirement income is now based upon the performance of the investment that *you* choose.

Unfortunately, even after tremendous educational efforts by employers and financial services companies regarding investing, too many people continue to put too much of their retirement assets in low-yield, traditionally "safe" investments—due to lack of knowledge and/or the fear of loss. Lack of knowledge and irrational fear cost millions of people billions of dollars in future retirement income. And Latinos are more likely than most to suffer such losses.

Now, here's the test:

- Do you know how much invested money you will need in order to assure that you can retire with your desired lifestyle?

- Do you know how much you need to save at what average return on investment in order to accumulate that much money?

- Do you know how your 401(k) or Keogh plan or IRA money is invested now?

- Do you know how much of a return your retirement investments generated last year?

I know of many Latinos who have the financial knowledge to pass this test. Sadly, I know many more who have not learned the basics of compounded returns to placing money into investments with varying degrees of risk. How about you?

It used to be that we could not trust those who ruled us; we could not be sure that if we placed our wealth into the form of money investments that it would not be confiscated in the future. So we lost the sense that money can increase for us over time if we invest it. We came to trust in land and real estate and other things that are called hard assets. As a result, today we tend to be very conservative about money and the risks it may be exposed to. We have much lower rates of checking account and credit card usage. (More than two-thirds of all Americans hold credit cards; less than one-third of Latinos have them—according to the January 1997 issue of *American Demographics*.) We have limited experience in the world of investing and in matters financial, hardly benefiting from the tremendous increase in stock prices over the past six years—because few of us own stocks. Yet we live in a new world in which these things come to matter more and more. In order to reach the goals that we all aspire to for ourselves and our families, we need to let go of the obstacles that block our way to leveraging our future earning power.

We Latinos find ourselves today at a unique junction between our history and our future. Our future is now! We need to capitalize on the opportunities this junction presents to us. *¡Sí!, se puede.* Let me show you what I mean.

Our History

We are a young people today. Many of us are not even thirty years old. We have not had much time to build up wealth in our lives. We need to start now.

We come from countries that lost much of their wealth. That means that we start out with less wealth than some other groups. That means in turn that we need to grow our wealth faster.

We have a priceless heritage. Our parents and other family members, and their parents before them, worked incredibly hard and sacrificed themselves to give us our priceless heritage: a strong work ethic, great family values, and as much education as they could afford. We have the psychological and educational levers for success.

We are not really immigrants; we are reclaiming our own place. Our civilization existed in the Americas long before Anglo America began. Many of our families have even lived in the same place for as much as four hundred years—a place that became the United States. So, for many of us, we haven't moved; the country borders have.

Our Future Right Now

We have the fastest growing middle- and upper-class groups in America. That's right. Right now. Forty-four percent of us are middle class; twenty percent of us are already affluent. Our future is to continue that growth, right up to the point where LatinoAmerica becomes twenty-five percent of the total population of the United States.

We have more businesses than any minority group in America. Latino men and women are achieving phenomenal success in business. Nearly one million Latino-owned businesses exist today. Many of us are becoming truly wealthy, even building skyscraper banking institutions; and Latino business owners are helping the rest of us with employment and careers. We can all move up in the financial high-rise building together.

It's becoming hip to be Latino. Our cultural contributions to America are no longer merely looked down upon. Take a look at what's going on in Miami (Chapter One). The value of our cultural capital can only go up.

What we lack is accumulated *wealth*. We tend to think too much about our present earned income and not enough about building up wealth. There is nothing wrong with being wealthy. Wealth is a word that stands for a beautiful idea. You can read more about it in Chapter Two. It used to be that nobody in Anglo America believed that Latinos would ever be anything but poor. That's wrong. It's no longer a question about *if* Latino Americans will ever succeed in this country; it's merely a question of *how fast* our rate of growth will be. The only thing that limits us is our relatively low rate of wealth creation. We don't yet create enough capital. That's why this book is so important for us all.

WHAT CAN THIS BOOK DO TO HELP CREATE WEALTH FOR ME?

You need four things to create wealth for your family:

The right attitude. The most important ingredient for success in life is the right attitude. It isn't inherited wealth; God knows, few of us have that. But did you know that over 10 percent of the people born poor in this country end up truly wealthy? Or that only about 10 percent of people born poor *don't* move up out of poverty? For that matter, about 10 percent of people born wealthy end up in or near poverty. Clearly, an inheritance doesn't do it. It isn't great intelligence. The B and C students in school usually do better economically than the A students. It isn't great skills. An employer will hire you and give you skills training—if you've got a right attitude. The same thing is true about creating wealth for your family; you need first of all the right attitudes about your opportunities for success as an Latino and about wealth itself. In Part I of this book, I'll give you a Latino attitude tune-up.

The right understanding for how life works. Too many of us don't really understand how things work; so of course, we make poor decisions in life. We become walking self-fulfilled prophets: We predict that we will not succeed in life, and we don't. I'd like to give you a highly visible symbol for success—the big city skyscraper. Personal life, work, wealth—they all have the dimensions of a skyscraper. As we come into life, we all live near an elevator in the skyscraper of life. We start at lower or higher floors, but we all have the choice to go to an elevator and push the right buttons to go up—or down. Sadly, few of us realize either that there is an elevator in the skyscraper of life or what floor we are on. In the great skyscraper of life, earning a living in a job, even if it is a very good one, means that you live in the *basement*. The highest level to the skyscraper of life is *independence,* largely defined as financial independence—having enough money power to meet any need. In this book, I want to make you aware of the skyscraper of life and the elevators in it, to help you figure out what floor you're now living and working on—and to show you how to push the right buttons so that you can go up in life.

The right building blocks. Wealth is created by using a variety of building blocks. You may be thinking right now that I mean various financial instruments such as mutual funds and common stocks. I don't. The basic building blocks for wealth are more fundamental than that: goal setting, planning, compounding, time, risk and reward, entrepreneurship, human capital, and generosity. And the right attitudes toward how we should value ourselves. Of these, time as a long horizon is probably the most difficult for Latinos to grasp. Part II of this book should help you expand your horizons, to learn the art of the possible.

The right strategies for future success. The future will not unfold in a manner identical to the past, but there are some underlying principles that will help us all develop the right success strategies as we enter the new millennium in America. Part III of this book shows you how to put all of your thinking together about creating new wealth for your family—and living well. *¡Sí!, se puede!*

SIX THINGS YOU CAN DO—RIGHT NOW

Create a financial plan for your future. Decide upon your priorities and goals, review where you are today, and make a commitment to take a first step forward. See Chapter Six.

Take control of your own money. Use a spending plan. See Chapter Six.

Start paying yourself first—not last. See Chapter Thirteen.

Eliminate bad debt. See Chapter Eight.

Start working at keeping your money—not just working at a job. Take steps to keep your wealth. See Chapter Ten.

Get straight about the difference between *saving, investing, and speculating.* Make the jump from saver to investor, and let the power of compounding expand your wealth. See Chapter Eleven.

Make money while you sleep—and still sleep well! Learn about risk and reward. See Chapter Eleven.

Cerro Rico
Transformed: The New
HispanicAmerica

CERRO RICO. Like a fearful apparition from the past, I can see with my mind's eye how it rose from a cold and barren high plateau in what has become southern Bolivia, the early morning sunlight forcing itself through a dense fog-wrapped summit. Not the tallest mountain by any means in this New World, it had an impact that bore down heavily throughout all Europe, Asia, and the Americas—like the weight of deep-laden treasure galleons wallowing eastward. It came to hold a title, the fabled Cerro Rico, or "rich mountain." With its fabled wealth, Imperial Spain ruled a previously unimagined empire, absolutely. Cerro Rico validated Cristóbal Colón and all his weary voyaging; it satisfied the subsequent explorers who had also set out looking for a short way to the riches of the fabled Indies and found instead a new world and a new history to write—and Cerro Rico.

Spain's future, as well as America's, changed forever in that fateful year of 1545 when silver was found at Potosí. Legend traces the place name to Potojchi, a Quechua Indian word meaning "to explode," because of the rumblings heard from deep within the belly of the mountain. Cerro Rico and Potosí did both explode, but not in a way the native peoples could have ever imagined. The explosion of silver wealth lead both to the rapid creation of Spanish imperial wealth and to the hubris that destroyed it all a relatively short time later. Fabulous wealth coming from the belly of Potosí gave birth to a vision among its European colonizers, a vision of building a bridge of silver from Potosí all the way to Barcelona. The frenzy surrounding the great wealth of Potosí eventually spilled into the form of the world's fifth largest city. By 1611, Potosí overran itself struggling to contain 160,000 inhabitants. Famous for its rich silver mines, magnificent colonial architecture, ornate churches, splendid theaters, and elaborate mint,

Potosí produced much of the wealth that the Spanish crown thrived on during the seventeenth and eighteenth centuries. Silver dug up at Potosí financed Spanish kings in their inglorious wars and extravagant courts.

Eventually, the decline in silver production in the eighteenth century, paralleling Spain's decline as a world power, abandoned Potosí once more to the country's barrenness. Historians' memories faded, and only antique maps remained to recall a former glory. After two hundred years of yielding their wealth, the mines grew silent, and the city itself became a shell of its resplendent glory. Potosí found itself in Bolivia, among the poorest of the newly independent South American states.

And all the great wealth, where did it end up? A tour of Spain in 1750 would have scarcely revealed any wealth at all. The former imperial nation of Phillip II had become, sadly, a second-tier, impoverished state falling prey to the superpowers of the day, first France through conflict and then Great Britain by virtue of the emerging might of the first Industrial Revolution. Two hundred years of fabulous production of wealth left no legacy, left scarcely a trace of the immense wealth engine of old. Everything settled back into a timeless rhythm.

Yet Potosí, though no longer living, can still speak. The lessons come through the ages strongly and clearly: Invest in a future; do not overspend recklessly. Focus upon tomorrow, or become yesterday. Once again, the image of Cerro Rico, the *new* rich mountain, rises before us, we descendants of native Indians and Spanish conquistadors. What will we do with this new wealth mountain of the twenty-first century that now faces us? The new HispanicAmerica: Will we abuse it in the short term, so that it fails us in the long term? Or will we make it into a true wealth engine serving us faithfully for generations to come? It is our choice.

The New HispanicAmerica? No, it's not a typographical error. HispanicAmerica, a once submerged group of poverty-stricken Mexican and Puerto Rican neighborhoods buried within a powerful United States, has risen into view, like long lost Cerro Rico. Like a string of new islands emerging from the ocean floor, its presence grows ever more apparent. San Francisco, Oakland, Sacramento, San Jose, Los Angeles, San Diego, Albuquerque, Houston, Dallas, Austin, Denver, Chicago, Miami, Washington, D.C., New York, and a number of others—vibrant Latino communities sweep from west to east like a broad rainbow across the United States. Los Angeles has traditionally been the largest center of Hispanic American population and culture; but now, Miami challenges it in the race to become not just the leading center of Latino life in the United States but the cultural core city for Latin America and even the entire Latin world. It is strange to think that capital cities of Latin America are located in the United States, but it is true.

Throughout all the islands of HispanicAmerica, business booms and night life pulsates to Latin rhythms; Latin fashion, food, and music drive a new American pop culture. Highly mobile Latino populations overflow their inner city roots; each year, the latest Latino additions to middle class America move to the suburbs. What's the most popular ethnic food in America? Mexican. Suburban families love Mexican food. Anglo kids learn to love Spanish phrases in school—not just inner city kids, but suburban kids as well. The most desirable second language for an American businessman to possess is not Japanese; Japanese comes in way behind. It is Spanish. Spanish has moved out of the barrios and into the boardrooms.

HispanicAmerica: much more than typography. The new Cerro Rico is emerging.

A View from the Top: Latino American Success

In This Chapter

- Learn who are the most successful wealth creators among Latinos.
- Learn why Miami represents a unique model for Latino wealth creation.

YOU MAY BE IN FOR A BIG SURPRISE
....

Now that you've started reading this book, you may be in for a big surprise. Chances are, you are one of the several millions of Latinos who have achieved the level of professional and financial success that puts you in the American middle class—or you aspire to that achievement. You may have even reached higher levels of affluence, such as your parents could not even have dreamed possible. The emergence of literally millions of affluent Latinos over the past twenty-five years is one of the great demographic events in modern America: Nearly one-half of Latinos are already middle class, and nearly one-half are affluent! But it has been a *stealth event.* While the so-called experts were wondering if Latinos would ever cease being poor, many of us quietly, and without massive government assistance, did the hard work that put us into the affluent category. It now comes as a great surprise to many people, Latinos included, because it is so unexpected, so unlike the stereotypes of Latinos that we all know and would like to forget. We see our own success; perhaps we are still amazed by it. We don't see how general it is becoming.

"WHEN THERE IS A WILL, THERE IS A WAY" .
....

In 1997, *Hispanic Business* magazine identified seventy-five Latinos with net worths exceeding $25 million. What do these individuals and families look like? Half of them have built their success upon business achievement; another ten percent or so have sold successful businesses to reach or exceed the $25 million level. One-quarter manage their families' financial assets; their wealth may be looked upon to

Did You Know?/¿Sabía Usted?

- HispanicAmerica has over 75 super-rich business people—men and women with net worths exceeding $25 million.

- Most wealthy Latinos have made their fortunes in consulting, high tech services, engineering, finance, investment banking, real estate development, and construction.

- The economy of HispanicAmerica is growing at three times the national average. By the millennium, it will exceed $500 billion.

- Over 10 percent of adult Latinos own their own businesses; the rate of Latino business start-ups is three times the American average.

- Nearly one-half of Latinos are *middle-class*, and nearly one-half of us are *affluent*.

- Latino food, music, entertainment, and idioms are redefining American pop culture. *It's hip to be Hispanic.*

- The new cultural and financial capital of the Latin World is—Miami.

some degree as "old money," even though it has also involved entrepreneurship. Entertainment figures and real estate investors make up the rest.

Notice that the overwhelming proportion of major Latino wealth holders have accumulated assets through recent entrepreneurial or executive leadership achievement. They are highly successful business owners and managers. While this book is not specifically about Latino business success, one of the unique and exciting aspects of our experience in the United States involves our willingness to take risks, to start and grow our businesses, to strive for personal financial independence through achievement. *Latino business owners represent our prime source for wealth creation.* They have become our most effective tool for shifting the public perception of Latinos in this country. They also represent the prime source for their fellow Latinos' advancement. Their vision and their dreams to create their own wealth can show the rest of us the direction we must take.

Let's have a look at a few of these people. Roberto C. Goizueta did not found the Coca-Cola Company, but he rose from the bottom to lead a most remarkable resurgence for this old line firm; under his direction, Coca-Cola stock increased in value over 2,200 percent. The Joseph Unanue family actually founded Goya Foods, purchasing the name from a moribund brand of Moroccan canned sardines for $1. Sixty years after its founding, Goya appears poised to move out of its Eastern markets to become a truly national food products company by penetrating California's Latino market. Both of these success stories have produced personal fortunes exceeding $400 million. More recently, Arturo Torres sold Pizza Management, a franchisee of Pizza Huts and Taco Bells, to PepsiCo a number of years ago for $100 million, and he has since founded two new ventures—Play by Play Toys and Veladi Ranch Steak Houses. Play by Play has license agreements for stuffed toys and pillows with Walt Disney Company; Veladi is an upscale restaurant chain.

Many Latino women as well as men are now starting businesses. Several of them recently sat around the table in a focus group I ran for this book. In the session, Martha Alvarez and Nila Jurado told me of their difficulties starting businesses from scratch. All the focus group members decried the lack of financial planning skills among Latino small business people. Martha Alvarez runs a cleaning services business, Nila

Did You Know?/¿Sabía Usted?

The *Wall Street Journal* reports on April 15, 1998, that Yemina, Bimbo, and Verde Valle have headed north. Having saturated Mexico with familiar U.S. brands, top U.S. and Mexican food producers are now rushing to satisfy the palates of the over 18 million U.S. consumers of Mexican descent. Recently, a flurry of deals have been cut among companies aiming to bring well-known Mexican brands to U.S. store shelves.

Jurado, a flower shop. Nila comes from a family of nine children—*all* of them now successful business people! Both women have struggled to attain modest success; both appear likely to achieve financial independence in the future. They attribute their ability to start successful businesses to the influence of their parents, people who gave them discipline and a work ethic—and who expected them to "do better than us." As Nila put it: "When there is a will, there is a way!"

Sadly, Martha recounts stories about her employees who have accumulated thousands of saved dollars in banks—but who do not know how to move beyond a savings account in the area of personal finance. A very successful banker, Mario Hernandez, described clients with over $80,000 sitting in savings accounts; they will not do anything more with their money. They come to Mario asking, "What shall I do with my money?" But, they only come to him because he speaks Spanish. Their distrust of financial institutions runs deep. Some will take his financial advice; many will not—preferring the safety of a savings account. I met Milton Ruiz, a CPA, many years ago and discovered we had much in common. I helped him organize his finances and set goals; and he helped me do my taxes. Now he is a trusted friend. Many Latinos, Mario tells me, only open a checking account when they reach the point of success where they have too many bills to draw postal money orders to pay! I am writing this book for the people such as Martha and Nila, for their employees, for Milton, and for the clients of Mario Hernandez—for you. We simply need to do better with the money we work so hard to earn. *¡Sí!, se puede.*

A CASE STUDY: IN MIAMI, IT'S HIP TO BE HISPANIC

As you fly into Miami today, the skyscrapers of Brickell Avenue capture the city landscape. Light flashes from their tall glass hides in the pure Florida sunlight. They symbolize the new city arisen from the past. On street level, the skyscrapers take form as the mighty ridged skeleton of an economic colossus; they house the financial giants of the American Spanish-speaking world—both for Latin America and HispanicAmerica. Many of them have Spanish names; they mark a transition from Anglo to Latino banking influence. Beneath their economic shelter, the New Miami grows like a healthy adolescent, spreading and flexing flesh and muscles. The old Miami was horizontal; a tourist haven for wealthy Anglos and Latinos alike, it lacked the backbone for a stand-alone economic powerhouse. Now it has one.

Sit within an upscale sidewalk cafe in Miami. What do you hear? Spanish. Anglo America's businessmen use it as do all the Latin nationalities that swell the swank streets of Miami's business and entertainment districts. The lingua franca for the crossroads of HispanicAmerica, Latin America, and Latin Europe, Spanish has become the cosmopolitan language of a vibrant new city reborn out of the doldrums of a former languid resort town. Spanish is in.

Listen to conversation in Miami. The air vibrates with talk of deals. Lincoln Road in Miami Beach, bounded by MTV Latino and Sony Discs, captures international communications attention. Fashion shoots for the new glossy Latin magazines keep camera crews busy, generating over $20,000 per day per team and making the city the world's third busiest fashion capital after New York and Paris. Telemundo network executives complete entertainment contracts that build up Spanish-language television in the U.S. and Latin America—helping make Miami the "Hispanic Hollywood."

Wealthy Brazilians and Italians buy multimillion-dollar condominiums here; Italians and French open new international business ventures. Huge trading deals help make Miami's port the surplus trade capital of the nation as exports surge more than $6 billion over imports. High finance deals in the boardrooms of Brickell Avenue skyscrapers absorb billions of dollars of new capital from all over Latin America. American multinationals such as GM and Disney locate their Latin subsidiary headquarters here, to be at the center of Latin economic life.

A modern-day Rome of the Americas, Simon Bolivar's dream capital displaced to the North, all Latin roads cross here—trade, communications, finance, the arts and entertainment. For economic advantage, for the deal, Latino regional jealousies get put aside, as though the city served as a vast neutral turf for rival nationalities. Secured by Anglo-America's property institutions, Miami pulses day and night to the Latin rhythms of success, like a huge economic heart.

Away from Miami Beach's Hollywood aura and Brickell Avenue's shafts of economic might, another Miami purrs away industriously, like a giant sewing machine in Hialeah stitching out the fresh dress of economic success for the city's tens of thousands of new immigrants

Did You Know?/¿Sabía Usted?

For the past two and a half years, television networks UPN and WB have been fighting each other for the title of "fifth network." But this rivalry is beside the point because the real fifth network is Univision. Univision reaches over 92 percent of Spanish-speaking households and scored higher ratings than UPN and WB last season. More impressive is that Univision now challenges the big four networks, winning prime-time ratings in Miami, and scoring well in L.A. and Chicago. Univision's success began in 1992, when two programmers based in Latin America, Televisia and Venevision, joined media mogul Jerrold Perenchio to buy Univision from Hallmark, the greeting-card company. The two Latin-American networks provide Univision with two-thirds of its programming, which saves the network in production costs. Univision, known for its *telenovelas* and Sabado Gigante, is always trying to stay ahead of the competition to stay the "fifth network" by developing new programming. Univision is also partnering with Home Shopping Network to launch a Spanish-language TV home-shopping service. Even as new competition looms, Univision has a reputation for having strong management; it is now headed by former Housing and Urban Development Secretary Henry Cisneros.

and recent refugees who arrive each year. They begin life here poor—poorer than the wives of Cuban exiles who worked the same machines while their husbands began an entrepreneurial miracle. They may now pull down the statistical averages—such things as per capita income—for Latinos generally, but they constitute the city's *most valuable import*. For Miami works like a huge economic pump, taking in immigrants at its mouth and eventually spewing many of them out into the sprawling suburbs—wealthy families. While in the pump, they will move from low-paid factory and service jobs, to perhaps construction work, to middle-management positions in fast-growing Latino businesses. Or they will start with one truck and build a construction company, brick by brick. Miami is an entrepreneur's city.

The power for the pump emanates from the skyscrapers of Brickell Avenue. In Miami's many banking businesses, capital deriving from all over Latin America gets lent to local Latino businessmen, both actual and prospective. Unlike mainline American banks, the Latin banks have a tradition of lending on the basis of personal relationships and the assessment of character. As a result, they make loans that mainline banks would never touch. The men and women they lend to then hire other Latinos, relying on personal relationships and character assessment. Character—rather than balance sheet—analysis appears to have worked for Latino Miami, producing the flow of loan capital necessary for a flourishing small business community. The Miracle of Miami may have resulted as much from this happy convergence of Latin capital and local initiative as anything else.

WHAT DOES ALL THIS MEAN FOR *YOU?*

If all this growth and excitement were only happening in Miami, we would still feel proud, but we would be disappointed in our limited success. But our success is not limited to Miami. Look at Westchester County, New York, for instance. Fourteen percent of the population in this affluent suburban area north of New York City—home to many wealthy stockbrokers and business executives—has now become Latino. Similar trends are showing up around other major U.S. cities with large Latino populations. HispanicAmerica is becoming wealthier, and it is moving to the suburbs.

Did You Know?/¿Sabía Usted?

By the year 2000 Latinos will have an annual buying power of $400 billion. Latinos are brand-loyal and have large families. In numbers, Latinos are growing five times faster than the rest of the population. Past studies have shown that advertising to Latinos in Spanish is more effective than a marketing approach in English, but that is changing. A recent Pepperdine University research study shows that Latinos will assimilate into American culture within one or two generations.

It is not just in Miami that Latino people help one another out with jobs and bank loans; it happens everywhere. We Latinos try to do business with other Latinos—because we want to help each other. We love our families, and we love our people. That helps makes us strong.

What does all of this mean for us? Right now is the greatest opportunity we will ever have to better ourselves in America, to make the lives of our families and friends richer in the good things that we enjoy together—good food and wine, high quality products, houses that we own. We are better able than before to afford to send our children to college and to provide for our parents who raised us and nurtured us. *¡Sí!, se puede.*

There is a problem hidden in all of this, however, and the problem makes this book important for us all. The problem is: Too many of us try to make all of the good things in life happen on just our earnings from work, our paychecks. That will never work. Well-off Anglo Americans cannot do it, and we should not try to do it, either. You see, we can only work so many hours, maybe seventy in a week. Then we must sleep, and we don't earn a paycheck while we sleep. But the smart Anglo Americans make money while they sleep, lots of it. This needs to change for us. Please read on, and I'll show you how to make this problem your greatest opportunity for success.

Look at Our Strengths

- We work very hard; we don't ask for handouts.

- We help one another; we are not selfish.

- We hire people and loan money to people on the basis of trust and character, not on that of how much skill or money they already have.

- We don't sit around and wait for somebody to hire us; we start and build up businesses.

- We love and support our families; that is the real strength for us.

Now, Let's Look at Our Weaknesses

- We live too much for today, and not for tomorrow, or next year, or dozens of years.

- We think that we can only make money while we work; we need to learn to make money while we sleep.

- We do not trust the very financial institutions that can help us become financially independent.

- We do not build up enough wealth to make our dreams for our families happen.

- While we work hard, we need to work smarter.

Read on. Let me show you how to change.

Creating Wealth

In This Chapter

- Understand the real nature of wealth.

- See how work and achievement are a source of wealth in this country.

- Visualize the first steps to becoming a working millionaire.

WHAT IS WEALTH ANYWAY?
· ·

> [Wealth is] the condition of being happy and prosperous; a felicity, a blessing.—*The Oxford English Dictionary*

> Wealth is not the same as income. If you make a good income each year and spend it all, you are not getting wealthier. You are just living high. Wealth is what you accumulate, not what you spend.—Thomas Stanley and William Danko, *The Millionaire Next Door*

Wealth is the good times and things in life that we can enjoy with our families and friends. Notice something very important; wealth is not silver or gold, or paper money; it is the condition of being happy or prosperous, a felicity and a blessing—to ourselves and to others!

I believe that we Latinos appreciate one aspect of life better than most. We love to share the good life with our family members and our friends. We do not fall easily into the Consumer Trap: the mindless pursuit of things that *cost* less but have sadly diminished worth or *value*. We have a reputation for buying the best brands when we shop; most of us live up to that reputation. We seem to instinctively know that buying less but buying the best yields greater contentment with life. We have, then, a finely tuned sense for one aspect of wealth, living well, but we often seem to miss the other side of wealth, the creation side. Let me explain.

Think of wealth as something filling a storage device—a device such as a community water reservoir, or a battery, or a data disk in your computer. In each example, something gets stored—water, or electricity, or information in these examples. Something can be put into the storage device, and something can be taken out. In all three examples, possessing a large, full store clearly benefits the owner(s) more

Did You Know?/¿Sabía Usted?

If you were meeting yourself for the first time, how much would you guess that you're worth? You'd probably make a quick appraisal based on your clothes, your jewelry, your car, maybe your home. Here's the question: Are you wearing clothes you can afford, or ones you hope to be to afford once you've moved up a rung on the corporate ladder? Is the gold on your wrist worth more than your 401(k)?

In other words, are you living above your means? Remember that instead of fooling others, you may be just fooling yourself. Bankable affluence comes slowly and increases for those who control their money instead of letting it control them.

The ability to be honest about money comes from knowing who you are—and knowing that your financial condition is only one component of who you are.

than having an empty store. Why? Water, electricity, and information stored in a usable form possess what we might call *potential*. Each thing has the capability of making life better for us when we choose to use the stored substance. While very important for us, water and information have limitations; both have specialized, even if critically important, uses. Electricity, on the other hand, can drive a wonderful variety of tools and devices to make our lives happier. Information may have very specialized uses, but it can be used again and again, without getting used up.

Think of what gets held in the wealth store as being both purchasing power (or *future value*) and finished labor. You see, thinking of the contents of the wealth store as just "money" is a bit too simplistic.

Money wealth is like electricity; it has vast potential for getting converted into many different enjoyments for us. Money wealth is also like information; properly treated, it can be used again and again but not used up. Or money wealth is like a garden that yields fruit one hundred fold; it grows even while we sleep to make us richer in the good things of life.

Notice that just like the contents of any other storage device, our store of wealth can be added to and drawn from. Think about economic life this way: the finished results of our labor may be either consumed immediately or stored for later use. We can spend a paycheck entirely or save some of it. When we store some of our labor in the form of a financial asset such as a savings account, we convert labor into future purchasing power. Whenever we feel the desire in the future, we can use stored wealth to command the work of others on our behalf—in any form we would like. This is why wealth is really all the good times and things we wish to enjoy with our friends. Not only that, when we use the right storage devices for our saved labor, the amount we have saved grows on its own! The garden grows fruit, even while we sleep!

Did You Know?/¿Sabía Usted?

One form of wealth storage device is real estate—say the house of your dreams that you wish to own some day. We Latinos feel very comfortable with real estate: It is real; we can touch it. There is nothing wrong with this—so long as we recognize that wealth stored in a house by itself, unlike money wealth, cannot be easily converted into other things that we enjoy. Wealth stored in financial instruments can—it is pure future purchasing power, good for anything. Our disinclination as Latinos to use financial storage devices for our wealth can really hurt us.

Did You Know?/¿Sabía Usted?

Did you know these facts about the economic elevator of life?

- Among the poorest one-fifth of Americans in 1975, in just fifteen years:

- Fourteen percent moved up to the second-poorest fifth.

- Twenty-one percent moved up to the middle fifth.

- Thirty percent moved up to the next-to-highest fifth.

- Twenty-nine percent joined the top fifth!

- Only one-half of one percent remained poor!

- The poorest families are five times as likely to move all the way to the top as to remain at the bottom!

- Of the richest one-fifth of Americans, over fifteen years 37% fell down one level.

- People in the second poorest fifth who remained there saw their real incomes increase 40% in fifteen years.

- The richest Americans made the smallest gains during this time; the poorest people made the largest gains.

The lesson: Some people go up fast; some, slow; some go down. Few remain the same. Or as it is said about the wealthy in America, "shirtsleeves to shirtsleeves in three generations."

Where is the economic elevator of life taking you?

Source: *Wall Street Journal*, February 14, 1997, editorial on University of Michigan research findings.

TIP

If you need to convert currency, you can do it on the World Wide Web at **www.oanda.com/cgi-bin/ncc**. Type in the currency you're starting with—say French Francs—and the amount and currency you want to change to—say Canadian dollars—and the equivalent comes up immediately. The site is updated daily.

The three central images of wealth should now be very apparent: putting our labor into a wealth store, setting wealth to grow by itself in the right storage devices, and taking money out to enjoy the fruits of the earth. Neglect of the third aspect makes us misers. Neglect of the first two makes us poor sooner or later. The trouble has been, for many Latinos, that we have desired the third aspect too much, without paying proper mind to the first two. We tend to bypass the wealth store altogether, and spend all the fruits of our labor immediately. When we do this, we miss the most important stage—the stage where the fruits of our labor grow while we sleep. Another way to picture growing wealth is like bread dough rising; in order for bread to rise, some dough and a little pinch of yeast must be put in beforehand. In terms of wealth, yeast is the miracle of compounding interest. Who knows, maybe that's why one American slang term for money is "dough"! Without it, we cheat ourselves of tomorrow while we live for today.

Understand the paradox of saving: Saving gives us more to spend—and nearly immediately.

HOW DID THOSE WHO HAVE IT GET IT?

Short of stealing it from others (capture), *there are only three ways to get wealth initially: blood, property, and achievement.* Anybody who has wealth today initially got it through one of these three means. Let me explain.

Some people in the past got their wealth through the good fortune to be born in a "noble" bed, through aristocratic succession. What comes to mind for some Latinos at this point is the image of South American plutocrats living on million-acre estates that have been in their families for generations, while peasants scrape away at a living on tiny plots of land. While this has been a sad part of Latino heritage, almost nobody in the United States gets wealth this way.

Other people have gotten wealth through property, through inheriting fortunes (largely in the form of money) from family. Historically, such wealth has been the property of merchants and whole families that have made their fortunes through trading. Relatively few people in America today become wealthy this way; those who do are as likely to lose it as to gain it. They have forgotten the meaning of hard work. "Shirtsleeves to shirtsleeves in three generations."

Most people in America today get started on becoming wealthy through achievement—through education, entrepreneurship, and professional promotion. What increasingly matters for high incomes is intelligence, imagination, hard work, and optimistic attitudes toward opportunity. Which one matters the most? The last, optimistic attitudes.

How do I know this? Recall the set of facts that began this chapter. What does it tell you? Over the next fifteen years, almost every family—99.5 percent of families to be exact—that is poor today can expect to escape poverty; 29 percent will become rich. This is extraordinarily

The Country That Squandered Its Wealth: a Story

Once upon a time, there was a country that was very rich in silver and gold; it brought in great quantities of wealth from its mines abroad, but its rulers used the wealth unwisely. They spent it all on wars and other foreign adventures. Eventually, the wars failed, and the people found themselves as poor as they had ever been; no, even poorer.

For many centuries thereafter, the descendants of those people mourned for the wealth that had been lost, for the spent silver and gold. They said, woe are we for our ancestors lost all our wealth. When people from other countries came to buy raw agricultural products, paying for them with fine cloth and manufactured products of wonderful design and construction, they continued to mourn that they had no silver or gold left to pay for them but had to work so hard to raise things to buy these wonders.

Then one day, a man came and told them that wealth was really not what they had been mourning for so long. Wealth, he told them, was merely the good things in life, which could be *created* by learning how to make better products for sales and how to trade. Bitterly, they laughed him to scorn.

good news for us, no matter how low we may have started. Clearly, poor people do not have a corner on education or exceptional intelligence; the improvement must be due to hard work and positive attitude. But hard work without an optimism to direct it toward opportunity is mere drudgery. When we have both, we grow in wealth. Clearly, there is no excuse for *any* of us, well off or poor, not to prosper.

Did You Know?/¿Sabía Usted?

Small businesses employ 53 percent of the private work force, contribute 47 percent of all sales in the country, and are responsible for 50 percent of the private gross domestic product. For more about small businesses, be sure to see the small business resource guide in the appendix.

We can get started on becoming wealthy this way—through hard work and positive attitudes. Actually reaching financial independence, however, also demands that we carry out the hard task of putting not just our selves but our *money* to work. The hard truth is this: No matter how you got your initial wealth—whether by blood, property, or achievement—you stand little chance to keep it, let alone make it grow, unless you put it to work. Believe it or not, that's how the millionaires of life have done it.

The Working Millionaire Next Door

The last thing you probably think about when somebody mentions the word "millionaire" is the word "work." Millionaires don't work, right? Wrong. You need to get rid of two dangerous misconceptions about millionaires: one, that they do not work, and two, that you will never be one. Both of these are lies.

In *The Millionaire Next Door*, Thomas Stanley and William Danko tell us the surprising things that they learned about studying real American millionaires—not the Hollywood variety. Real American millionaires are not the very few super-rich individuals that we read so much about in gossip pages and business magazines. Rather, they are the 95 percent of all American millionaires who have a net worth of between $1 million and $10 million. Why $1–$10 million? Because that is the range that one person can achieve in a working lifetime—if the person does the right things.

Look at what Stanley and Danko discovered about these everyday millionaires:

- The average American millionaire is a male in his mid-50s.
- Two-thirds of American millionaires are self-employed.
- Their average taxable income is $131,000.
- Their average net worth is $3.7 million.
- Ninety-seven percent of them own their own homes.
- Eighty percent are first-generation affluent.
- They live *below* their means.
- Eighty percent are college graduates.
- Education is a priority for them.
- They invest on average 20 percent of their household income each year.

Probably most of these findings have surprised you, perhaps even shocked you. Why? My guess is because they sound so much like most of us—except for the net worth figures. Even the annual income figure comes as a shock. Why do they make so little money? Because they save so much and shelter it from taxes. On the other hand, most of us could probably do all right on $131,000 a year.

These two authors have also found out some interesting things about ethnic peoples and wealth creation. They found that the longer the time that an ethnic group has been in the United States, the *less likely* the group is to produce a larger than average number of millionaires! The reasoning goes like this: The longer people get exposed to American consumption-based living, the less likely they will save for the future. After all, a high-consumption lifestyle can appear very attractive. Unfortunately, it can also utterly destroy our wealth creation habits. Another thing that they found relates to the most likely forms of employment for first-generation Americans: They tend to be self-employed—and that is in itself a great producer of wealth.

Did You Know?/¿Sabía Usted?

Who buys lottery tickets? You may think it's the poor, but when people who earned less than $25,000 were asked, "When did you last buy a lottery ticket?" the largest number said never. Meanwhile, more than 75 percent of those with household incomes above $50,000 a year admitted to bouts of lotto fever. Lotteries are most popular in Texas, Florida, and New York.

What does all of this mean for us Latinos? Well, since we make up most of the new arrivals in this country, and we are more apt to work for ourselves, we should make up an increasing proportion of the working millionaire set! No other ethnic group in America can be so well-positioned to do this, to build up a real legacy of wealth, passing it on to our families and communities.

Let me mention to you two other habits of these highly successful ethnic millionaires:

They know where their money goes. They know what they spend in the various categories of daily living, and so they can manage their spending (see Chapter Six) in order to create savings.

They spend time planning their financial futures. They are more likely than most Americans to actually set time aside to review goals and objectives, monitor progress to goals, and consult with professional advisors.

What these last two things should tell us is that working millionaires differ from most of us only in that they can control spending and plan investing in ways that most of us simply refuse to do. With some attitude and habit change, any one of us can achieve real wealth creation success.

TIP

Live below your means. Own less. Give yourself the freedom of not having to worry about all that extraneous stuff.

What the Working Millionaires Can Tell Us about the Work of Making Wealth

The lessons from the millionaire next door are clear: Work and millionaire can go together. Most of us can become millionaires—if we simply do the simple things that they do. Simple, but not necessarily easy. Hard work and the willingness to change unproductive habits matter greatly. So does a cheery attitude.

This book's special mission to my fellow Latinos is likewise simple: to help each reader take the first steps on the road to working millionaire status, or to accelerate a wealth creation process already begun.

The goal should become nothing less than joining the millionaires next door in America. Not easy, but very rewarding. *¡Sí!, se puede!*

WEALTH PRINCIPLES

In America, nearly everyone has the opportunity to become wealthy. If you are unhappy with your wealth status now, don't feel sorry for yourself. Find out in this book what you're doing wrong, and fix it.

Wealth is all the good things and times that we can enjoy with our families and friends. Becoming wealthy does not mean that we have to suffer or be stingy; it does mean that we have to be careful, and we have to learn to think ahead and change some negative attitudes.

Wealth has aspects of both pleasure and effort to it. We Latinos tend to be very good at the former and neglect the latter. We need to change this. It takes real effort to acquire the habits of spending control and saving, and to put in the effort to make our money work for us.

Wealth is originally gotten in America through achievement—not through inheritance. Don't fall into the trap of feeling bad because our Spanish history cheated us out of a money inheritance. Remember, the values our parents gave us, such as hard work and perseverance, can be made to be worth far more than a money inheritance.

Wealth gotten is not wealth kept—unless you put your money to work. In this book, we'll show you how to do it.

Architecture of Latino Wealth

In This Chapter

- Deepen your sense of your financial goals.
- Learn how to choose financial professionals.
- Learn about the three spheres of influence money has on your life.

THE CITY OF WEALTH—A STORY
....

Lo que empieza mal, termina mal.

Many years ago a small village existed on the shores where a big river drained into the ocean. Since time immemorial, people had lived in that village, a scattering of rude huts grouped about a communal space with room for a great fire and for dancing and other rituals. The village never grew very much; the number of huts remained about the same. Sometimes a few got added, and then perhaps a famine or a disease came along and swept people away. People wept; the village contracted a little.

And so it went from century to century of unrecorded time—until one day an amazing thing happened. Some other people visited the village; they looked like the villagers, but they had very big canoes. They brought wonderfully crafted cloth and jewelry for trade, the likes of which the villagers had never seen. They came looking for the fruits that the villagers usually raised in abundance. Trades got made. The canoes left deeply laden with lush fruits, and the villagers rejoiced in their newly gained wealth.

As the years passed, the villagers traded again and again with the strangers, who soon became familiar to them. The villagers learned to build large canoes and venture forth upon the deep ocean, even so far as the homeland of the strangers. There they found a City of Wealth— huge dwelling places two stories tall, actually built of hewn stone!— and gracious public gardens and beautifully laid out parks and walks. The strangers had so many good things! They showed the villagers all of these, and also how they stored their surpluses from all their labors.

They used tiny bits of gold, but also papers showing obligations—who owed what things to whom.

The villagers returned from these voyages of discovery utterly fascinated with what they had been shown. A god began to visit them in their dreams telling them that they too might have many of these good things, if only they learned how to get them. What is it that you really want, the god of the dreams kept asking them. What is it you *really* want? They realized that they could have many things in the future, but they had to decide upon *which*.

The Lesson

What lesson comes to us from this simple story? *Few of us know what we really want: what is important about money to me?* So we dwell in huts rather than palaces. Money itself, as I've said, consists of a storehouse for our unused wealth—the good things of life that we choose not to use up now but to save for later. Money only exists to allow the person holding it to do something with it; money itself has *no real value!*

Why do you want money? An obvious question—perhaps too obvious. Here's an exercise for you to do, right now.

A Little Money Exercise

Ask yourself the question: *what is important about money to me?*

Now think hard about this, and have a pad of paper and a pencil handy. Begin to list the *reasons why* money is so important to you. Your answers may include some of these:

- The ability to provide for my family, my children, my parents
- The resources to send my children to college

- The freedom to travel

- The good things in my everyday life

- The ability to give money to church or charities, or people in need

Dig deeper now, and ask yourself *why* the ability to use money in each way is important to you, and write down what you find out.

What would I like to see happen as the result of my using money for this reason? *Picture the result.* Write down the goal you picture next to the reason.

What people would I like to make happy as a result? *Picture them.* Write their names down.

How will I feel when I achieve this goal? *Picture yourself.* Name your emotions and write them down.

Do all of this with great care. It is important.

Now let's talk about the purpose of the exercise that you've just done. The purpose is to connect you in a deep, emotional, personal way to the money that you can have in the future. The exercise has the power to take you beyond the fears, insecurities, and guilt that usually get in the way of any serious discussion of money, personal finances, and planning for the future. When you do this exercise carefully and thoroughly, you escape, maybe for the first time in your life, the power of these emotions gripping you and holding you back. You see, financial independence begins not with somehow getting a lot of money, but with determining the goals for your life. Money follows goals, and not the other way around!

TIP

Learn the language of business. Keep a notebook at your side, refer to the glossary in *¡Sí!, Se Puede,* read business publications, and watch the business news.

To go from day to day through life without planning, without setting goals, is easy. You need no skill; no effort is required. On the other hand, the exercise I've just given you is hard. The painful truth is that unless you go through such an exercise, nothing can ever change for you. You may already have decided to skip over the exercise and read on in this book; tomorrow, you may be telling yourself right now, tomorrow I'll do it. Let me tell you about tomorrow. Tomorrow is a date that exists only in the calendars of fools. Or you may be thinking that it's already too late in life to start planning a future. It may be late, but it does not have to be too late. As Og Mandino wrote in *The Greatest Salesman in the World*, there's an immeasurable distance between late and too late. Between late and too late, you can see miracles happen in your life.

THE NEW CITY OF WEALTH AND HOW IT GREW—A STORY CONTINUED

The small cluster of rude huts about a common space seemed like an unlikely prospect for great growth and wealth. After all, nothing had ever changed there for ages. But inspired by their dreams, the villagers realized first that they needed skills they did not possess, so they invited artisans and tradespeople from the City of Wealth to come to their village. They told them, just tell us what you will need, and we'll do whatever we can to please you. At first, the villagers' efforts seemed tiny. They built a pier at which ships could unload and load. Gradually, a regular pattern of streets appeared, fine new stone houses grew out of the ground, and, amazingly, water got piped to all the houses. A large new marketplace was built, roofed over against the hot sun and frequent rains.

The newcomers demanded schools for learning and the growth of knowledge about how to make and do things; they also asked for schools for the creation and preservation of beauty. Gradually, the schools they imagined came to pass; the arts and the sciences flourished in them. Huge buildings, much bigger than the villagers had ever imagined before, had to be built to hold all this knowledge, and the villagers willingly built them.

The villagers had established a council early on to direct the affairs of the village. Under its wise leadership, peace reigned throughout the village and its surroundings. The council did not become greedy and make huge demands for taxes upon the people, and it administered justice fairly. Pretty soon, the tiny, impoverished village had become a bustling wealth engine, a great city in fact. Bankers created money for the city coming to be, and banks grew up to protect the individual citizens' wealth and to lend it to others who would build the city even bigger. Everyone prospered.

Eventually the land in that city became so valuable that the bankers had a great, tall building erected, far surpassing any other. Story upon story, it rose seemingly into the clouds themselves. A skyscraper. At its very top worked men and women who had become financially independent; they had created enough wealth for themselves that they had the money for any good thing that they wished. They had come a long way from their ancestors' primitive huts.

Nothing good happened for the villagers in the story until they began to answer two simple questions: What do we really want, and why do we want it? Once that got decided, they began to make progress—even without any money. Eventually, they needed to create money to use to store their surplus wealth. Before they set their first goal, nothing in life improved for them. When they had set one simple goal—to build a pier—that got them started on the road to a brave new life. As early needs arose, they set goals and planned to make the goals happen. They grew richer. Eventually, they created a self-sustaining wealth engine, so that there would always be enough money for every good thing that they wanted.

GETTING OUT OF LIFE IN THE NO-PLANNING ZONE

Think about goals as a do-it-yourself building project. You want to build your own new dwelling place—call it Prosperity House. When it's finished, you will live in a suite on the top floor, but right now you don't even have a basement. You haven't planned for it. You start out living in a rented apartment—no planning for the future there. The apartment may even be pretty plush, but it is just an apartment. You take life as it comes; it's easy, but it doesn't offer much convenience, and the future looks about the same as the present and the past—pretty dull. *Unfortunately, too many Americans, Latinos included, live life in the no-planning zone.* What can you do right now to propel yourself into a better future? Start planning.

The first thing many of us try is what gets called "New Year's Resolution" planning. Constructed out of thin air, resolutions quickly fade into the reality of hard work. Next comes what I call occasional planning: planning and saving for some important occasion—Christmas, a vacation, a wedding. Not surprisingly, occasional planning rarely meets more than occasional needs. It's not an effective approach to wealth creation, however, for the overwhelmingly obvious reason that it is almost always undertaken with the full intention of spending what's saved when the day of the occasion arrives! Sadly, it leads right back to the same place—economic dependence, lack of personal control over your destiny, and limited choices for you and your family.

How to Choose a Stockbroker

When selecting a stockbroker (many now call themselves Financial Consultants or FCs), you should first decide how much advice you want:

Full-service brokers charge a commission of three to five percent on every transaction. Many are willing to negotiate and charge a discounted commission, rather than lose your business. Most can charge 20 to 30 percent less than the top rate. The only way to find out is to ask. Remember that the broker gets paid for selling product and executing transactions. Be wary of brokers who churn your account to generate commissions. Don't trust your memory, but take notes of conversations with your broker. Be sure, also, to confirm that your statements are accurate. The best way to evaluate your broker's performance is to compare it to the S&P 500, which is a measure of 500 leading stocks. If your money is consistently performing worse than the market as a whole, find another broker. Before handing over any money to a broker, check with the North

How to Choose a Stockbroker (Cont.)

American Securities Administrators Association, the National Association of Securities Dealers, and your state securities commission. You should be able to get a printout of your broker's professional profile and history. Be sure to ask the following questions, when interviewing a potential new broker:

- How long have you been in the industry?
- How long have you been with this firm?
- What is your educational training?
- Can you provide me a certified history of your investment and research recommendations? Of your firm's?
- Where do you find your recommendations?
- What industries and companies does your firm follow?
- How often will I receive a statement?
- What are your commission rates?
- What other types of charges will I be assessed (such as account management fees)?
- What is your investment philosophy?
- How many clients do you serve?
- Will you give me client references?
- Have you ever been subject to any professional disciplinary actions, or criminal convictions?

Discount brokers charge commissions equal to 50 to 70 percent less than those for a full-service broker, but they do not offer any advice or recommendations.

The next floor up in Prosperity House from the ground level of occasional planning is *needs planning*. I call this "feel good" planning because after you do some needs planning, you feel better about some particular area of your overall financial situation. Examples of such needs-based planning schemes? Retirement, college, funeral expenses. This type of needs-based activity—feel a need and buy a product to meet it—forms the heart of the financial services industry. Large banks, insurance companies, and stockbrokers all peddle their wares on a needs-based approach in order to sell you their services as "financial advisors." There's a problem with this approach, however: It treats our lives as collections of unconnected needs, ignoring the fact that all facets of our lives have an interconnected and interdependent nature—just as family life itself does. Planning for needs focuses our attention upon life's minimums—not its maximums. Which would you rather achieve? Focusing upon needs alone forces us to "settle" for less than what we can really achieve.

My experience has shown that people are willing to work hard and make sacrifices for just two things—needs and wants. However, *we receive our greatest satisfaction in accomplishing those things that get us what we want*. Needs-based planning will never, never get us what we truly want, and that is the great misfortune attached to it.

Think about it. A bigger or a nicer house, more property, a trip to Europe, a new kitchen, a college education, the time and skill to paint landscapes or play or write beautiful music—none of these are things that we need. But without some of these wants reaching fulfillment, we live our lives in a sadly deprived, shrunken state. We're not living life on the ground floor but just scraping together enough for life's few, meager occasions. Rather, we're living just high enough above the ground to see people all around us fulfilling more wants than we do.

Do You Need a Financial Planner?

Here are 10 questions to help you find out. Put a check mark next to the statements that are true for you:

1 ____ I live from paycheck to paycheck.

2 ____ I'm deeply in debt.

3 ____ All of my investments are in money markets or certificates of deposit (CDs).

4 ____ I have no idea what my net worth is.

5 ____ I'm worried I won't be able to help my kids pay for college.

6 ____ I've received an inheritance and have no idea how to invest it.

7 ____ I don't think I'll have enough money to retire comfortably.

8 ____ If I were to die or become disabled, I'm not sure my family could maintain its current lifestyle.

9 ____ I have some money to invest, but I keep putting it off.

10 ____ During the past year, I have experienced one or more of the following changes: a new baby, adoption, marriage, disability, inheritance, divorce, responsibility for an aging parent, layoff, early retirement.

If you answered "yes" to any of these questions, you're due for some financial planning.

How to Choose a Financial Planner

A financial planner can help you develop a usable strategy to meet your financial goals. When choosing a planner, look carefully at how that person is paid:

Commission-only planners make their money by collecting commissions on the investments they recommend. These planners make money only if you buy their products, so be wary of being steered toward investments that pay them high commissions.

Fee plus commission planners charge a fee to set up your plan and get additional commissions if you buy their products.

Fee-offset planners cost more up front, but they won't get any kickback or commission on your investment.

Salaried planners are paid by the banks, credit unions, and financial institutions that offer advice to their members. While these planners don't get any kind of commission, they aren't likely to encourage you to withdraw your money from their institution for the purpose of investing it elsewhere.

Remember, there are no statutory professional, educational, or licensing requirements for financial planners. That's why you're reading *¡Si!, Se Puede* to find your way through the confusing maze of options. You can look for certain letters after a planner's name that signifies that she has received some training. Fewer than one out of five of the nation's planners have gone to the trouble to meet professional standards. Those who do may have the following letters after their names: CFP (certification from the Institute of Certified Financial Planners) or ChFC (certification from the American Society of Chartered Financial Consultants). Credentials don't guarantee excellence, but they don't hurt.

How to Choose a Financial Planner (Cont.)

To help you determine if the financial planner you are considering is the one for you, remember to ask the following questions:

- How are you compensated?

- What is your investment philosophy? Conservative? Aggressive?

- What do you specialize in?

- Can I have a list of references?

- What type of follow-up may I expect?

- What professional training have you had?

- What is your education?

- Do you research the products you recommend?

- How frequently will we meet?

- Will you personally work on my plan?

What Else Is There?

Right now, you may wonder: What else is there? In fact, a whole other realm of planning exists. I call it *holistic planning*, because the goal of such planning is to look at the whole, big picture. Holistic planning has a different goal—*creating wealth*, not just meeting needs. It focuses upon something needs planning seems to have forgotten: *the overall efficiency of your money,* of your personal financial system. Or to put it another way, *every need, and want, that you have ever known or felt in your life has one common denominator—money.* So why not focus directly upon maximizing money, instead of trying to deal with needs, and wants, piecemeal—one at a time?

The Common Denominator Game

Try this as a little exercise. If you could have the most important financial goals in your life met, what would they be? Take a minute and write down some of the possibilities. In working with my clients, most have focused upon these key lifestyle issues:

- Retirement
- College funding
- Buying a home
- Caring for parents
- Taking a trip
- Starting a business

You may have listed others. Which are most important for you? Write them down. Notice the obvious: The one common denominator for all them is the need for money, an adequate amount of cash to fulfill them.

What would happen if you created a personal financial system than made your money work more efficiently? In general terms, you would achieve a whole new planning architecture; you would be able to lay the plans for a tower of wealth, able to meet any need. As Latinos, we're starting out late and are now behind in the race to build up wealth in America. We need a new architecture to enable us to catch up.

TIP

Trust your gut. If you're uncomfortable with a financial proposition, or with a financial advisor, there is probably a good reason why. You can't get something for nothing, and you should be leery of someone who promises the sky with little effort on your part. Your best bet is to follow your instincts. Dr. Spock told new parents, "You know more than you think you do." So do you, with your investments.

How to Find a Financial Planner or a Money Manager

You may want to find someone to help you manage your money. Financial planners and money managers both provide investment advice, but a financial planner takes a more global approach to your finances.

The following organizations can refer you to a financial planner in your area:

The International Association for Financial Planning (800-945-4237)

The Institute of Certified Financial Planners (800-282-7526)

The National Association of Personal Financial Advisors (888-333-6659, **www.napfa.org**)

If you need to check out a potential broker:

The National Fraud Exchange (800-822-0416) will do a comprehensive background check on an advisor for $39.00.

The Council of Better Business Bureaus, Inc., (703-247-9310) will send you several consumer brochures, including *Tips on Financial Planners* for $1 and a self-addressed stamped envelope.

How to Find a Financial Planner or a Money Manager (Cont.)

A private money manager may be a good bet when you have significant assets to manage. A money manager will put at your disposal someone who is trained to deal with large sums owned by individual investors.

If you want to start your own investment club, contact:

The National Association of Investors Corporation (810-583-6242, **www.better-investing.org**)

When you follow up on a recommendation, know the history of the firm, the level of experience they bring to dealing with individual investors, and what their performance has been. Remember, U.S. businesses are obsessed with credentials (CPA, CFM, CTE, CCM, CMA, and so on). Business acts as if a credential anoints the holder with special skills, but such credentials mean little more than that the individual passed a standardized exam, which in most cases is multiple choice. They do not reflect the real world, and they are not a complete indicator of an individual's knowledge. They are an attempt to give the user a "brand label," and while they do not hurt the credential holder, they do not guarantee competency. Be sure to look beyond the "brand label" credential and find someone who has the experience to suit your needs.

Continuing professional education is necessary throughout one's professional career, but credentialized programs that arrogantly set themselves up as defining competency are not needed in today's constantly changing and complex global business environment.

How does holistic financial planning differ from traditional planning? Holistic planning says that money is money. We only need to look at *the three spheres of influence* that money has on our lives. Think about this for a moment. Some things in life threaten our well-being—both personal and financial. They're covered by the *security sphere* for financial planning. We'd all like our money to grow rapidly. That's the *growth sphere*. Last, almost all of us have borrowed money in the past; we'd like to reduce, or even eliminate, those borrowings. The weight of them threatens us. That's the *debt sphere*. The first two spheres are positives for us—security against life's harms and growth in wealth. The last one is a negative. We wish to increase the first two and shrink the third. Here's what a holistic model for maximizing money efficiency looks like.

Things above the line add to our well-being; things below the line subtract. Grow the top things and shrink the bottom things, and you can generate a tower of wealth. It's a neat, simple, and powerful architecture. Let's take a look at each sphere.

The Security Sphere

The security sphere encompasses all the facets of *protection* that we require in our lives; it's our shield from life's harms—to ourselves, to our families, and to our abilities to earn a living. Let's face it; most of us do not possess enough money to buy such protection directly; even if we did, using our own money for protection would erode our ability to create wealth. This is one of those areas in life where we're better off using *other people's money* (OPM). We can buy protection cheaper than we can provide it for ourselves. The major way in which we can use OPM for personal protection is through insurance.

Our own attitudes can condemn us to great losses. Consider auto insurance, for instance, something we must all have by law. Do you realize that your automobile policy is very likely the most valuable protector of your present and future wealth that you can possibly possess? An auto accident or theft can come upon you like a thief in the night—and literally steal nearly all your wealth. Yet how many of us really understand all the coverage items in our policies and the specific ways in which they *protect our wealth?* Does your policy contain the protection that you really need? Do you pay too much for too little coverage? That's an important question that few of us address—because we think of auto insurance as a legal obligation, rather than as a prime security barrier around our wealth.

The same *efficiency* principle applies to homeowner's, liability, and life insurance policies as well—how much do you get in protection,

How to Lower Your Auto Insurance Rates

- Maintain a good driving record. Drive carefully and defensively.

- Resist buying a third car or naming your child as the principal driver of a car. Rates are lower when a child is considered an occasional driver.

- Raise your deductible. If your current deductible is $0 or $250, consider raising it to $500.

- Check rates before buying. The cost of insuring a new car is usually higher.

- Reduce your coverage. Be careful before doing this, however. Protect against theft. Get a security device or have your car's serial number etched on the windows.

- Shop. Get quotes from several companies and compare rates and coverage.

- Ask about discounts. If you are retired, have air bags or safety devices, are an association member, have been with the same firm for years, or have multiple lines of coverage, you may be eligible. You won't know unless you ask.

for how little money? Make your money work more efficiently here, and you'll have more money left for the growth sphere in your financial planning. I'll tell you more about how to take charge of your insurance situation later in this book.

The security sphere goes beyond insurance to include all money that we hold in so-called *guaranteed accounts*—accounts such as bank savings, CDs, and money market accounts. People tend to put their "rainy day" money, emergency fund money, or even long-term savings into such accounts if they are unwilling to take any chances with it. We Latinos may tend to put money into such accounts exclusively because either we want the guarantees, or we don't know what else to do with our money, or we get too confused by all the choices available. Later in this book, we'll get into the remedies for this sort of overly cautious saving.

The Growth Sphere

Welcome to the sphere where dreams get made, stars are born, and high returns become expected almost as a birthright. The growth sphere is where the action is for people who want to see their wealth growth rapidly. Welcome to the world of stocks, bonds, mutual funds, real estate, and some other more esoteric investments. It can also include such very speculative investments as commodities and limited partnerships. Of course, the growth sphere operates on a very different principle than the security sphere. There, the principle is *guarantees*; here, the principle is *change*. Not everybody wins playing in the growth sphere. Think of it as a high-speed elevator in one of those tall Miami skyscrapers: It goes up very fast, but it can go down fast as well.

An important part of holistic financial planning involves maximizing the efficiency of your security sphere money, so that you have more money to put into the growth sphere. But where should that money go, and how risky is it to put money there? These questions frequently trouble us.

Early in 1998, something truly astounding came about—American households generally now have more of their wealth invested in stocks than in real estate. Federal Reserve statistics showed that stocks, or equities, now made up 28 percent of total household wealth, compared to 27 percent for real estate. The equities figure has doubled since 1990. And families now hold less cash as a percentage of total wealth, cash declining from 17 percent in 1990 to 12 percent now. More and more money is being put to work. It's no coincidence that during this same period—1990 to 1998—American households have experienced the largest average gains in the stock market's history. Today, 40 percent of American households hold mutual fund investments, which of course do not offer guaranteed gains. All of this should tell us something about how American households grow wealthier every year.

What about Latinos? Recent studies indicate that we own very few investment products. We still think that our final investment goal should be owning real estate. The reasons for this may include lack of information and personal experience in investing in equities, mistrust and fear of anything that is not either substantial (as in real estate) or guaranteed (as in bank accounts), and last, a certain cultural apathy toward planning for long-term goals.

We Latinos need to wake up to the reality that guaranteed investments only guarantee us the same life that we have right now; nothing can get any better financially. The experience of the general American population shows that we can do much better when we take advantage of the above-average rates of return available to us in the equities markets. *¡Sí!, se puede.*

The Debt Sphere

Most of us know altogether too much about the debt sphere—except for how to reduce its size! Included in the debt sphere we find home mortgages, auto loans, student loans, credit card balances, store charges, overdraft charges, and many others. The list goes on and on. That's the problem—there's no shortage of debt in our economy. The size of our personal debt spheres is the most important obstacle to wealth creation—much more important than savings rates, lack of knowledge, and fear of loss. The financial services industry promotes the extension of debt every day through offerings of new credit cards with higher limits and "teaser" interest rates. It does so for one very simple reason—it's so profitable for the industry, and so hurtful to us. Make no mistake here, excess debt is the most effective way to strangle wealth creation for each one of us.

Think about it this way. Over our lives, things will in all likelihood not remain stable, the same. Instead, things tend to go into spirals; you can either spiral up (wealth creation) or spiral down into a deadly plunge that sucks the energy right out of our wealth engines and creates a vicious cycle of payments to creditors. We become blind to the opportunities we have to use money in a more effective manner.

Debt affects more than just our ability to create wealth. It affects our confidence, our sense of worth; it destroys our optimism; it breeds fear. It can ruin relationships and health. Yet no amount of debt is hopeless. Being in debt does not constitute a black mark on our souls, though many who become mired in debt may feel that way. Getting free of debt's clutches begins with recognizing its sources: How did I get into debt in the first place?

Life comes with no guarantees. As much as we may seek guarantees in "secure" investments (those that offer us no real returns), we cannot escape every harm that life may bring us. Debt sometimes seizes us through life's unexpected, and unwelcome, events. The other way that debt strikes at us comes from *inside* of us. Misfortunes strike from the outside. The unwillingness to live within our means comes from within. The desire for the good things in life outruns our knowledge that we need to first earn the right to those good things, if we are to keep them.

Good news! No matter how you got your debt sphere to grow, you can reduce it. You can go from the status of debtor to that of wealth creator. I'll show you how as you proceed through this book.

PUTTING IT ALL TOGETHER

As we have already seen, Latinos are far behind in wealth creation, for reasons that we've already discussed. No point in crying over spilt milk. We now need to begin to look to our future and figure out how we can fulfill our needs and wants as we live it. It's not an overwhelmingly difficult task. We need to do just two basic things:

1   Put a greater share of our money assets into equity-based investments such as stocks and mutual funds, and

2   Develop a holistic approach to our total money management.

Once we create a holistic means to plan our financial lives, we can then focus upon the specific steps that take us toward real wealth creation. Part II of this book will lead you through these steps.

The Foundations of Latino Wealth

In This Chapter

- Deepen your historical perspective on Latino strengths and potential.

- Begin to conceive a new model for Latino wealth creation.

A GLITTERING PAGEANT—FOR THE LOST

> The record clearly shows that Hispanic peoples are responsible for laying the foundation for much of American industry and civilization, yet their contributions have often been maligned, ignored, or forgotten. —Nicolas Kanellos, author of *Hispanic Firsts: Five Hundred Years of Extraordinary Achievement*

> Siente orgullo en quien eres, en tu cultura, en tu lengua.... Te irá muy bien y podrás integrarte perfectamente en ambas culturas y en cualquier cultura en este mundo.—Lionel Sosa, President and CEO, KJS Marketing Communications

The red and golden banners snap briskly in the warm, arid wind. In color and pattern, they signify the rule of Phillip of Spain. Far from the courts of Madrid, they have been planted this day in an out-of-the-way corner of the New World. A lawyer named Manuel Gullon de Oñate has traveled all the way from Spain for the great ceremony, the unveiling of a large bronze statue. The scene conjures up images of tall Spanish galleons and soldier-adventurers triumphantly claiming yet another new colony for the mother country. Somberly clad priests will stand by to give the benediction. From the lively flags, the year might be guessed at as early in the glorious sixteenth century, when Spain seemed poised to capture the whole world's wealth.

Nothing of the sort. Just this year, on April 28, 1998, a group of men and women gathered in New Madrid, New Mexico to watch the twentieth-century descendant of a sixteenth-century conquistador unveil a statue to his four-hundred-year-old ancestor. The statue points northward, beyond the Rio Grande that Don Juan de Oñate had crossed for the honor of Spain in the New World. Some of the people present to observe this Spanish descendant of the great adventurer may also carry his bloodline, for they are mostly Latinos who have lived here all this time.

While Don Juan de Oñate occupied himself with laying claim to vast territories in the Americas, Jamestown Plantation still lived as a dream in the minds of several English merchant adventurers. It would not be settled for ten years yet, and even then, it would cling precariously to a scrap of Atlantic-washed lowland. Don Juan de Oñate had reached far into the great American hinterland. Meanwhile, Plymouth had not yet even been conceived in the minds of the Pilgrims.

So much of our Latino past has been buried with Don Juan de Oñate, and other heroic figures like him. Sadly, the winners get to write the history books, and Don Juan de Oñate's achievements eventually got buried under a huge mass migration of English speakers sweeping over the Appalachian Mountain ranges and into the great plains where our ancestors had until then lived uninterrupted lives. Like most Latinos, I grew up oblivious to these significant facts of United States history—until my research for this book ultimately led me to Don Juan de Oñate and New Madrid.

WHAT GOT LEFT OUT OF HISTORY 101

When I studied U.S. history in both high school and college, I took pride in my growing knowledge of America, warts and all. After all, I am an American, too. Sadly but understandably, History 101 never taught me anything about what I discovered during the course of writing this book. Now I know hundreds of stories about the impact of Latino life, our culture, upon America. These newly discovered stories tell about our courage and vision, and about our impact upon the cultural, business, and inventive growth and development of the United States—our country. I did not realize that many of us never even moved to the United States, as my family did; the United States moved to them!

Did You Know?/¿Sabía Usted?

One of the reasons so many men and women have immigrated to the United States is to give their children a first-class education. What they are not likely to learn in the classroom, but should, is how to shop without getting ripped off, how to handle finances without making dumb errors, and how to be a savvy consumer in an ever-changing marketplace.

Schools teach how to earn a living, but not how to get the most for your hard-earned money. You can't get out of high school without knowing what an amoeba is, but many high school seniors cannot balance a checkbook. That's why you are smart to arm yourself with information, including what you are learning in *¡Si!, Se Puede.* Teach your children well.

Why should any of us really care about these long lost stories? I think they matter very much to each one of us. Do you know the real message that they send to us over the centuries? They tell us that once upon a time, the character that we have inherited provided the basis for achieving an extraordinary way of life, rich and cultured. We need to know that our spiritual ancestors made a vast engine of wealth creation work for them; we stand as inheritors of a unique heritage as makers of new wealth. We do not start from scratch in America, but rather from the strong position of reclaiming a lost inheritance. Once through extreme misfortune and even folly, our wealth got lost, stolen, wasted, or spent. But it is redeemable. Our imperative must be to continue to build upon the last few decades' momentum. Yes, the environment has changed radically since the sixteenth century; the stakes have become much higher, the pressure and complexity, much greater. Once we understand the full nature of our inheritance, that we possess all the essential components for making new wealth once more, we can rebuild our legacy of economic success. Then we can indeed move forward with great confidence *y orgullo*, to realize our own dreams for creating wealth.

I'd like you to take a look with me at the strong foundations for building a tower of new wealth that we Latinos possess, right now.

Foundation One: Nuestra Historia

Beginnings. In the late fifteenth century, a largely unknown man named Cristóbal Colón finally concluded a search of many years for capital to fund his new business. That business we could call The Indies Company, Inc. Mr. Colón intended to make a fortune by discovering a short route to the fabled spice islands of the Far East. The individual who funded him? Queen Isabella of Spain, the modern world's first female venture capitalist. Of course as we all know, Mr. Colón ran into a rather large land mass blocking his way to the spice islands—a roadblock that changed history, forever. We also know that Queen Isabella did very well for Spain from her high-risk overseas investment venture.

What really matters about running into this big roadblock is not the story we so often hear, the one that conjures up all those images of conquistadors. Of course we have all heard about the excesses of the Spanish Conquest. Sadly, that's usually about all we hear. What we don't hear is what matters: the examples of successful individuals triumphing over all odds to build an amazing new civilization in America so many years ago. In his book called *Hispanic Firsts: Five Hundred Years of Extraordinary Achievement,* Nicolas Kanellos tells us this stirring story of forgotten accomplishments made by the original settlers of what has become the United States. He gives us an extraordinary collection of true heroes and heroines for HispanicAmerica today.

A key area of early Latino life that he focuses upon involves the business and commerce leaders of our nation. After all, these men and women became the original wealth creators of the New World. Their story stands as a story of superb achievement:

In 1598, the leading Spanish colonizer and future governor, Juan de Oñate, introduced livestock breeding into the Southwest of what is today the United States. The new cattle breeds that he created became critical to the growing silver-mining industry's success in northern New Spain (Mexico today).

Tomás Menendez Marquez built the largest cattle ranch in Florida and developed an early trading business with Spanish-settled Cuba.

In 1690, Captain Alonso de León brought the first cattle to the Spanish mission as San Francisco de los Tejas, creating the cattle industry in East Texas.

In 1760, Captain Blas María de la Garza Falcón formed what would become the largest cattle ranch in the Americas—the King Ranch of Texas.

In 1763, meanwhile, Francisco Javier Sanchez became the first native-born Hispanic American to achieve large-scale success as a merchant and entrepreneur.

María Hinojosa de Bali became Texas's first cattle queen, controlling over one-third of the present Rio Grande Valley.

Patricia de la Garza de León helped found the city of Victoria, Texas, and became one of the richest women in Texas.

María Gertrudes Barcelò, one of the first female entrepreneurs on the American frontier, began operating her first business in 1825, later opening the Wild West's first gambling casinos!

Texas's first real estate developer was Henry Castro, who also lent money to Sam Houston to support the Texan independence movement.

The first Latino real estate developer in the Southwest was Leopoldo Carrillo, who got listed as the wealthiest man in Tucson, Arizona, in 1870.

In 1882, Bernabe Robles became the first Latino millionaire by taking advantage of the Homestead Act. He eventually controlled over one million acres of land and owned large parts of Tucson.

Individual efforts such as these established and built western civilization in the frontier lands long before the forces of "manifest destiny" drove Anglo explorers, adventurers, and settlers westward from the Appalachians. While the sources of this original Latino wealth got rooted in the land, rather than in industry, these Latino entrepreneurs took amazing risks, aimed to achieve formidable goals, and thought very long term indeed. If you doubt this, just recognize that building a well-bred cattle herd is not a get-rich-quick sort of business—nor is it for the faint-hearted to undertake. Creating large-scale ranching enterprises out of arid scrub and wasteland offered challenges as awesome as those faced by the latter-day builders of railroads over this land.

We must see it as inevitable that the great Anglo expansion westward would, in the end, derail the initial entrepreneurial efforts of these first Latinos—even though Anglos and Latinos lived harmoniously together at first in Texas. Too many land-hungry Easterners poured through the Appalachian Mountain gaps. Once through, nothing would stop them. Finally, the 1848 Treaty of Guadalupe Hidalgo created eighty thousand new Latino U.S. citizens overnight, ending three hundred thirty years of Spanish rule. While this treaty completely changed the future political and economic development pathway for the region, it did not erase our very real accomplishments. Latino pioneers had already transformed huge wilderness expanses into a vibrant economic entity possessing major urban centers—*San Francisco, San Diego, Los Angeles, San Bernardino, San Antonio, Santa Fe, Saint Augustine, Colorado, Texas, Florida, California y Montana.* The names that represent supreme achievement still live on.

Nuestras Fuerzas: Our Strengths

Whenever a people become overrun by larger forces in history, and those people still survive and even thrive as a cultural group, they must possess tremendous inner resources. Of course this has been true for Latino peoples—both those who have lived here for centuries and those who only recently arrived. We have all known this for a long time. We possess a resiliency that has seen us through some very hard times.

Do you know what has just begun happening? In the last few years, non-Latino journalists and commentators have begun to take note of the power and strength that we possess. What has gained particular attention has been our tendency toward economic self-sufficiency through our own entrepreneurial actions. We do not like to ask anyone else for help, certainly not the government. What we have accomplished, we have achieved on our own. Now, after many years of living nearly invisible lives, we're getting noticed by political leaders and by major corporations eager to focus upon our success. The best sign of this is the growing desire of financial services giants to invest our money for us!

TIP

Invest in what you know. Buy stock in the company you work for, unless it's not managed well. You know as well as anyone on Wall Street how well it's run. This is one of the smartest ways to get into the market, and it's how people like Warren Buffet and Peter Lynch do it.

Observers of American culture have just now discovered that education, hard work, and strong family values set Latinos apart from some other ethnic groups. These things turn out to be good predictors of economic success in the future. A 1998 editorial page piece in the *Wall Street Journal* went into great detail about how well Latinos are doing in America today. The writer of this piece described the usual combination of Latino attributes: hard work and strong family values. The writer added the somewhat atypical Anglo view that Latinos know or desire to learn English. Finally, he included the observation that Latinos wish to become full-fledged Americans. Clearly, he had become quite enamored of us, and thoroughly appreciated the qualities that we show. The title of this piece, however, made for the most interesting reading. It said, "How Hispanics are Americanizing"! I believe that it was unintentional, but the title does suggest that the writer saw Latino success as coming from our adopting Anglo-American virtues—hard work, family values, and patriotism. My explanation differs from this title's suggestion: We have possessed these virtues all along.

In his book *Exito Latino*, Augusto Failde describes his findings from research into the most successful Latino executives and entrepreneurs. Here is what he learned: Those positive qualities and values that we most identify with as Latinos—*the importance of family, pride, courage, passion, compassion, language skills, loyalty, cultural sensibilities, and adaptability*—turn out to be precisely those necessary for success in America today.

Obtaining FDIC Information

The Federal Deposit Insurance Corporation offers a free consumer newsletter that focuses on how to raise financially responsible kids, how to limit unsolicited credit card and insurance offers, and how to avoid investment swindles. To get on the mailing list for the quarterly *FDIC ConsumerNews,* call 800-276-6003, send an e-mail message to **publicinfo@fdic.gov,** or write to the FDIC's Public Information Center, 801 17th St. NW, Room 100, Washington, D.C. 20434. You also can check the Web site at **www.fdic.gov/consumer/consnews/.**

We live in a complex and fast-paced world that changes constantly; it constantly poses new challenges and obstacles to success. Sometimes, it almost seems governed by technology and machines, although most business leaders will admit that the ability to form close relationships in business is even more critical. While business has not gotten done on a handshake for a long time, the ability to form positive and mutually beneficial relationships offers one key to success. Notice, for instance, how so many big business mergers end in failure when personal conflicts (usually over power) erupt among chief executives. Latinos appear as noteworthy exceptions to this sort of behavior; we possess the seemingly innate ability to form lasting, healthy relationships, in business as well as in our family and personal lives.

Think about it. The courage, compassion, and adaptability of our Latino pioneers from centuries past allowed them to transform a wilderness into a new order of civilization. These same qualities help us today in building a new culture of wealth within our own communities. We know that we have to embrace risk and adapt to the changing financial strategies that match success with changing conditions. What worked before for us now needs to change. We can do it! Our cultural sensibilities and language skills position us perfectly to take advantage of the new globalization of business and commerce. The Latin world in both Europe and America has become much more important. Remember, more people now speak Spanish worldwide than any other language! Latin America has emerged as an engine for this new global growth pattern. Clearly, our language skills and comfort in dealing with Latino culture allow us to take advantage of these exciting new trends.

But wealth does not get created in a vacuum. It requires fertile soil, maintenance, and care. It requires just the qualities that define us as Latinos: discipline, hard work, intelligence, courage, passion, love, flexibility, patience. Remember, we are all spiritual inheritors of Francisco Javier Sanchez, María Gertrudes Barcelò, and Bernabe Robles, to mention just a few. We have only to create our own *personal vision* of wealth, and then follow along the pathway to success.

TIP

Don't try to keep up with the "Joneses." Thousands are busy buying things they don't need but feel they need to keep up with their neighbors. Remember, we live in a consumer society where spending and consumption are encouraged. Before you buy something, ask yourself twice if you need it. If it's a big purchase, sleep on it and see if you still want it the next day. Those who spend with impunity are among the 1.5 million Americans who declare personal bankruptcy each year.

In the following chapters, I will give you a new model for Latino wealth creation, building upon this strong foundation that we already possess. We need nothing less than a whole new architecture for the wealth tower we will construct. That architecture will focus upon building up—maximizing—the performance of those money assets that we already hold, or will earn in the future. It will also focus upon the bigger picture, upon understanding why we need to combine all the various components of wealth creation if we are to see this magnificent tower of wealth rising up in front of us. Having inherited a strong foundation, let us act wisely and forcefully now so that we can recreate the wealth that our ancestors once built. *¡Sí!, se puede!*

Financial Elevators: How Wealth Goes Up... and Down

In This Chapter

- Learn the essentials of interest on investments.
- Consider the effects of taxes, inflation, and debt.

MAKING MONEY WHILE YOU SLEEP

En que tiempo agarra, tiempo le sobra.

Smart money people talk about "making money while you sleep." That means, of course, putting the money you already have out to work for you so that it earns more. Everybody should know that money in various forms of savings accounts earns interest, and that some stocks earn dividends—a special form of interest. Money earns a return that we can call *generalized interest,* so we can speak here about any financial investment we make earning interest. This is so even for a stock that does not pay a dividend: When the stock goes up in value over time, that's a form of generalized interest. But very few of us *think with clarity* about what this really means. It turns out that the concept of *compounding interest* is one of those everyday terms that, when explored, becomes a marvel. Albert Einstein in fact saw compound interest as one of the most amazing mathematical properties of the universe. Let's go on.

The first thing we need to see with clarity is that all financial planning—whether rainy day, needs, or holistic wealth maximization—relies upon earning generalized interest. All financial investments earn some sort of interest, or we would not hold them. Our goal should be to earn as much generalized interest as we safely can from our total mix of financial instruments. Again, this is pretty obvious when you think about it; but many of us split our money up into various needs-based investments and then fail to see that in this way we do not earn as much generalized interest as we can.

The next thing that we must see with clarity is why we earn this generalized interest when we make financial investments.

Did You Know?/¿Sabía Usted?

Rubin and Rosalinda Montalvo, Owners of Cantinflas Restaurant & Bar in Greer and Greenville, South Carolina, are an interesting study in success. Thirty-seven years old, Rubin, from Veracruz, Mexico, is a 1985 graduate of the National Polytechnic Institute in Mexico with a B.S. in Engineering. He also received a B.A. in International Marketing and Business Administration from Harvard University in 1988. He worked for international corporations for 12 years, including Fluor Daniel, based in Greenville, South Carolina. Rubin lived in Spain while working for Fluor but had a rental house in Greenville, South Carolina, for use when he was in the U.S.

In 1993, while on vacation, Rubin stopped through Greenville to check on his house and, through a mutual friend, met his future wife, Rosalinda, who had been working in Atlanta for several years but moved to Greer, South Carolina, to help with her father's business. She grew up in the restaurant business, as her father owns a chain of popular Mexican restaurants in South Carolina.

Rubin and Rosalinda were engaged seven days after they met.

After working for so long in international business, and for other people, Rubin decided the next step in his career was to open his own business.

He wanted a business that could provide a fast return on his investment, and he initially thought about opening a franchise, which would cost $40,000, but changed his mind after talking with Rosalinda.

Rosalinda, with all her years of experience in the restaurant business, knew how to own and operate a restaurant but was weary of the restaurant industry. Together, though, they decided that owning their own restaurant would be the best investment for them. An added benefit was that Rubin would no longer be on the road. They used their combined savings, credit cards, and lots of prayer to get things started.

Did You Know?/¿Sabía Usted? (Cont.)

In May, 1995, they opened Cantinflas Restaurant & Bar in Greer, South Carolina. Rosalinda—who is a vegetarian—wanted to make the menu different, and she developed a menu with unique appetizers, drinks, and entrees that brought new flavor to the Greenville scene.

Initially, Cantinflas was open seven days a week with only six staff members, including Rubin and Rosalinda.

Success came quickly as Cantinflas was named a "Best in the Upstate" award by the *Greenville News-Piedmont*.

Rubin and Rosalinda opened a second Cantinflas in downtown Greenville, in the booming Main Street area in February 1997. It, too, has received "Best in the Upstate" awards.

As of this writing, the Montalvos were planning to open their third Cantinflas in the summer of 1998 on Greenville's east side.

They manage the enterprise together, with Rosalinda handling payroll, accounts payable, interior design, and the menu, while Rubin manages the restaurants and books the entertainment. Rubin said that he has always planned financially and that he and Rosalinda have diversified their financial portfolio by investing in real estate. They have as much capital in their businesses as they do in rental properties.

The Montalvos are great partners because she has all the experience, and he is a businessman. They recommend that anyone thinking of starting their own business do the following:

1   Don't play copycat. Be original. Invest in a unique idea.

2   Believe in yourself.

Did You Know?/¿Sabía Usted? (cont.)

3 Know that you're never going to have enough money to begin with.

4 Work with a partner, but it's better if you do things on your own.

5 If you get into a partnership with friends, be careful because you do not know what might happen. You could jeopardize a relationship.

6 Invest in something else (real estate, stocks and bonds, or the like). Always have a "Plan B."

THE PRICE OF ANYTHING

The cost of something is what you give up to get it.

There is a price to anything you buy or sell. It is exactly equal to what you have to give up. Every day of our lives we face trade-offs. When you buy something, you judge that the trade-off—money for a product—is worth it to you. When you sell something, it's just the opposite—you give up a product to get money. The price is the dollar amount that exactly balances off what you get and what you give up.

Now, what about saving? Does the same economic law hold? Yes! You give up the use of your money for a time, and you get *more* money back in the future in return for lending it out now. Or you borrow money now, and you have to give back *more* money later. What exactly balances what you give and what you get in each case? Again, it's a price. You see, *interest is the price paid for the rent, or use, of money*. When you rent a piece of property, you get paid a price for that rent; the same thing is true for money. If you didn't get paid, you would rather use your property yourself—whether it's a building or money. Of course, the price to rent something differs from a purchase price in one important way: A rental price is due each time period that you let someone else use something of yours, or you use something of theirs, whereas a purchase price gets paid just once.

TIP

Pay yourself one percent. If you begin saving one percent of your take-home pay and increase it by one percent each month, by the end of the year you will be saving twelve percent.

Getting paid each time period for the use of your money in that time period creates an opportunity for us, the *most marvelous opportunity in the world* for our financial futures. Each time period that you get paid for the rent of your money, you have a choice. You can either spend that rent, or you can invest it as well—add it onto your current money investments. When you add it on, rather than spend it, your next time period rent gets even larger—by the price of money times the added amount that you have saved and invested.

Most of us do not fully grasp the reality of this marvel. It seems like so little difference to us, and it is, until you begin to look at the reality over a considerable time period.

INTEREST AS A FINANCIAL ELEVATOR

Recall for a moment the idea that the wealth you have is the financial equivalent of what floor you reach in a skyscraper: The higher in the skyscraper you go, the more wealth you have gained. Let's review. Up at the top, in the penthouse, is financial independence—you don't even have to work if you don't want to. At the bottom, in the cellar, is just working for a wage or a salary—even if it happens to be a big salary. *Without saved wealth, you still live in the cellar.* How do you go up skyscrapers? In elevators, of course. Well, think of wealth skyscrapers as having elevators, too. Do you know what the elevators are in a financial skyscraper? The things that take you upward in wealth? *Interest,* of course!

Some of us have been in buildings only a few stories high, old buildings with creaky elevators. They don't go very fast; they seem to take forever to reach the top—and the top isn't very high off the ground. On the other hand, some of us have been in high-speed elevators in skyscrapers, the kind that go shooting up so fast that they nearly put your stomach down inside one of your legs. In just a moment, you've gone up twenty floors, or even more. Now imagine that you have a choice between riding in the creaky old elevator and the space-shot skyscraper elevator. Which elevator would you rather ride in? Think of the creaky old elevator as a passbook savings account and the skyscraper rocket of an elevator as a high-technology growth stock, and you get the difference. Obviously, you'd choose the fast elevator— whether it's in an actual building or in our imagined wealth skyscraper.

What matters in both cases—the speed of an elevator and the speed at which your wealth grows? Two things. First, how fast the elevator is going. That's the obvious one. A financial elevator driven by a ten percent motor will build up your wealth faster than one driven by a five percent motor. Higher interest rate, higher wealth. But the difference between the ten percent motor and the five percent motor *is not* that the first one goes up twice as fast as the second. That would only be true if you rode in a *simple interest* elevator—one in which the interest you earn does not get added to your principle. Let's look at a *compound interest* elevator.

The second thing that matters has to do with *acceleration*. When you get in a modern elevator in a skyscraper, you can feel it going faster and faster as it goes up. It doesn't just speed up a little and then run at that same speed. It's more like a fast sports car; hold the accelerator down, and it just goes faster and faster. Now, which sort of financial elevator would you rather go up in—a simple elevator that runs at the same speed all the time, or a compounding elevator that makes your wealth increase at a faster and faster rate?

Did You Know?/¿Sabía Usted?

Value investing is an approach that is widely used today by individual investors and portfolio managers. The approach was formulated in 1934 with the publication of *Security Analysis* by Benjamin Graham and David Dodd. Graham is credited as being one of the "fathers" of value investing. Graham's approach focuses on the concept of an intrinsic value that is justified by a firm's assets, earnings, dividends, and financial strength. Focusing on this value, he felt, would prevent an investor from being misled by the misjudgments often made by the market during periods of deep pessimism or euphoria. Graham outlined his philosophy for the lay investor in his book *The Intelligent Investor*, first written in 1947 and periodically updated.

Graham felt investors should view themselves as the owners of a business, with the goal of buying a sound and expanding business at a rational price, regardless of what the stock market might say. And a successful investment, he said, is a result of the dividends produced and the long-range trend of the average market value of the stock.

Did You Know?/¿Sabia Usted? (cont.)

Graham felt that individual investors fell into two camps, "defensive" investors and "aggressive" or "enterprising" investors. These two groups are distinguished not by the amount of risk they are willing to take, but rather by the amount of "intelligent effort" they are "willing and able to bring to bear on the task." For example, he included in the defensive category professionals—a doctor (unable to devote much time to the process) and a young executive (interested in finance but not yet familiar with investing).

Graham felt the defensive investor should confine his holdings to the shares of important companies with a long record of profitable operations and that are in strong financial condition. By "important," he meant a company of substantial size and with a leading position in the industry, ranking among the first quarter or first third in size within its industry group.

Aggressive investors, Graham felt, could expand their universe substantially, but purchases should be attractively priced as established by intelligent analysis. He also suggested that aggressive investors avoid new issues.

Graham summarized his own philosophy by stating that intelligent investing consists of analyzing potential purchases according to sound business principles. This includes: an understanding of what you are doing, making your own decisions, ensuring that you are not risking a substantial portion of your original investment, and sticking to your own judgments without regard to market opinion.

"You are neither right nor wrong, because the crowd disagrees with you," he said. "You are right because your data and reasoning are right. In the world of securities, courage becomes the supreme virtue after adequate knowledge and a tested judgment are at hand."

Let's take a simple example. Imagine that you have $1,000 to invest, and that you also have a choice between putting it into either a five percent simple financial elevator or a ten percent one—elevators that go up at the same speed year after year. How long will it take your money to double? Well in the five percent elevator, it will take 20 years; in the ten percent elevator, 10 years. In the case of simple financial elevators, double the interest motor speed, and you double the speed at which you double your wealth. That's the first effect.

Now suppose that you can invest that $1,000 in either a five percent simple elevator or a five percent compounding elevator. In the simple elevator, we already know the result: Money doubles in 20 years. You receive $50 at the end of each year. It's sort of like driving along a superhighway at a constant 50 m.p.h. It might be a pretty trip, but it's also pretty slow to get you to your destination—here, it's financial independence, remember. What happens if we put the same $1,000 into a five percent compounding elevator? Now, you will earn $50 the first year, the same as before. But in the second year, you will earn five percent on $1,050—or $52.50. In fact, your annual interest will *increase at an increasing rate* each year; your wealth elevator has an accelerator pedal! Now your money doubles to $2,000 in 14.4 years, instead of 20! Each year your wealth has increased, at an increasing rate: $50, $52.50, $55.13, $57.88, $60.78, $63.81, $67.01, $70.36, $73.87, $77.57, and so on. That's the second, the compounding effect.

So we've learned that financial elevators have both speed and accelerators. Let's add the two gains together: The simple five percent elevator doubles money in 20 years. The compound ten percent elevator doubles money in 7.2 years. The total gain? Your money doubles in nearly one-third the time when you both take a little more risk to get into that ten percent elevator and get the extra boost from compounding. That result is a true marvel.

Let me give you one more example, to show you that the compounding financial elevator is one of the *world's greatest inventions*: Just suppose for a moment that you are twenty-five years old, and you decide to take the $1,000 that you've saved in life and put it into a 30-year bond that pays nine percent compound interest. What do you suppose that your $1,000 investment will be worth when you're fifty-five? Well, if you'd only gained simple interest, you'd have your $1,000 back plus $2,700 in interest—$3,700. But because your interest compounded, you'd have $13,268—ignoring taxes. *Four times as much!* Keep this little miracle play in mind, because we're going to look at some important lessons it can tell us.

The Rule of 72

The first thing that we've learned is that you cannot tell how fast your wealth will increase by simply looking at the generalized interest rate. Fortunately, it turns out that, build right into the universe, a simple rule exists to help us out: to calculate how often money doubles, divide the interest rate into 72. For instance $72 / 10 = 7.2$, the number of years it takes money to double at ten percent compounded interest. See, Albert Einstein didn't call compound interest a marvel for nothing!

Unfortunately, the government understands the rule of 72 also and helps itself to some of our wealth gains. Let's look at the tax man next.

Silent, and Not-So-Silent, Taxes

Remember that we just talked about the idea of a compounding financial elevator—a marvelous invention that can lift you literally out of poverty and into financial independence. The rule of 72 tells us how fast—*in an ideal world* in which the tax man never comes. But the tax man does come for us all, and that's like having a brake put upon the speed of our financial elevator, dragging it down. Now the tax man comes with two forms of tax.

The first form is what we might call not-so-silent taxes. We pay all sorts of taxes on our income, including Federal and State income taxes and Social Security taxes, and interest earnings are income—about 28–35 percent for the average American. These taxes are not silent, because we can all hear ourselves groan out loud as we file our tax returns and pay up. Remember our nine percent bond? It just earned us six percent, after taxes. The tax man makes us run faster to stay even—unless we figure out ways to beat him at his own game. This is because the way that most of us pay the taxes on our interest earnings is by taking money that we'd rather use on something else to give to the government. Usually that gift takes one of these forms:

- A lower tax refund

- Higher withholding payments

- A check on April 15

That means, of course, that we now have *less money to save for the future.* Later in this book, we'll get into specifics about how to *postpone* the arrival of the tax man, in ways that will help us over the long term.

You may be wondering about the other tax, the silent one. What is it? *Inflation.* Right now, inflation may be fairly small, but in the past, it has robbed some of our relatives and friends of a great deal of money that they could have used as they grew older. And there's nothing to say that inflation may not steal from us in the future.

How to Predict Economic Downturns

By following economic indicators in the financial press and watching for the same signals as the economists do, you can spot the signals that mean the caution flag should rise. The five indicators that follow are what economists call coincident indicators. They do not forecast the future, but they tell what is happening in the present. Why not use the highly publicized leading indicators? Because they are not dependable.

- *Consumer price index.* This is the principal fever chart of inflation. Compare it with retail sales and personal income for the same month to determine whether those indicators are staying even with the inflation rate or falling behind it.

- *Monthly retail sales, published monthly.* Remember it takes a sales increase of 0.6 percent to 0.7 percent monthly just to stay even with inflation. If the increase in dollar sales is less, unit sales have declined. If retail sales in dollar figures actually decrease from month to month, consider that to be a strong negative indicator.

- *Total employment, released monthly.* This is the number of people employed, which reflects labor demand. It's more meaningful as a recession indicator than the rate of unemployment, which reflects the labor supply.

- *Personal income, released monthly.* This should go up by at least 0.6 percent to keep up with inflation. Any smaller increase is a negative signal because it shows consumer buying power is falling.

- *Industrial production index, issued monthly.* It's a negative if the index declines. But it may be a negative if it rises. Here's why: Suppose industrial production rises while retail sales for a month are up less than 0.5 percent in dollars, which means no real change in unit sales. That shows that factories are producing more goods than stores are selling and means inventories are building. Sooner or later, production will have to be cut in order to bring inventories in line.

Inflation comes like a thief in the night: We do not see the theft, but afterward we feel the loss. The government has not voted it into law as it has income taxes. But over time, our money's value declines as the cost of living rises. How does this happen? Think back to the idea of trade-offs. When you save and invest money, you let someone else use it in return for paying it back later, plus the price of renting money— interest. When you get paid back your money, however, you get back less than you lent in the first place. Inflation has made the dollars you get repaid with worth less than they were when you lent your money.

Inflation, then, is like an elevator going *down* in your wealth tower. It works against the upward movement of your compound interest elevator. If you receive six percent for your money when inflation runs at six percent, the two movements exactly balance one another out. You then come out even—except that the tax man sends you a bill for the six percent interest that you receive! You come out a loser in this case. What's the simple rule? Take the interest rate for your investments and subtract the inflation rate. That gives you the *real* amount that your wealth increases by. Remember, *you have to subtract the tax elevators going down from the interest elevators going up.*

BIG CHEESE, SMALL CHEESE
••

Some things in life are big cheese: Their effects upon us are large. Others are small cheese. How does big cheese, small cheese enter into your personal financial planning? It's just a matter of *time*. If your period of investment—your *financial planning horizon*—happens to be short, say one to three years, then the interest rate that you receive does not matter quite so much. When you think long, the interest rate becomes big cheese. Remember, you just saw that the difference between nine percent and six percent over 30 years comes to about $7,500 per $1,000 that you invest initially. That's big cheese!

Now, it turns out that big cheese matters a lot for us Latinos, much more so than for Americans generally.

The Younger You Are, the Farther Ahead You Can Think

Whenever we do financial planning, one of the most important things we think about is the length of the planning horizon: how far ahead should we see and plan? What will we need or want money for in 5 years, 10 years, 20 years, and so on? We Latinos happen to be a very young people in America. Our average age is under 30; in fact, the U.S. Census Bureau reports that some 58 percent of all Latinos are under 30 years of age. By contrast, only 42 percent of non-Latinos are under 30. This means that the average Latino should have a 50-year planning horizon! Sadly, most young Latinos plan for far shorter periods—if at all. We will all die someday, of course, but the younger you are, the farther ahead you can think.

TIP

By the time you're 50, you should have saved two times your annual earnings.

Sadly, too, most uses of these population statistics emphasize that we have high fertility rates, large numbers of children, and also lower-than-average educational attainments: the numbers are used to put us in a negative light. Let's instead look at these numbers in a positive light: Our young people have lots of time in which to become wealthy! *Time* is on our side. All we need as younger Latinos is a wake-up call. *¡Sí!, se puede!*

The Biggest Downer in the World

We started off in this chapter by considering how wealth gets earned—through the miracle of the compounding interest elevator. Such elevators can really lift you up in life; as they rise ever upward, you can have every good thing that you want. Except there's a big downer in all of this—far worse than the tax man coming. It's that sphere of financial life that we all hate—debt.

Debt is the biggest, most powerful downward-moving financial elevator in the world. The miracle of compounding that increases our wealth at an increasing rate works in reverse, as a growing evil, when the financial elevator goes down. Now what you *owe* grows greater every time period—period after period. It can be as though you are aboard an airliner plunging ever-faster toward earth—until you abruptly crash to a halt in bankruptcy.

Do you now understand more vividly and graphically why your debt sphere must be gotten under control at all costs? Otherwise, you crash and burn.

LET'S REVIEW WHAT WE'VE JUST LEARNED

Compound interest accelerates wealth creation because it gives you *interest on interest*.

The rule of 72 tells you how often your money doubles—a quick rule of thumb for judging how good various interest rates are for you.

Taxes and inflation are the biggest eroders of our wealth; they come upon us like a thief in the night.

The younger you are, the longer the compound interest elevators of life will work for you. Start your wealth creation plan for the future *now*!

II

The Seven Building Blocks: Creating Latino Family Wealth

Más vale que sobre que no falte.

The skyscraper symbolizes the new wealth of HispanicAmerica. Even big buildings get built one block or piece at a time, however. That's how each wealthy Latino has done it, one block at a time. Block gets added to block, until eventually *you* have achieved financial independence.

Building your own tower of wealth requires the discipline of putting into place the basic building blocks. They resemble the foundation for a tall building. It only takes *seven blocks* to create a firm foundation for family wealth creation:

- Your personal inventory statement
- Expanded cash flow
- Reduced debt
- Maximized protection
- Enhanced yields
- Increased growth
- Giving back

Each of the next seven chapters deals with one basic building block. By the time you've finished all seven, you'll know exactly what to do to change your financial future.

Taking Stock: Your Personal Inventory

In This Chapter

- Create your own personal and family information and goals statement.

- Identify your housing situation and plan.

- Identify your occupational situation and goals.

- Create your own personal balance sheet—your net worth statement.

- Create your own spending plan and income statement.

REMEMBERING WHAT YOU'VE ALREADY LEARNED
··

Cada quien construye su propio destino.

Let's do a quick review. In Chapter Three I described a new approach to personal money management—holistic financial planning. In holistic planning, we abandon the old world of planning for individual needs for the new world of planning for what we want. Instead of many, individual money needs, we begin to think in terms of just three interdependent categories: safety or protection, growth, and debts. Money is money, no matter what need it fulfills. Maximize your money gains, and you can take care of far more than your needs: *you can begin to fulfill your wants.*

A key thing about this new world is that in it everything is interrelated; each element of our whole money system impacts the other elements: Because money is money, bad debt reduces growth money, and money invested inefficiently in protection reduces growth money as well. Minimize bad debt, buy protection efficiently, and you have the maximum money for growth. Here we have the basis for a wealth creation plan that will enable each one of us to accomplish all that we want to in life, a plan leaving us firmly in control of our own financial destiny, with peace of mind and pride in our accomplishments.

Wouldn't *you* like to be there? Sadly, most of us Latinos have not even begun to put such a wealth creation plan into place. In fact, the most commonly asked question that I encounter when I talk about this plan is this: *Where do I begin?*

IN THE BEGINNING: THE FIRST BUILDING BLOCK

I've already invited you to ask yourself why money is important to you. Hopefully, you've identified some of the things you want money to achieve in your life. Very good, but what now? Beginning a great endeavor in life, with any chance of success at all, involves the action of *taking stock*:

- Where am I now?

- What do I have to work with?

- What plan of action will get me to my goals?

None of us start this process of financial planning for future wants with a clean slate financially. Most us of start with debts—often much more than we'd like. We all also begin with a number of assets, many of which we do not even recognize that we own—such as knowledge and skills, and most important of all, determination. So let's do some stock-taking. This will be a very real exercise that you can do as you read this chapter, step by step. Have a pencil and a pad of paper ready.

TIP

Keep a financial notebook. Write down smart tips you come upon (like telling everyone you know to buy *¡Sí! Se Puede*). Like a good pen, or an umbrella, good ideas tend to get lost, so keep track of them.

Step One: Where Am I in My Life? Personal and Family Information and Goals

Clearly motivations for people differ, depending upon our individual situations. The most important situation is the one that you face every day.

Single, married, married with children, or something else?

Traditionally, of course, single people had to concern themselves only with their own needs and goals, while married people had each other and their children to plan for. Today, however, things have become thoroughly mixed up. Single people are not necessarily in their 20's and living alone; some are single parents, some are sons and daughters caring for parents or siblings. A variety of human relationships exposes people today to a rainbow of financial planning choices and imperatives:

Whom do you need to plan for?

Who depends upon you today?

Who may depend upon you in the future?

Some important things to take stock of

If you are married, is this your first or second?

If you have children, how many and what are their ages?

Are your parents still living?

If so, what are their ages, and what is their health status?

Are you named as a guardian for any other children, or older adults?

In a sense, these are the very obvious questions, so why mention them here? They are mentioned not because you are not aware of them, but because *the answers are often so hard to face*. Behind these questions may lie oceans of pain or anxiety. But if we are to face up to our financial planning needs and wants, we do have to take this inventory. You can start right now; take your pad of paper and a pencil and write down your answers as you go through these questions.

TIP

If you are a new parent, get your newborn a Social Security number. This will let you claim your new bundle of joy as a deduction and open an account in his or her name for savings bonds and other financial gifts.

Did You Know?/¿Sabía Usted?

Indexmedico (**www.indexmedico.com**) is a free, bilingual site where doctors, medical professionals, and the public can research medical information and technology and link to hospitals and institutions. Indexmedico provides short Spanish summaries of information from medical journals and research studies. Patients who have questions can direct them to a doctor on staff who will respond within five to ten days.

Step Two: Where Do I Live? Where Do I Want to Live? Housing Situation and Plans

We Latinos have become the fastest-growing group of home buyers in the country. First-time home buyers make the majority of our purchases. For example, a recent study found that Latinos accounted for 16 percent of home purchases in Houston during 1996, up from 8 percent in 1992 (*Houston Chronicle*, November 9, 1997).

Do you own, or rent?

If renting, do you want to own, and if so, by when?

What specific plans have you made to purchase a home?

What do you know about the process of buying a home—about qualifying for a mortgage, using a real estate broker, securing insurance?

How much money have you saved for a down payment?

How good is your credit?

If you own a home, how do you feel about where you live?

Do you plan on staying where you are now for a while, or do you plan on "moving up" to a larger, nicer house?

If so, when?

What additional resources will you need to accomplish that move?

What kind of mortgage do you now have, and why did you choose it?

What kind of mortgage should you consider when you purchase your next home?

Write down your answers to these questions as they apply to you.

Step Three: What Do I Work at Now? What Will I Do in the Future? Occupational Information and Goals

The main machine that drives our wealth creation process is our ability to earn income from the work that we do. That's obvious. What's less obvious is how our ability to earn more over our working lifetime can dramatically increase the amount of wealth that we create. Why? The extra income that we earn above our basic needs can then take a ride on the interest elevator that we talked about in Chapter Five. In that way, even an extra $1,000 per year earned and saved can easily become more than $100,000 over your working lifetime. It can become the source for college for children, or for the good life in retirement for you and your spouse, for instance.

Some of us work at jobs that provide us with all that we could wish for: *interesting work, good pay and benefits, a positive career track,* and *good opportunities for advancement and professional development.*

Unfortunately, most of us do not. We Latinos often find ourselves working simply to produce an income, with little chance for advancement and career growth; others of us find ourselves not earning enough income, or we find ourselves at risk of losing a job due to inadequate skills and experience. Later in this book, we will take up the matter of these job skills and career opportunities shortcomings that we experience. Right now, we all need to look at the following things:

- How do I feel about my job?

- Will I stay at my present job for the foreseeable future?

- What is my current income?

- Will my income be likely to increase over the next five years? Ten years?

- What benefits am I receiving, or paying for, at work?

Remember, you need to actually write down your answers to these questions. If you haven't been, now is the time to begin. Get a pad and pencil and start. Believe me, you'll be glad you did.

Step Four: Putting Together My Personal Balance Sheet

The corporation you work for keeps a balance sheet to determine the value of all of its assets and liabilities. We can do the same thing for ourselves in order to help us review and understand our financial situations. Our personal balance sheet, or *net worth statement*, will then become our *scorecard for measuring how much we have created so far in our lives*. It's called a net worth statement, of course, because it tells us how much we're worth financially after taking account of our liabilities, and our debts. We're going to list every asset, everything of value, that we own, giving each item a dollar value at a given time. Then, we'll list liabilities, the money we owe. The difference is our net worth.

In the appendix to this book, you'll find a model balance sheet for you to use in determining your net worth. Please turn to page 399 in the appendix and complete your own net worth statement. While your net worth is the most important number on that page, you will also want to look at the things that make up your net worth. For instance, how much of your net worth is *liquid*—readily available for you to use as money? Obviously, real estate is not too liquid, but money invested in a mutual fund is very liquid. Also, how efficiently is the rest of your net worth working to make you more money? Ask yourself some questions, and again write down your answers:

What do I like about my bank accounts? Mutual fund investments? Government or municipal bonds?

What don't I like about these investments?

How important to me are the guarantees that come with these investments? Why?

How did I choose the mortgage that I have on my home?

Am I currently prepaying anything on my mortgage?

How much credit card and other unsecured debt do I have?

How did I take on this debt?

What interest rate am I paying?

Your personal balance sheet and your answers to these follow-up questions will not only give you a better picture of where you are financially today, they will also provide you a much deeper understanding of how you got to this point and how you feel about your money holdings today. You may find that you have uncovered questions about the financial decisions that you've made so far in life. Ultimately, you will come away with deeper knowledge and clarity about what you have done so far that will help you put in place a more effective wealth creation plan.

Read the fine print in a prospectus, brokerage agreement, insurance policy, retirement plan, or annuity. Yes it's boring, but it's important. If you don't understand it, find someone who does.

Step Five: Creating a Personal Spending Plan and Income Statement

Corporations use income statements to show in detail their sources of income or revenues and their expenses of doing business. Think of yourself as a corporation for a moment. How well is your business doing? Do the revenues exceed the expenses, so that you're making a profit? Or is your personal business running losses? Right now—do you even know? Here, we'll be creating a personal income statement.

For most of us, the closest we come to an income statement is our monthly bank statement. If we balance our checkbook, our bank statement gives us a pretty good gauge on what we took in for the month, and what we spent. Sadly, for many Latinos, this does not work—because many of us distrust financial institutions. Strange as it may seem to most Americans, we Latinos tend to avoid even getting a checking account, until postal money orders become too inconvenient! Clearly, we need to begin by paying attention each month to what our bank statement tells us.

Our bank statement has this advantage: It keeps accurate track of our deposits and expenditures by check. Unfortunately, it also leaves a big hole in any personal financial analysis. Let's take a look at this big hole.

For most of us, the big hole does not come on the income side. Most of us who have a checking account work, get paid, and deposit (or have automatically deposited for us) our paychecks in the bank. For those of us with second jobs, side businesses, or rental incomes, we usually deposit those as well, so they also get reflected in our bank statement. The problem—the huge hole—lies in our expenses. The big culprit here is the ATM machine. It's so convenient, and the resulting ease of access to our money makes it seem as though we've taken the padlock off our accounts. The ATM machine gives us the nearly unlimited freedom to drain our accounts of money—*leaving us with no trail to trace where the money went!* Then we find ourselves in total confusion wondering where it all went—usually a few days or a week before payday!

TIP

Weddings, christenings, birthdays, anniversaries, Christmas, and other special events can lead to overspending. Set a budget, and don't let emotions control your spending.

A spending plan is not a budget

I know of only one solution to this problem that threatens us all with a big negative hole in our finances—a *spending plan*. No, you did *not* hear me say a *budget*. Don't panic! Budgets, after all, are pretty scary things: They remind us of our human limitations; they restrict and ration our pleasures. They take away freedom. Budgets are something that we place upon ourselves as a *future discipline*—and then find that we cannot keep. Budgets resemble New Year's resolutions; they readily evaporate in the cold light of reality. They frequently leave us more discouraged than when we sat down to do them in the first place. There is one irreducible problem with all budgets: *They offer us no positive reward for changing our behavior.*

So what's the difference between a budget, then, and what I'm telling you about—a spending plan? *A spending plan is a simple, powerful wealth creation tool.* Let's start by listing some of the things that a spending plan can do for each one of us. Spending plans:

● Recover the cash that seems to sift through our fingers every day: spending plans create cash!

● Give us control over what we spend and how we spend it.

● Give us structure and discipline on a daily, even hourly, basis.

● Give us control over the powerful emotions that drive our spending habits.

● Force us to answer the most critical question in our personal financial lives.

What is that most critical question, you may be asking right now? Here it is:

Do I really *need this, or want that?*

And the matter does not stop here. If I answer "yes, I really do need or want this thing," then I should ask:

"Can I wait to get it later?"

Most of us have heard of the term *"impulse buying"*—but we usually fail to see how it applies to us personally. "Can I wait to get it later" can become *the most important question that you ask yourself in the everyday business of life.* If you can make asking yourself this question into a habit, you will find that you have started a new business—the business of creating surplus cash for yourself nearly every day of your life. You will find that this simple question will reinvigorate your motivation to handle money wisely. After all, most of us get into financial difficulty because we allow fleeting, momentary desires to overrule our intellect, just for a moment at a time. This question can become pure salvation for you: Can I wait to get it later? Let's take a look at the implications for you behind this simple question.

The ten reasons for a spending plan

1   To find out what you're spending money on

2   To get out of debt

3   To live within your income

4   To handle a personal emergency, or life change—such as divorce, loss of a job, or a disability

5   To find out how much you can *really* save *now*

6   To be able to buy what you want

7   To teach your children an important lesson about money

8   To gain control of your financial life

9   To determine your most important priorities

10 To implement your wealth creation plan

Go back to the matter of an *accurate* personal income statement. The reason why most of us have so much difficulty putting together such a thing is very simple: We don't know where we spent our money! Our bank statement does not tell us where we spent all of our money, only how many ubiquitous checks we wrote to "Cash" and how many ATM transactions we fell prey to making. Let me show you, right now, how to fix this problem, in a way that can become a permanent fix—not just a temporary bandage over a bleeding checkbook. Beginning the process of putting in place a spending plan can cut off your flow of red ink at the source. *You* determine your own goals, priorities, and needs. The spending plan makes it all happen, automatically.

Let's start by playing a little game. It's called: *"Where did my money go last month?"* Use your bank statement as your handy guide as you try to navigate the maze. Write down all the information your checkbook tells you about *what you specifically spent your money on.* Add it all up to get your total specific expenditures. Now take your total income and subtract your total specific expenditures. What do you end up with? Chances are, the two totals will not be the same. Your total expenses may turn out to be much more than the specific expenditures you can identify. Why? ATM charges and checks made out to "Cash." Where did all that cash go? Can you tell how much went for clothes, gasoline, fast food, meals out, dry cleaning, photo development, newspapers and magazines, perhaps cigarettes and/or beer or other alcoholic drinks? If you can, you're doing better than I ever could!

How to Stop Credit-Card Rip-Offs

When you travel, limit the amount of cash you carry, and carry travelers checks. Keep your receipts separate. If you lose the checks, you can get them replaced. If you lose your wallet, or if it is stolen, don't be fooled by a "Good Samaritan" phone call telling you your missing credit cards have been found. It may be from a thief seeking time to run up charges. Don't carry infrequently used cards, and consider cutting them up. Make photocopies of all your cards, and keep them at home or in a safe place.

When you check your statements each month, be on the lookout for hotels and restaurants that throw away the ticket you sign, substitute another one with inflated charges or tips, and then forge your name on the inflated ticket. It happens most in Las Vegas.

For a simple way to prevent credit-card rip-offs, pick a number and make sure that all of your credit-card charges end in that number. For example, if your number is 3, and your dinner bill comes to $30.00, then instead of adding $4.50 to the tip, add $4.53. When your statement comes at the end of the month, check to see if all the charges have 3 as the last digit. If not, compare charges to your receipt and report discrepancies to your card issuer.

THE FIRST THING TO DO: RECORDING YOUR DAILY EXPENDITURES

The spending plan is a tool to help you answer the question: "where did all my money go?" It will first of all tell you what you have spent money on and where you have spent it. Here's how to begin:

Get yourself a small pocket notebook a begin carrying it with you every day. Record in it every purchase that you make, on a daily basis. *Every purchase*—including the 75-cent cup of coffee, the 50-cent newspaper, and the 85-cent role of candy. Add the $5 cab ride, the $10 lipstick, and the $8.25 lunch. *Nothing is trivial*—because it all adds up.

TIP

> If you have trouble with a product, most companies will work with you to make you satisfied and keep you happy. Call the-toll free number, or mail a written complaint. Do something about it, don't just sit there and fume. For help, see the consumer protection section in the appendix.

Let's take a look at an example that will show you what I mean. Alfredo buys a cup of coffee, a donut, and a newspaper each day on his way to work. The coffee costs 75 cents, the donut, 25 cents, and the newspaper, 50 cents—for a total of $1.50. No big deal, you may think. But look what Alfredo has spent over one year: $1.50 × 5 days per week × 50 weeks = $375. Now, if Alfredo happens to smoke, this will add, let's say, $2.50 per day for a pack of cigarettes. Now when we annualize his expenditure we have: $4.00 × 5 days per week × 50 weeks = $1,000. In addition, Alfredo always buys a take-out lunch from a local shop, at a daily cost of $7. Now his annualized expenditure becomes: $11 × 5 days per week × 50 weeks = $2,750.

In this simple example, Alfredo has spent $2,750 in a year—*all without thinking about it*. And let's be real, this sort of pattern of expenditure does not exaggerate anything—there are many Alfredos in this world. Please recognize that I am not placing judgment upon Alfredo for *what* he chose to purchase. It may very well be that these daily purchases please him immensely. What I am placing judgment upon is the unthinking manner in which he makes these purchases. Every one of us continually makes trade-offs in our economic lives. We ask ourselves such questions as: Would I rather purchase a vacation, have more savings, or make a home improvement with part of the $2,750 that I currently spend on everyday incidentals? The key point? Alfredo has denied himself this basic economic choice, because he has no plan for spending his money.

A Snapshot Daily Spending Record

Item	Cost
Newspaper	$0.50
Coffee	0.75
Cab	5.00
Lunch	8.00
Magazine	3.50
Candy	1.25
Groceries	21.75
Wine	9.75
	$50.50

All it takes to regain your personal freedom of choice is a pocket notebook and the discipline to record every purchase every day. Once you have developed this habit, you will never, never again take $100 from an ATM machine and wonder the next day what you did with the money.

THE SECOND THING TO DO: SUMMARIZING WEEKLY EXPENDITURES

The second step involves recording your daily spending information *and your checkbook expenditures* onto a weekly record sheet—by spending category. Here's what such a record looks like:

Weekly Record

June 1–7	Amount
Mortgage/taxes	$1,455.00
Groceries	124. 46
Clothes	62.40
Entertainment	21.50
Laundry	14.50
Telephone	87.90
Transportation	26.50
Meals	96.40
Papers & Magazines	8.95
Utilities	196.00
	$2,093.75

Notice that you will probably combine some daily purchases into bigger categories on your weekly record. For instance, that morning cup of coffee might get added to the take-out lunch and totaled into "Meals," and newspapers and magazines might get combined. This is O.K. because you always have the daily records to look back at if you're uncertain about what made up any spending category.

Get Organized!

Your financial life will be a mess unless you know what you own, where it is, and what it's worth. Buy a filing cabinet. Also buy an emergency fireproof file box, or rent a bank safe-deposit box. Keep these items in the safe-deposit box:

- Birth, marriage, and death certificates and family records

- Divorce or separation agreements

- Adoption or custody papers

- Title papers to real estate, car, boat, and so on

- Mortgage papers and deeds

- Stock certificates, bank, investment, and credit card account numbers

- Insurance policies

- Contracts and legal agreements

- Military discharge papers

- Copies of credit cards

- Car registration

- Copies of your tax returns

- Copies of passport, Social Security cards and official identification

- Photographs and log of possessions. Better yet would be a video.

- All home improvement receipts. When you sell your home, add these expenses to the cost basis (the figure used to determine a gain or loss on your home). Over time, this can mean thousands in tax savings.

Get Organized! (Cont.)

Do not put these things in a safe-deposit box:

● Your will. Keep it at your attorney's office, with only a copy in the safe-deposit box. The reason is that safe-deposit boxes are sealed at death until the IRS sees what's inside. This could prevent relatives from getting into the box right away to see if a will exists.

● Money or other valuables on which income tax has not been paid. This is illegal, and your heirs may be taxed at your death.

THE THIRD THING TO DO: CREATING A MONTHLY SPENDING RECORD

The third step involves transferring your weekly numbers to a monthly record sheet. This monthly record will now contain *every* dollar and cent you spent for that month—whether by check or by cash. Here's what a monthly record might look like:

SPENDING RECORD FOR JUNE

	WEEK 1	WEEK 2	WEEK 3	WEEK 4	TOTAL
MORTGAGE	1,455.00	---	---	---	1,455.00
GROCERIES	124.46	138.50	116.40	162.55	541.91
CLOTHING	62.50	---	38.50	16.45	117.45
ENTERTAINMENT	21.50	16.00	9.45	31.50	78.45
LAUNDRY	14.50	7.50	9.50	---	31.50

SPENDING RECORD FOR JUNE

	WEEK 1	WEEK 2	WEEK 3	WEEK 4	TOTAL
TELEPHONE	87.90	---	---	---	87.90
TRANSPORTATION	26.25	26.25	26.25	26.25	105.00
MEALS	96.40	18.50	26.25	46.50	187.65
PAPERS & MAGS	8.95	7.50	7.50	7.50	31.45
UTILITIES	196.50	---	---	---	196.50
TOTALS	2,093.96	214.25	233.85	290.75	2,832.81

Let's take a minute right now to review what we've accomplished. Why? Well, this may look suspiciously like a *budget* to you, and it's not. Remember, a budget is a future promise that you make to yourself. In it, you state how you intend to spend money in the future. Because such promises rarely reflect our present behaviors with money, they almost always get broken. A spending record, on the other hand, tells us what our current spending habits actually are. Unlike most budgets, a spending record gets based in financial reality, and it becomes the basis for creating both an accurate current income statement and a revised spending plan.

If the numerical calculations that appear above scare you, or you don't want to spend time adding up numbers, and you have a computer to use, consider doing your calculations on a computer spreadsheet. You may also wish to consider computerizing your personal finances. For less than $100, you can purchase a package called Quicken, or one of its competitors. Once you have invested the time needed to set up your "books" on the computer, you will find that the savings to you in time and reduced errors will be tremendous. But a word of warning: No computer in the world can do the most important part of this overall exercise for you, that is, recording your daily expenditures.

Getting Aid from Your Computer

If you want to use your computer for more than just playing Solitaire, consider using it to manage your finances.

TurboTax (**www.intuit.com/turbotax**) can file your taxes online.

Kiplinger Tax Cut (**www.conductor.com/lalas/taxcut/taxcut.htm**) will take you through an interview that includes a "refund monitor" that automatically changes your bottom line every time you make an entry. It will also check for omissions and flag deductions you may have forgotten, and it will compare your deduction and taxes to national statistics.

SecureTax (www.securetax.com) does what the software products do, but it's entirely Internet-based, and there is nothing to install.

Or Go the Low-Tech Route

While there are lots of high-tech ways to get your financial life in order, here is a low-tech way: Take a loose-leaf three-ring binder, and create separate sheets for each of these items: safe-deposit box (where it is, where the key is kept, what it contains); life insurance policies, with numbers, agent, and where the policy is kept; name, address and telephone of your accountant and attorney; where your wills are; a list of all bank accounts, including types of account; a list of all credit-card numbers, where the payments are sent, and emergency telephone numbers. Make a new sheet every time you acquire a new asset, and list the item, where the paperwork is, and payment information and account numbers. Put your binder in a fireproof box.

THE FOURTH THING TO DO: CREATING YOUR PERSONAL INCOME STATEMENT

Congratulations! Once you've reached this point, you've accomplished one of the most difficult tasks in spending planning: You've accurately determined where all of your money currently goes. Now, it's an easy thing to make your monthly spending record into a monthly *income statement*. All you have to do is figure out your monthly income, add that to the top of your monthly spending record, and subtract total monthly spending from income. Hopefully, there is something left over when you're done—a personal monthly "profit"! That "profit" may very well be necessary for meeting infrequently occurring, large expenditures, such as property taxes, that only come due annually, semiannually, or quarterly. As you continue recording expenditures, month by month, you'll eventually have a good record of your *annual* spending, allowing you to create an annual income statement as well.

Only one question remains. How long should you continue recording all of your everyday expenditures? You do not have to become a slave to such dull work. But you do need to keep recording expenditures daily until you have captured the unconscious pattern of spending that you have never before recognized.

THE FIFTH THING TO DO: CREATING YOUR PERSONAL SPENDING PLAN

From the spending record that you have created for yourself through the preceding steps, you have now achieved *spending freedom*. Because you now know where every dollar gets spent, *you can begin to make real choices as to how you would like to spend your money in the future*: you can identify the trade-offs that you would like to make. Remember, the fundamental reason that you undertook this exercise was to discover the hidden money available to you that you never realized you had. Now you can use that money for implementing any one of the ten reasons for a spending plan that I gave you a few pages back. You may, for instance, use the information that you have created to help get yourself out of debt, or to significantly lower your debt. Gaining mastery over your debt sphere will then allow you to begin creating real savings for you and your family. Remember, that's the key to implementing your own personal wealth creation plan, driven by your newly created or expanded growth sphere.

So look at the results from recording expenditures and totaling them up by week and month, and begin making the spending trade-offs that will help you achieve your overall money goals in life. Then make a new spending plan that reflects the trade-offs that you would like to begin to live out. As you implement your new spending plan, you may find it helpful to keep recording daily expenditures—especially until you have created new spending habits. And remember those two most important questions to continue asking yourself:

Do I really need this, or want that?

Can I wait to get it later?

LET'S REVIEW WHERE WE'VE COME

This chapter of *¡Sí!, Se Puede* has challenged you to take a thorough personal inventory. By now, hopefully, you will have taken stock of your

- Personal and family information and goals
- Housing situation and plans

- Occupational information and goals

- Personal balance sheet and net worth statement

- Personal income statement and spending plan

As you review the hard work that you have accomplished, you will begin to see your real priorities in life, as well as your financial problem areas. By learning where your money is going and how much you have left over after your expenditures, you can now begin to determine what you can do to achieve personal, family, and housing goals. For instance, an examination of your occupational situation may lead you to consider new alternatives—whether that means career advancement, switching careers, or perhaps even a return to college or university for more education. Or your personal balance sheet may make you feel very unhappy about your lack of net worth, something that may motivate you to make important changes that will increase your net worth in the future. *¡Sí!, se puede!*

The value from this personal inventory statement lies in the clarity that it provides about where you are in your financial life, what you want to achieve in the future, and whether or not you are on track to achieve what is important to you. Without a clear understanding of your current situation, *your commitment to the wealth creation process, quite frankly, is suspect.* Your personal inventory statement also provides you and your family with a *benchmark* that you can use to measure your future results as you move ahead in your wealth-creating activities. As you reach each individual goal and make progress toward reaching others, you will update your personal inventory to reflect your accomplishments—increases in net worth, changes in incomes, and realized spending objectives. And all the while, you will keep control of your money, remaining fully conscious of how it is coming in, where it is going out, and how your wealth-creating activities are contributing to your lifetime goals. *¡Sí!, se puede!*

In the next two chapters, we'll continue this basic work that you have already done, by putting into place two more basic building blocks: cash flow expansion and debt reduction.

Before moving on, please make sure you are ready with your responses to the exercises in Chapter 6.

Expanding Your Cash Flow

In This Chapter

- Decrease your expenses, without decreasing your enjoyment.

- Use six tips for reducing expenses that will save you more than $3,000 a year.

- Review when to refinance your home mortgage.

- Use specific ideas for increasing your income.

- Determine whether you should start your own business—become an entrepreneur.

CASH MAKES THE WORLD GO ROUND
. . . .

En el querer está el poder.

In the Chapter 6, we talked about the idea of looking at your personal financial life as though you were running your own business—call it *Me*, Inc. Let's continue thinking that way for a moment. For most of us, *Me*, Inc. is not very much like IBM; *Me*, Inc., is more like a small family business, not very large. Now what's the most important thing in the world for any small business? *Net cash flow!* Small business people know that they must have *positive* cash flow almost all of the time; survival depends upon it. Cash inflows must exceed cash outflows. Selling products or services does not really help a small business at all, unless it results in cash coming into the business on a timely basis—more cash than is going out. *Managing* cash flow becomes critically important for the small business owner. Without adequate cash coming in, bills and salaries cannot be paid, and product cannot be produced or bought. Disaster looms.

Sadly, most *Me*, Inc., owners, even many who do in fact operate their own small businesses, fail to manage cash flow. Many of us fall into the trap of thinking that business rules somehow do not apply to our personal financial situations. Remember, you *do* run a small business, *Me*, Inc., and unless you treat that small business well, it will turn around like a wounded dog and bite you! Each of us possesses a personal cash flow. In Chapter 6, you have already learned the first step in managing it: creating your own personal spending plan and income statement. The spending plan determines where our money goes. If we want to have more money to spend on something we want, or to pay down debt or save more for the future, we can begin by trading off unimportant everyday expenditures, thereby gaining "free" money for the things that we would like. That is one lesson from Chapter 6. But what if we want more money than trading off can gain us?

There are only two ways in life to increase our personal net cash flow:

- Decrease expenses.
- Increase revenues (incomes).

> One of the best things about doing your taxes is that you see the truth behind the numbers: how much you've gained on investments, how much you've donated to charity, what you are paying in property taxes. It's a good reality check.

Now, small business people become very adept at both of these activities. As an owner of a *Me*, Inc., business, you can also become a highly creative manager of your own cash flow. Let's look at some of the ways that this can be done, starting with decreasing expenses.

> If you itemize your taxes, many investment expenses—subscriptions, safe deposit boxes, transportation to meet your broker or accountant, investment fees, and *¡Sí!, Se Puede*—are deductible. Be certain that you deduct everything allowable.

Seven Steps to Handling an IRS Audit

1   Answer only the questions you are asked. Auditors don't have the right to ask you about anything that isn't in your audit letter. If you prattle on, you're likely to divulge something you shouldn't.

2   Be professional and don't expect any sympathy if you show up for an audit with a box of receipts and a bad attitude.

3   When you go to the audit, bring the receipts and a calculator tape or spreadsheet showing the total. Frequently the auditor will glance at the tape and okay it.

4   Never contradict your form, and always have an explanation that justifies any deductions or expenses. Even if they don't accept your story, admitting you lied ruins your credibility for the rest of the audit.

5   Unless your audit letter asks for one or two items that you can easily address with receipts, it pays to hire an accountant to represent you. Find one who has earned Enrolled Agent credentials from the Treasury Department because it's likely the local auditor will know him or her, which will ease negotiations.

6   Don't use cash. Canceled checks and credit card statements are your best receipts, since you can easily get duplicates for an audit. Maintain a separate business checking account and credit card.

7   Even if the audit letter tells you to bring your bank statements and tax forms from prior years, leave them at home. Many auditors use these documents to fish for other problems. If the auditor persists, buy some time by saying it will take a few weeks to find them, and call your accountant.

MAKING MONEY BY DECREASING EXPENSES

Think back to creating your spending plan for a moment. That activity was all about clarity. It required you to think differently, attaching importance to the smallest expenditures. Increasing cash flow by decreasing expenses requires the same kind of thinking. Here, it means trading off reduced or eliminated expenditures for cash that you can keep. Once more, a little can add up to a lot, over time.

 **TIP**

> See if your employer offers a Flexible Spending Account (FSA). If you have a child under 13, or an ill parent, an FSA lets you set aside up to $5,000 of your before-tax salary in an account to be used for babysitters, day care, camp, after-school programs, and adult care. You don't pay income tax on the amount in your FSA, but you lose any amount you don't spend.

For example, let's just say that you currently earn $40,000 a year, and you find it impossible to save any money. Assuming that your earnings will not increase, what options do you have?

- Do nothing, and save nothing, or

- Seek alternatives for what you are spending your money on.

Clearly, the first option will not be satisfactory, if you set a goal to save money. So let's examine the second and see how it differs from the spending plan technique that you've already learned. Again, an example will be helpful.

TIP

Never shop without a grocery list, or when you're hungry. You'll wind up buying more than you need, and you'll most likely get more junk food than you need.

The Small Cheese: How the Little Things Add Up

Imagine that you have created a spending plan for your $40,000 income. That plan shows that you currently spend $200 a month on cabs in the city. You realize that you might cut back on the use of cabs, perhaps by sometimes taking the subway or by walking when the weather is nice. In this manner, you figure that you can save half of your cab expenditures, or $100 a month. In Chapter 6, we suggested that you might make a trade-off—fulfilling some want. Let's say it's your desire to go to the ballet, which happens to be the great artistic love of your life. You could use the cab fare savings to go to the ballet. Or you could use the cab fare reductions to generate extra cash for savings. In this way, you actually increase your net cash flow by decreasing an expense. You do it by *seeking an alternative to a current expense.*

TIP

The average newspaper coupon is worth 85 cents. Use five a week and save $195 a year.

What kinds of alternatives to current expenses are there? Here's where you can become a creative owner of Me, Inc. The table that follows gives you a sampling of the many creative ways that people have developed to increase cash flow by creating an alternative to an expense:

Some Other Ways to Create Alternatives to an Expense

- Bartering services such as baby-sitting

- Car pooling

- Buses/trains, instead of cabs

- Walking instead of buses/trains

- Going to the movies, instead of the theater

- Renting a video, instead of going to the movies

- Instead of buying popcorn and soda at the movies, bring your own

- Entertaining at home, instead of taking guests out

- Traveling by train, instead of by plane

- Attending a state or city university, instead of a private one

- Wearing last year's evening dress one more year

- Writing letters instead of calling long-distance

- Keeping your daily spending record scrupulously

- Cutting down the frequency of nonessential services such as lawn maintenance and car washing, and doing them yourself

- Eating meals at home, instead of out

- Brown bagging your lunch

- Stopping smoking, or drinking

- Giving gifts of personal services or things you've created rather than buying them

- Borrowing books, tapes, and videos from a public library, instead of buying or renting them

- Deferring nonessential medical treatment

- Using parks and public facilities rather than private clubs for sports and exercise

- Using museums, galleries, aquariums, and free public events as part of your entertainment

- Repairing, or have repaired, damaged items such as clothing or appliances

- Reupholstering rather than replacing furniture

- Increasing the deductibles on your auto and homeowner insurance policies

- Consolidating credit card debt

- Refinancing a mortgage

- Fixing a leaky faucet

- Insulating and weatherizing your home

- Eliminating ATM use, especially if not from your own bank

Do these ideas sound silly to you—too much trouble for not enough payoff to make a difference? Let's take a test, using just six of these items.

Test One: Brown bagging occasionally. Spending $5 a day for lunch every business day costs you about $1,250 a year. Bringing your own lunch just two days a week saves you $500 a year. Save it.

Test Two: Raising your auto insurance deductibles. If you are a safe driver, why give the insurance company most of the benefit? Increasing your deductible from $250 to $500 could save you around $150 a year. Save it. In just a little over a year, you will have made up the deductible covering the accident, which, hopefully, you will never get into in the first place. And with the larger deductible, you'll have an incentive to drive even more carefully!

Test Three: Refinancing your home mortgage. If you currently hold a ten percent, 30-year mortgage on a $100,000 home, and you refinance at eight percent, you could save some $1,600 *per year* over the life of the loan. Save it.

Test Four: Lowering your credit card interest rate. Moving $7,700 of debt from a card charging 20.3 percent interest to one charging 14 percent could save you $485 a year in interest payments. Use the savings to pay down your indebtedness!

Test Five: Fixing a leaky faucet. It sounds incredible, but fixing a leaky faucet, if you live in an urban area, will both cut water consumption and save you $300 a year! Save it.

Test Six: Weatherizing your home. If you live in a colder climate, you can save on heating and cooling costs simply by using caulking and weather stripping, and by making sure that your heating equipment runs efficiently. You could save $300 a year. Save it. And you could save much, much more if you chose to have your uninsulated house insulated or your outdated heating system replaced.

Look at the results from taking these six simple actions. Your annual savings could easily amount to $3,335 *every year!* From Chapter Five, which dealt with financial elevators, you have already learned that the total value of these savings over, let's say, 15 years at ten percent will slightly exceed $105,000! Do you still feel that fixing a leaky faucet is trivial? And the ways to make money by creating alternatives to expenses are by no means limited to the list I have just given you. Examine your own spending plan, and start thinking up your own creative ways to make money—without increasing your income.

Because bank card offers change every day, it's best to get up-to-date information on what is available. For $4, Bankcard Holders of America (703-389-5445)—a nonprofit consumer credit education and advocacy organization—will send you a list of 50 card companies that offer credit cards with low interest rates and no annual fee.

IntelliChoice (**www.intellichoice.com**) provides dealer prices and ownership costs on many car makes and models.

Small Cheese to Big Cheese: Refinancing Home Mortgages

Clearly, some alternatives to expenses are small cheese—a few hundred dollars a year each. Even so, the small cheese items add up to big cheese, as we've just seen. One big cheese item on the menu is so important that I'd like to explore it further with you now, before we go on to the income-increase menu. That item is *refinancing your home mortgage.* As you saw above, nearly half the total money gain from six alternatives to expense came from this single item—refinancing.

Cancel your private mortgage insurance (PMI) if you have over 20 percent equity in your house. When you have this much equity, it's expensive and not necessary.

Over the past several years, the mortgage financing marketplace has been a very busy one, as hundreds of thousands of homeowners have traded in their old eight to eleven percent mortgages for ones with lower interest rates. These people have been saving hundreds of dollars a month on their mortgage payments. Is this a good move for you? If so, how do you go about doing it?

Interest on a home mortgage or a home equity line of credit on your residence is tax deductible. Interest paid on car or credit card loans is not.

Clearly, refinancing makes sense if interest rates are substantially lower than when you first obtained your mortgage. The question is, how much lower? Conventional wisdom used to say that refinancing only makes sense if the new rate that you can get is at least two percent lower than your existing rate. That two percent was believed to be the minimum interest savings that would compensate for the costs of refinancing—closing costs, points, and possible prepayment penalties. But is conventional wisdom right about this? Probably an even smaller rate difference should trigger a closer look at refinancing. See the mortgage refinancing tool in the appendix of this book for details.

Refinance your mortgage when interest rates are low. Make sure, however, that your savings are not eaten up by fees for the application, appraisal, title insurance, and other legal and transaction costs. The rule of thumb used to be that you had to lower your rate by more than two percent to justify the refinance, but that doesn't hold true any longer. Use the refinance worksheet on page 386, or contact a mortgage specialist.

MAKING MONEY BY INCREASING YOUR INCOME

Think back to the beginning of this chapter. If you wish to generate more cash for *Me*, Inc., you have only two choices: Decrease expenses or increase revenues. We've now considered the ways to increase cash by creating alternatives to expenses. How about increasing revenues—our incomes?

Most people seem to sit around and complain about how little money they make. Some people take a different approach. They search for ways to make more money. What sort of things do they come up with? Well, to begin with, let's recognize that things have gotten more complex today than they were for our parents. It used to be that you worked a 40-hour week, and if you needed or wanted more cash, you took a second job evenings or weekends. What can we do today?

Barter what you have for what you need, if you have a "trade" skill to trade and would welcome the additional income from that time or skill. Examples and budgets are easy to follow and will enable you to increase your ability to barter (check out **www.barter.com**.)

The first step in any extra income plan is to determine how much you need or want. From your spending plan and balance sheet, you have already analyzed where you stand financially. Where are your financial gaps, and how big are they? Can you close the gaps by creating alternatives to spending, or do you need or want to seek more income? And very important, returning to your personal inventory once more, how happy are you in your current occupation? If you do not see your current occupation as one that you wish to continue in permanently, perhaps you should allow your desire for more income to push you to investigate career choices—perhaps even to having your own business.

Next, you can look at the nature of your additional cash needs. Are those needs temporary, or permanent? If you need a one-time sum of money, you can do such things as:

- Sell something you own that has marketplace value. Perhaps you do not desire to keep it anyway.

- Liquidate an asset, such as a savings account.

- Hold a garage sale. You may be surprised at how many hundreds of dollars your garage sale may bring you.

- Call in a debt owed you by somebody else.

If, on the other hand, you find that *Me*, Inc., requires hundreds of additional dollars each month, you could do such things as these:

- Take in a boarder or a roommate.

- Put in overtime at work.

- Take a second job.

- Do private tutoring.

- Leverage a skill or expertise that you possess.

- Start a home-based business.

Each one of these options can produce additional income, with varying degrees of likelihood and commitment. Only one of these choices, however, represents something new and exciting for Latinos. That's the home-based business.

The decision to start a business, whether home-based or not, has gotten made by nearly *one million* Latinos in the recent past! In fact, according to *Hispanic Business Magazine,* nearly two-thirds of the richest Latinos in the United States have earned their fortunes through starting and running their own businesses—through *entrepreneurship.*

Entrepreneurship Can Begin at Home

Let me give you some more facts about becoming an entrepreneur right in your own home. According to the research and consulting firm Find/SVP, approximately 18.3 million self-employed Americans currently work at home. Of that number, 8.7 million say that they operate home-based businesses. What do the other ten million do? Well, it turns out that the difference is simply a matter of perception—of how you see what you're doing at home. Many self-employed people see themselves as just that—self-employed. They do not see themselves as running a business. Actually, their situation is no different from how you and I choose to see our financial lives. Do you just work and pay bills, or do you run *Me,* Inc.? When you begin to see yourself as running a business, not just employed or self-employed, great things can begin to happen for you. You may wonder why; what's the difference?

The move toward home-based businesses has been growing very rapidly in recent times, for two simple reasons: First, corporate America has been downsizing itself to more profitable employment levels. That means that a lot of Americans have turned to home-based work of necessity. Those cushy corporate jobs just aren't there anymore. Maybe that's bad news. But second, there's a lot more opportunity now to make a lot more money at home than ever before. This is great news! But where does all this new opportunity come from, you may wonder?

Partly, it comes from the reality that all of us today feel more pinched financially and short of time. We'd like to find ways to buy things at

Six Steps to Turning Your Job into a Career

- Identify three prospective mentors today.

- Make a list of five questions to ask each prospective mentor.

- Set up appointments with each mentor to discuss his or her approach to the industry.

- Prepare a 30-second verbal résumé for association dinners, meetings, and social events.

- Practice delivering your verbal résumé before you attend each event or meeting.

- Before you accept your next position, initiate the salary negotiations by stating a range that's above a predetermined "walk-away" point you have set for yourself.

better prices and with less time wasted shopping around. It turns out that people running home-based businesses can help others meet those money and time needs. Partly, it comes from the technological revolution now going on in America, centered upon the personal computer and such things as fax machines, e-mail, and the Internet. These new things allow home-business people to communicate and operate far more effectively and efficiently than ever before imagined.

Just as technology has influenced the direction of home-based business people, these people are also influencing the direction of technology. According to *Entrepreneur Magazine*, 15 percent of all adults in America

Did You Know?/¿Sabía Usted?

About 41.5 million U.S. adults are currently using the Internet.

About 15.9 million U.S. adults tried the Internet in the past year but no longer use it.

About 23.8 million U.S. adults say they want to get Internet access in the next year.

This is according to the American Internet User Survey (**www.cyberdialogue.com**). For more on doing business on your computer and on the Internet, see the appendix.

today say that they own a home business. These Americans are *five times* more likely to be on the Internet than adults who do not own their own home businesses.

Did You Know?/¿Sabía Usted?

The following Web sites are either bilingual or entirely in Spanish:

PC World Online, a computer buying guide, **www.pcworld.com.mix**

CityConnection, Inc., which runs its Manhattan site at **www.cityconnection.com**

The Latino Entrepreneur

You may be surprised to learn that we Latinos possess unique strengths as home-based entrepreneurs. How can this be? We are relatively young and family- and friends-oriented. That means that we have many personal relationships that offer each one of us selling opportunities. We like to buy from fellow Latinos. That means that we have a natural access to the fastest-growing niche market in America today—*us*. Our own people. We trust each other more, perhaps deservedly so. We like to buy from people we know. We like to buy excellent-quality products backed up by a familiar face. All of this favors our selling products to each other, right out of our own homes.

We also have a natural access to international Latin American markets. Many of us have friends and relatives in Latin countries. We also have the support of a growing network of local Latino Chambers of Commerce, and other organizations focused upon Latino entrepreneurial development. Some of these appear in the appendix to this book. So what are you waiting for? *¡Sí!, se puede!*

A Brief Guide to Getting Started

If you want to investigate starting your own business, home-based or not, what should you do? Obviously, I cannot tell you everything in a page or two in this book, but here's an overall plan for you to follow:

Step One. Determine your aptitude for running your own business by answering a few simple questions, such as these:

- Do I have the willingness to assume the responsibilities of business ownership?

- Can I effectively set goals for my new business and take actions to reach them?

- Do I have the necessary determination to keep at something when success does not come to me immediately? Can I keep at an activity for at least one to two years, even when it is not paying off?

Should You Be an Entrepreneur?

To help you answer this question, the SBA has devised the following quiz. If you answer Yes to six or more of the questions, you fit the profile. If you fall short of the mark, you will know what skills to work on before you take the plunge:

1   Do you have organizational abilities, personal drive, and leadership qualities?

2   Are you able to endure long hours?

3   Are you psychologically ready to take risks?

4   Are you prepared to wait months before you make a profit?

5   Do you have expertise in the business you want to start?

6   Have you carved a market niche and identified customers?

7   Do you know how to sell products or services and set a profitable price?

8   Can you raise money to start and keep the business's cash flowing?

9   Do you like to think ahead, then work to make it happen?

For more on entrepreneurship and small business, see the appendix.

Do you want to know truthful answers to these questions? Take a careful look at what you have done with this book. If you have done what I've recommended you do for *Me*, Inc., chances are you have some of what it takes to run your own business.

Step Two. If you give yourself a passing grade on Step One, begin to plan your business activity:

- Choose an area of business that interests you.

- Develop a business plan (just as you have now developed a personal financial plan).

- Put that plan in writing.

- Begin to put the plan into effect.

Step Three. Determine how you will finance your business:

- From personal savings?

- Through a loan from a friend or family member?

- Out of current job earnings?

- From earnings of another family member?

- With a bank loan?

Step Four. Develop in detail how you will sell your product.

Step Five. Do it. Begin operating and managing your business.

A word of caution: Do not try to be a "Lone Ranger" if you choose to start your own business. Seek the help of others. Read books on entrepreneurship. Remember that nothing worthwhile ever got built in a day, or without great effort and sacrifice. Be forward-looking.

ACTIONS YOU CAN BEGIN TODAY
TO INCREASE YOUR CASH FLOW

- Run your personal financial affairs like a business, and you will see profits you never imagined.

- Make money by substituting a low-cost or no-cost expenditure for a high-cost one.

- Create an extra $3,000 a year in new cash to you by following the six money-saving ideas.

- Create new future wealth and present cash for yourself and your family by knowing when to refinance your home mortgage.

- Earn extra income to increase cash flow, in surprising as well as obvious ways.

- Start your own home-based business, or other business enterprise.

Lead Us Out of Temptation: Dealing with Debt

In This Chapter

- Learn how to determine whether you have a debt problem, and if you do, where to get help.

- Learn the difference between good debt and bad debt.

- Learn how to get out of bad debt—*completely and forever*.

- Learn the mechanics of reducing your debt.

- Learn the critical role of credit bureaus in your life.

THE DEMONS WE FACE IN OUR LIVES
. . . .

El que nada debe nada teme.

There are three financial demons that we all face:

1　Taxes

2　Inflation, and

3　Debt

They threaten to eat up the wealth that we might otherwise have for ourselves and our families. The first two, however, differ fundamentally from the last, in that the government directly imposes them. We cannot do very much about them. The last one we impose upon ourselves. Unlike the first two, which we always recognize for what they are, this third demon possesses a real allure: Just look at all the wonderful things we can have right now, rather than having to wait until we can pay for them! "Pay for it as you use it!" "Have it now!" "Enjoy life!" "Delay payments!" These become promises that merely mark our path down a slippery slope. They lead to a big trap, and then, the demon shows his real colors—*blood red*. The slide into the bog of debt always begins when we refuse to see the real harm of it.

TIP

Never shop with a friend who is a bigger spender than you.

Sad to say, we Latinos face greater danger from the debt demon than do most other Americans. Why? First of all, we usually face bigger barriers in obtaining credit: We frequently have lower incomes, immigrant status, and less knowledge about how to obtain credit. We also see seemingly wealthy Americans buying wonderful things with credit cards, so we tend to see the world of credit as a brave new world that we want to enter. Like everyone, we can become easily hooked on the American consumer culture, and because we tend to have lower incomes, less experience handling credit, less knowledge of alternative behaviors to credit purchases, and fewer assets to fall back upon, we can easily get into big trouble.

PUSHING THE DOWN BUTTON

The real problem with debt is not the money that we borrowed; it is the *interest* on it. Think back to Chapter Five. There you learned that compound interest works like a high-speed elevator in a skyscraper: it can zoom you quickly to the top. Do you know what else a financial elevator can do? It can take you just as fast, or even faster, to the basement. Just push the down button. That's what you do when you take on debt foolishly. You begin to *pay* interest, rather than earn it—and very likely at *three times* the interest rate. If you do not pay the interest due each month, the unpaid interest compounds, and your debt grows bigger, just like a cancer out of control. How much out of control? Remember, by the Rule of 72, at let's say 18 percent, your money would double in just four years. But with credit cards, it's not your money that's doubling so fast, it's your debts!

Let me give you an even more graphic example of what is called the *negative power of compound interest*. A $1,500 car repair bill placed on a credit card at a 19.8 percent annual rate will take 22 years to pay off if you only make the minimum payment each month. Let's face it, by the time you pay off such a loan in this manner, the car that you had fixed will be long dead!

TIP

> Buy a car that is two or three years old. You'll save because it's suffered its greatest depreciation. By the same token, buy the smallest house on your street. It will be easier to sell than the most expensive house on the street.

Reality Check: What's Your Relationship to Debt?

Let's do a little reality check. Everybody has some relationship to debt. Like all relationships, it may be a healthy one, so-so, or really sick. The debt demon, then, is really a sickness. People tend to fall into one of these three categories. We either:

- Have enough cash flow and/or wealth, and don't worry about debt,

- Have an uneasy relationship to debt, fearing that it may get out of control, or

- Have become overwhelmed, buried, by debt.

Where do *you* fall?

Most of us probably fall into one of the last two categories, which means that we tend to live our lives centered around concerns over debt. Wouldn't it be nice to join the people in category one: those who don't worry about debt? That's what this chapter of *¡Sí!, Se Puede* is all about—treating a developing or real sickness. Of course, before a sickness can be treated, it must be diagnosed.

When we start to run into trouble over debts, we're often the last to know. The reality of our growing difficulty becomes so unpleasant that we'd rather not face it. If you're uncertain about where you stand in your relationship to debt, take a look at this list of symptoms for trouble with debt.

Symptoms for Diagnosing Debt Disease

Patient shows the following symptoms:

- Avoids opening letters or bills.
- Avoids balancing checkbook on a regular, monthly basis.
- Fails to pay bills.
- Puts only a minimum amount down on new purchases.
- Takes frequent cash advances on credit cards.
- Shows expanding balances at department stores.
- Uses multiple credit cards showing frequent overdue amounts.
- Has a history of canceled overdue accounts.
- Displays ignorance of money matters.
- Has no savings or investment accounts.
- Bounces checks regularly.
- Borrows from one account to pay another.
- Makes only minimum payments on accounts.
- Receives letters from collection agencies on a regular basis.

None of these symptoms appear very pleasant to live with. But remember, a good diagnosis is the first step to a complete cure! We all need to reach a point of total honesty about our debts. Only then can we begin to take the proper remedial actions that can free us from the threat of a cancer that can literally eat us alive. The beginning point for reaching complete clarity about our current relationship to debts is looking at parts of the personal inventory that we've already completed in Chapter Six—the personal balance sheet and income statement.

TIP

Carry only one credit card. Pay with cash as often as possible. You're more likely to spend less and just buy what you need.

Putting Debt into Perspective

A cancer is just a normal living cell that has run out of control. Strange as it may sound to you, *there is such a thing as good debt!* There is also such a thing as bad debt—debt that has run out of control. To put your present debts into proper perspective, begin by going to your personal balance sheet. From there, list all of your debts by category and amount. Your categories may include such things as:

Mortgage

School loan

Auto loan

Home improvement loan

Home equity loan

Store charge accounts (list them individually)

Credit card charge accounts (list them individually)

As you write down each category and amount down, put it into one of two columns—"Good Debts" or "Bad Debts."

How do you know which column each debt belongs in? Let's begin with definitions for these two kinds of debt. *Good debt is investment-related borrowing. It is debt secured, or backed up, by some asset. Bad debt is everything else.* Your home mortgage is secured by your house; your auto loan is secured by your car. What about your school loan, if you have one? That is investment-related debt—secured by your increased ability to compete in the job market and earn more money. You can actually calculate the "return" on a college degree by comparing the average lifetime earnings of a college graduate to those of a nongraduate. The result will astound you. If your home improvement or home equity loan has increased your assets, then it is a good debt as well. *All other debts are bad.*

Good debts are "good" for just one reason: They allow you to gain an asset that earns you a return—so that the return on the asset offsets the interest you must pay on the loan. For instance, your house goes up in value, most of the time, and that gain helps offset the interest you pay. What about your car? It goes *down* in value each year. Yes, but it allows you to be more efficient in your job and career—so that even though it depreciates, your money earnings appreciate because of it. If you borrow money for a car that is strictly used for pleasure, it is bad debt.

So go ahead and list each debt that you have in the proper column. Next to each debt account, write down the amount owed, the interest rate, and the minimum monthly payment. If you currently make a larger-than-minimum monthly payment, write that down as well. Last, total up both your good debts and your bad debts—both the amounts owed and the monthly payments. Your good debts should exceed your bad debts. If not, it is a big trouble sign.

Did You Know?/¿Sabía Usted?

You've heard the pitch, "Own your own home? Need cash?" Home equity loans have become a flexible means for homeowners to get their hands on cash, but remember that they are really a second house mortgage.

Home equity loans involve borrowing against your home's equity. You can take the money in a lump sum or use a credit card or checks to slowly draw down the amount of equity. The money is considered a loan, and the interest is usually lower—perhaps by as much as one or two percentage points—than it would be for a routine personal loan. Some lenders will even lend at prime rate. Sounds like a great deal, but there are pitfalls. Remember, you are using your home as collateral on the loan. This may make sense if you're house-rich and cash-poor, but if you lose your job, encounter unforeseen expenses, or overextend yourself and can't repay the loan as planned, you could lose your home.

Really need that cruise? You should consider how you plan to use the money before taking out a home equity credit line. Avoid unnecessary purchases, which can slowly erode the lifetime equity in your home. Is a vacation really worth putting your house on the line? Would you take out a personal loan to go on the same vacation?

Forget the smoke and mirrors. When it's payment time, your house is going to cost more if you borrow money by taking out an equity loan. Even those deals that consolidate your monthly payments so that you'll pay less each month don't tell the whole story. What lenders fail to mention is that you'll be making payments for a longer period of time, so your total interest payments will go up.

Did You Know?/¿Sabía Usted? (Cont.)

Sometimes you're better off starting over—and instead of taking out a separate home equity loan—refinancing the existing mortgage. This depends on the interest rate you are paying. If you bought your house when rates were high, and if the interest on your existing mortgage is lower than current rates, you should keep your mortgage. A rule of thumb has been that you shouldn't consider refinancing unless the current rate is two percentage points below what you are paying, but your situation is unique and you should consult with an advisor before refinancing. Also, see the refinancing tool in the appendix.

TIP

Rule of thumb: Monthly nonmortgage debt payments should not exceed 10 percent of *monthly gross income.*

Let's get more precise about how much debt you should have. A key measure is how much you are spending each month on *nonmortgage* debt. Your nonmortgage monthly debt payments should not exceed 10 percent of your monthly gross income. For instance, if you earn gross pay of $4,000 each month, you should not be paying out more than $400 on nonmortgage debt expense. Otherwise, you are diverting too much money from more productive uses—uses that could create future wealth for you.

What to Do If You've Pushed the Down Button

When you have dug yourself a hole in the ground, the first thing to do is stop digging.—Margaret Thatcher

Sadly, we can easily get overwhelmed with good ideas for saving and investing more money, while getting out of debt remains a wasteland. After all, lending institutions make a lot of money on our debt. It is not in their interest to tell us how to get out of debt, or how to avoid debt in the first place. The first thing to do if you've gotten yourself into too much bad debt is to stop getting any further into debt. Period. This can be the hardest thing in life for somebody hooked on debt. "Who is this guy kidding?" may well be the initial reaction. You see, debt can become a way of life.

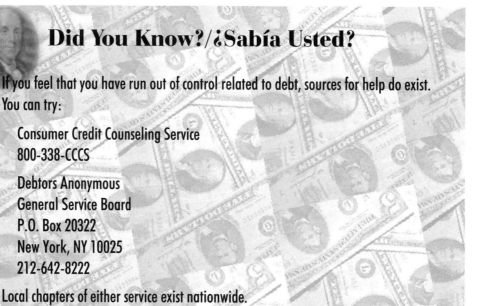

Did You Know?/¿Sabía Usted?

If you feel that you have run out of control related to debt, sources for help do exist. You can try:

Consumer Credit Counseling Service
800-338-CCCS

Debtors Anonymous
General Service Board
P.O. Box 20322
New York, NY 10025
212-642-8222

Local chapters of either service exist nationwide.

Try this experiment. Tomorrow, just for one day, don't dig yourself any deeper into debt. Don't use a credit card for anything; put the card(s) away somewhere at home before you go out. Don't accept any service or product that you cannot pay cash for. Don't use a store charge card. See how you feel at the day's end. You may surprise yourself and find that you feel elated. And you should. You've accomplished something very difficult. Now try it again, the next day. Then the next. And keep going. While you do this, record each cash expenditure that you make. Keep working on the spending plan that you began in Chapter Six. For the first time in a long time, you will begin to find your actual spending under control. You can make a month without overspending. You begin to experience financial freedom—and *choices* over how you spend your money. You begin to learn that you do not need to rely on debt.

TIP

> Save your bonus. You got along fine without it. Have it automatically deposited into your checking account, and then invest it in a money market or growth fund.

Just look what happens when you cease to rely on debt:

You will spend less. It will become less convenient to spend using a check or cash as your medium of payment, and your spending plan will determine what you actually buy.

Your total debt will shrink. When you stop digging yourself further into debt, each monthly payment that you make will actually reduce your overall indebtedness. You will soon find that you have more money than ever before.

You will feel great—in control of your financial situation. Your confidence and enthusiasm about your financial life will grow, perhaps daily.

Of course, enthusiasm and these early efforts at controlling your own money can easily wear off, and you can quickly become discouraged without some more powerful tools to help you carry on.

DEBT REDUCTION—THE MECHANICS OF HOW TO DO IT

Yes, it is possible to get completely, and forever, out of bad debt! Here's how. Begin by:

Restructuring your present debt. This means moving your debts out of higher interest accounts and into lower interest accounts. You can do this by:

- Shifting credit card balances to lower-rate cards
- Consolidating credit card and other high-interest loans into a single lower-rate loan through either a credit union or a home equity loan

Make one-time payments against your debt from proceeds of tax returns, sales of personal items, or savings.

TIP

Apply for a loan when interest rates fall. They cost less, and rates will eventually go back up.

Increase your monthly payments, even if only by $15 per month. This move works just like prepaying your mortgage to reduce your long-term interest payments—except that here you save 20 percent interest rather than something like 8 percent interest. This makes the impact very powerful indeed. For example, if you only make the minimum payment on a $3,000 credit card balance, it will take you over 30 years to pay off this debt! If, on the other hand, you add just $15 to each monthly payment, you will achieve a zero balance in 5 years. What a world of a difference!

 **TIP**

> Add just $25 a month to your mortgage check, and with a 30-year, eight percent mortgage, you'll save $23,337 over the life of the loan. Prepay $100 a month and you'll save around $62,000 in interest.

This represents one very simple, powerful means for reducing your debt to zero. Here's another:

In his book called *How to Get Out of Debt, Stay Out of Debt, and Live Prosperously,* Jerold Mundis comes up with the idea of "the ideal repayment plan." This plan gets constructed on the framework of the personal spending plan that we've already gone through in Chapter Six. As you will recall, the spending plan had you identify the specific categories of personal expenditure that each of us has and then assign a dollar amount to each category on a weekly and a monthly basis. The ideal repayment plan simply adds a new category to your spending plan—the debt repayment category.

Whether you owe $15,000 or $50,000, developing a repayment plan based upon what you can afford to pay down within your spending plan will provide you with discipline and a structure for controlling your debt. In this plan, you determine a repayment amount that equals what you now pay creditors plus your surplus cash. The spending plan helps you identify where you can come up with free cash; in the ideal repayment plan, you develop an efficient way to spread that cash over your various debt accounts. Here's an example of how this plan can work:

Get out your spending plan; the complete listing of your debts that you have already prepared; and a calculator, pad, and pencil. O.K.? Now:

Figure out how much you can pay toward your debts each month, without depriving yourself. Let's just say that you can find a way to direct $400 a month toward debt repayment.

List your creditors and the amounts that you owe them each month.

Add up your total debt.

Use a calculator to figure out each creditor's *share* of the total. The formula is: Creditor's Amount / Total Debt = Creditor's Share.

For example: Imagine that Jesús and Marta owe the following amounts:

Creditor's Amount	Divided by Total Debt		Share of Debt
Bank credit line	$5,000 / $10,750	×100 =	46%
Credit card	$3,000 / $10,750	× 100 =	33%
Store charge	$1,500 / $10,750	× 100 =	14%
Doctor's office	$750 / $10,750	× 100 =	7%
Total debt	$10,750		100%

Now multiply each creditor's share by the total amount that you can spend each month on loan repayment:

Creditor	Share	Of Total	Creditor's Repayment
Bank credit line	46%	$400	$184
Credit card	33%	$400	$132
Store charge	14%	$400	$56
Doctor's office	7%	$400	$28

Now begin to pay each creditor this payment each month.

Notice these important features of the ideal (or proportionally balanced) repayment plan:

- It allows for a steady elimination of debt that is within your capacity to pay.

- It is fair to all creditors.

- It provides a share basis for making additional payments as money becomes available.

Hopefully, the total amount that you have available for debt repayment will exceed your monthly minimum amounts due. In the case of Jesús and Marta, their $4,800 annual loan repayment amount is more than double their $2,032 annual interest charges, calculated at 18.9 percent. In this happy case, keep paying the same monthly amount, and watch your debt disappear. Of course, sometimes life will not allow you to proportionally balance your repayments. Some of your debt accounts may be charging you sky-high interest; you may have past-due accounts; your telephone or electric bill may get cut off. In these cases, you have to adjust your repayment plan to meet these unpleasant realities. Whatever you do, *no more charging!*

When you get your debt reduction machinery running properly, you will next want to pay attention to your credit record. Why, you may wonder? Wasn't the idea of all of this to get on the road to eliminating debt? Yes, but remember that the debt that you wish to zero out is your bad debt—debt that is not investment-related for you. At some future time, you will find that you need to take on some good debt—such as the new or late model car that will get you to a better job on time. Then your credit record matters, because without a good credit record, you will find that you have to pay bad-debt interest rates for good-debt borrowings—because the financial industry still sees you as a credit risk.

Your Credit Record and What It Means

Your credit record shows your past performance on paying your bills. Credit records and something called "credit scoring" are being used more and more today—even for normal transactions and employment searches. For this reason, you must understand your own credit report and make sure that the information it contains is true. Your rating will become especially important if you are new to a community, recently divorced, or seeking credit in your own name for the first time. Your credit record comes from information put together by creditor subscribers—the department stores, banks, and other institutions that have issued you credit. These subscribers report to credit bureaus how much credit you have with them, how much you have used up, and how promptly you have paid your bills. Any company that you apply for credit with may get a copy of your credit report and use it to make a decision about your credit application.

A typical credit report will contain this information:

- Your name, current and previous addresses, Social Security number, year of birth, current and previous employers, and spouse's name if you are married

- A listing of your bank cards, charge accounts, and mortgages, including how long you have had them

- The date of your last payment for each account

- Your maximum credit lines on each account

- The current balances that you owe on each account

- Current payment status and amounts past due, if any, for each account

- The type of loan each account represents

- A delinquency record on payments

- Special problems—including repossessions in the past

- Court liens and judgments

- Your legal relationship to each account

- A listing of any disputes

- A listing of institutions that have requested copies of your credit report

Now it may seem to you that with all this detailed information being recorded, few mistakes would get made. Just the opposite happens to be the case. Your credit record can easily become distorted, due to a number of factors. The most important one is simply general accuracy.

Did You Know?/¿Sabía Usted?

Whether you are looking for a loan to expand your business, or just want to finance a car purchase, it is important to have a clean credit report.

Eight steps to beating a bad credit report:

1   Don't avoid bill collectors. Companies are interested in getting their money, not reporting you to a credit agency. If you can't pay a bill on time, call the company to see if you can work out a payment schedule.

2   Use your full name. Credit bureaus sometimes mix up credit information on people with similar names. To minimize the chance for error, use your full name, middle name included.

3   Check your credit before you go for a loan. Three to four weeks before meeting with a loan officer, contact one of the three major credit bureaus listed in this chapter for a copy of your report. Then fix any errors and address any issues. In addition to TRW, Equifax, and Trans Union, you can also check with:

Dun & Bradstreet, 800-333-0505

Experian (**www.experian.com**), 800-682-7654 (recorded information only)

800-422-4879 (if you've been denied credit)

800-353-0809 (to get off mailing lists)

The Federal Trade Commission (**www.ftc.gov**), 202-326-2222

Did You Know?/¿Sabía Usted? (cont.)

4   Check your credit three to four weeks before you go for a loan. Don't go to a credit doctor. The repair clinics you see advertised, especially on late night TV, are a scam. If there is inaccurate information on your credit report, you can remove it on your own.

5   Recheck your report. Errors have a way of coming back into your report, even after they have been "corrected." After having a mistake corrected, wait three months, then order another report.

6   Know the limit. All delinquent accounts must be removed from your credit report after seven years, except bankruptcies, which can stay on for ten years.

7   Ask why you were turned down. If you're denied credit, you have the right to ask the lender where they got the negative information on you.

8   Save your canceled checks for at least seven years. The only way to successfully dispute a company's contention that your payment was delinquent is to show proof.

Credit reports are produced by computers; errors can be made that a human observer would readily recognize, but that now slip through unseen. Billing disputes you may have gotten involved in that are not treated correctly also lead to errors. If you are a married woman, much of your credit performance may be reported, unlawfully, under your husband's name. In addition, many things that would normally show up on a credit report will not if some of the institutions that you do business with do not subscribe to a credit reporting system.

TIP

Never co-sign a loan unless you're willing and able to pay off the entire debt. If your partner defaults, you're left holding the payments. If you don't make them, the fact will go into your credit report and you could be sued for collection, or your wages could be garnished.

According to the Consumers Union, 48 percent of consumer credit reports are inaccurate! Nearly 20 percent contain significant errors that could adversely affect your access to additional credit. To check out your own credit report, you need to write the various individual credit bureaus, requesting copies. Three major credit bureaus exist today, and they do not share requests for information. So you must contact each separately. They are:

TRW

National Consumer Assistance Center
P.O. Box 949
Allen, Texas 75002-0949
800-682-7654
www.experian.com

Equifax Credit Information Services
P.O. Box 740241
Atlanta, Georgia 30374-6241
800-685-1111
www.equifax.com

Trans-Union Credit Information
Consumer Disclosure Center
P.O. Box 390
Springfield, Pennsylvania 19064
316-634-8440
www.tuc.com

You are automatically entitled to a copy of your credit report within 30 days of being denied credit. If you want a copy and have not been denied credit, the bureau may charge you a fee (up to $10).

If you find an error in your report, highlight it and attach an explanation for why it is an error. Send the original credit report back to the bureau with a request that they investigate and correct the error. Make sure to keep a copy of everything you send for your own records. If the credit bureau refuses to agree with you over the item that you challenge, you must then submit proof for why their records are incorrect and request that they make a correction. When your report gets corrected, make sure that the corrections are recorded at all three bureaus. If this sound like quite a lot of work, it is. On the other hand, credit record errors have become so common and so potentially harmful that everyone should update these records at least every few years.

TIP

Avoid credit clinics that charge hundreds of dollars. Use only a nonprofit consumer foundation for help with credit card debt problems.

Did You Know?/¿Sabía Usted?

Your teenager should know the value of a good credit history. The sooner your child starts to establish a good credit history, the easier it will be for him or her to have access to future bank loans. State regulations on giving credit to minors vary, but you should minimally be able to get your child a credit card. Remember that you are ultimately responsible for the debts, but teaching your child how to manage debt responsibly is a valuable lesson. Be sure to set the following guidelines:

- Let the card be used only for purchases agreed upon in advance.

- Set monthly limits to the amount your child can charge.

- Insist that she save all receipts of purchases.

- Require her to pay for credit purchases with earned income and to use her allowances for daily expenses. This builds in an incentive for a teenager to supplement income for major purchases.

From Debt Management to Wealth Creation

Chapter Three offered you a great way of thinking about your financial life—a holistic approach that links together the three areas or spheres of each person's financial world: *security* or *protection, growth,* and *debt.* Building your own powerful wealth creation engine demands that you make all three of these spheres work together efficiently. Two of these, security and growth, are positive spheres of influence; debt is a negative sphere of influence. And debt becomes the major reason why most Latinos' wealth creation engines do not run correctly. The malfunction usually comes from a lack of knowledge about the power of coordinating security, growth, and debt into one smoothly running machine.

To understand this relationship better, let's look at an example of how good debt management can lead to overall wealth maximization. To do this, we'll return to the situation of Jesús and Marta. Assume that they have a total nonmortgage debt of $10,750 that costs them $400 each month to serve, or keep current. They pay an 18.9 percent average interest rate on this debt.

Jesús and Marta also have savings and growth assets—a $10,000 CD (certificate of deposit) paying 4 percent, a money market account for $21,000 paying 5 percent, and a passbook savings account of $7,000 earning 2.5 percent. Their debt-to-savings position, then, is:

		Rate
Debts	$10,750	18.9%
Savings	$38,000	2.5–5%

They happen to have their CD with the same bank that has issued them their $5,000 credit line loan. Their debt–to–CD savings cash flow looks like this:

- A $10,000 CD at 4 percent pays Jesús and Marta $400 each year.

- $10,750 in loans at 18.9 percent cost Jesús and Marta $2,032 each year.

A simple and effective holistic strategy would be for them to use the CD to pay off their loans. Then they can take the $1,632 net gain ($2,032 less $400 in lost CD interest) they make in their first year and invest it for long-term growth. Better yet, they can now take the $400 per month that they used to use to pay down their loans and invest that long term. If they invest $400 per month for twenty years at an average eight percent return, they will then have $237,230 for retirement or other purposes. On the other hand, the reinvested CD would have only grown to $21,910 over the same 20 years. Look at the results from this very simple strategy:

Jesús and Marta's 4 percent CD has in effect been turned into an 18.9 percent account—simply by paying off high-interest debt, thereby saving many thousands of dollars in interest payments.

Jesús and Marta take back control of $400 per month of their own income, instead of turning it over to creditors. That regained control will be worth $237,000 in the future.

They have also learned an important lesson in life: All aspects of your financial life need to be coordinated and integrated for maximum wealth generation. Strategies that benefit financial institutions do not necessarily benefit us. Notice that it is possible to make a 4 percent CD earn 18.9 percent—without any sleight of hand. The potential cost of not using their money effectively came out for Jesús and Marta at $215,000 over 20 years. It could be even greater for you.

Surprisingly, many of my Latino clients make just this sort of basic financial error. Jesús and Marta are by no means "deadbeats." They have a good general financial position, yet this one mistake was costing them many thousands of dollars. What about you? If you have high-interest-rate consumer debt and also low-interest savings accounts, look closely at what paying off debt with savings could do for you. *¡Sí!, se puede!*

TIP

Get Smart (**www.getsmart.com**) offers information on credit card and home mortgage deals, as well as mutual funds.

SLAYING THE DEBT DEMON— STARTING RIGHT NOW

Sit down today and use my simple method for determining how badly the debt demon threatens you:

- Identify how much good debt versus bad debt you have.

- Begin to get out of bad debt today.

- Develop a system for getting out of bad debt forever.

- Make your credit report work for you, not against you.

Making Your Savings Accounts Perform like Financial Elevators

In This Chapter

- Learn how traditional savings accounts work as wealth *reducers*.

- Learn the real reason for having savings, and how much you need.

- Understand the features of the various savings products that you can put your money into.

- Learn how to gain one percent more on your savings without increasing your risk.

- Read about five yield-enhancing strategies to increase your savings rate of return.

El que guarda siempre encuentra.

Let's go on now from the debt sphere and begin looking at the most basic thing that we all do related to both the security and growth spheres of our personal financial lives: *saving*. It turns out that we will always feel some conflict over how we handle our savings. Why? We would like two things at the same time: security and high earnings on our money. Unfortunately, the way the world is, these two desires cannot be fully met at the same time. Either we choose security and give up some earnings, or we choose higher earnings and give up some security. In this chapter you will learn something about the fine art of balancing these two desires, to get the best of two different worlds.

CHARITY FOR YOUR LOCAL BANK

Each year, I advise many Latinos about financial matters. I am still astounded at how many of these good people have chosen to make charitable contributions to their local bankers. *You may very well engage in the same activity—helping out your local bank, at the expense of your family and yourself.* These Latino contributions to banks are made *unknowingly*; we don't even realize that we give many millions of dollars to bankers every year—for free. How can this be?

Whenever you put your hard-earned money into a conventional savings account at a bank, you make that bank a gift. Of what sort? Your gift is the difference between the passbook or statement savings account interest rate and the next lowest yielding savings instrument, a competitive money market account. How big is your gift? It's currently the difference between approximately two percent and five percent, or a gift of about three percent on your money to your banker every year—small cheese, until you remember that at three percent, your money would double in 24 years. Sadly, many Latino people have made three percent gifts to their bankers for time periods this long. They have lost, badly.

It's not just Latinos that make these free gifts to bankers. In the United States today, in spite of the great numbers of mutual funds and other higher-yielding investments available, Americans still have over $1.3 trillion in low-yielding savings accounts—making a gift to banks of some $80 billion or so each year! Do the bankers love us? You bet! When we lend them our money cheaply, they can lend it at competitive rates and make a lot of money on the difference—the "spread" as it's called. When a bank can pay us two to three percent for our money and lend it out at as much as twenty-one percent, the shareholders rejoice. They're getting rich. But what about us?

We Latinos, unfortunately, are far more likely than the average American to put money into low-yielding savings accounts. Why? We do not like risk; we are what is called risk averse. We tend not to be very well-informed about various forms of savings accounts. We like the convenience of shopping at a local bank, just as we shop at small, local "mom and pop" stores. We confuse a familiar face at our local bank—perhaps a Latino face—with security. Large banks and other financial institutions, perhaps out of town or out of state from us, will pay us much more for the use of our money, but we often do not see this. So we lose out. I believe that when Latinos realize just how big our losses are, we will begin to change. So let's look at the *full* cost to us of these gifts to bankers.

What is the full, or *real*, cost of putting your money out at passbook savings account rates? During April 1998, the passbook savings account

Did You Know?/¿Sabía Usted?

Banks make a lot of money selling you blank checks. If you are buying them from your bank, you may be paying double or more what you could be. Checks In The Mail, P.O. Box 7802, Irwindale, CA 91706 (800-733-4443), has interesting designs and offers a full line of computer checks. You can get 300 checks and 200 deposit slips for under $40—a big savings when you consider that some banks charge $70 or more.

rate has been about 2.5 percent. Not a great gain, but things get worse when the demons of taxation and inflation finish their work. Let's use 28 percent for the overall tax rate on your savings and 2 percent for the inflation rate in the economy. The real gain is now not 2.5 percent but rather a *loss* of 0.20 percent. Here's the simple calculation:

2.5% minus 28% of 2.5%, or 0.70%, equals *1.8%* (the loss from taxes). 1.8% minus 2% equals *0.2%* (the loss from inflation).

Some of us lose 0.2% every year for many years. No wonder the bankers love us. We are so generous to them.

What if instead of putting our money away in savings accounts, we were to put money into certificates of deposit (CDs), an equally safe investment but one paying about three percent more than a passbook account? What would be our gain? Again, let's do the simple calculation:

5.5% minus 28% of 5.5%, or 1.5%, equals *4.0%* (the loss from taxes). 4.0% minus 2.0% equals *2.0%* (the loss from inflation).

Now instead of losing 0.3%, we're gaining 2.0%. What would be the effect upon an initial $10,000 if we left it in each of these investments for, let's say, 30 years? Well, invested at a real rate of 2.0%, $10,000 would become just under $20,000 in 30 years. (Remember the Rule of 72.) Invested at a real rate of –2.0%, the same $10,000 would be worth only $9,138 in 30 years. We'd lose some $11,000 over an equally safe, very conservative investment. That's big cheese.

In what follows, I'll give you the right information, so that you can make the most of the money that you feel you have to keep in banks.

If you have more than $100,000 in a combined savings and checking account, do business with more than one bank. FDIC insurance only covers bank accounts up to $100,000.

And watch out for bank mergers. If you have accounts at two banks that merge, only $100,000 will be protected after six months. Move any amount over $100,000 to another bank, or open an account in the same bank in the name of another family member.

WHY HAVE SAVINGS ACCOUNTS?

If savings accounts are such a bad deal, why have them? Whatever you do, don't jump to the conclusion that the act of saving money is a bad thing.

That would spell financial ruin in the long run. What we need to do is determine how much of our total money savings we need to have in savings accounts—and how much we can instead put into other investments that earn us bigger returns.

Why do we have savings accounts? Each one of us will give our own reasons, of course, but people generally put money into these accounts for the following reasons:

- Security, or protection from loss (FDIC insurance)

- Liquidity, or ready access to our money

- Yield, or an interest rate greater than that earned by cash (which is zero)

These are worthy reasons. They do raise one big question, however: How can I get the most yield, while still having the security and liquidity that I desire?

TIP

Simple interest is not the same as annual effective yield. Simple interest is the annual rate without compounding, while the annual effective yield is the return after compounding. For example, a one-year five percent CD has a simple yield of 5% and an annual effective yield of 5.13%.

To answer this question, we need to look at the *uses* that people generally make of their savings accounts:

- Emergency funds

- Savings for large purchases

- A temporary place to put spare cash

- Long-term savings

Let's examine these uses.

Emergencies that require money in a hurry can, and sadly often do, happen to us all—injury, illness, job loss, uninsured property loss, unexpected bills for services. Some form of savings account makes sense to cover these unexpected needs. By keeping an amount of liquid savings equal to two to three months' normal income available at all times, you secure yourself and your family against real hardship should something happen to you or your job. If we assume that Jesús and Marta together earn $75,000 per year, they should reserve $12,000 to $18,000 in short-term savings as insurance against an emergency—job loss. That way, all lesser emergencies will also be covered. What they should not do is accept an interest rate on all this money that loses them money—and makes a gift to the bank. Bankers should have to work for their money, too.

TIP

Rule of Thumb: You should at all times hold readily available money equal to two to three months' income.

Let's take a look at the ways that you can earn more interest on the money that you feel you *must* hold in secure, liquid accounts. Any money that you do not feel that you absolutely must hold in this form should be invested in the growth sphere of your overall financial plan. We'll talk about what to do with the rest in later chapters of this book.

MAKING THE BANKERS EARN THEIR MONEY
··

The first thing to do when making any economic decision is to know what your choices are; then, you can choose the best option in your given circumstance. What kind of choices do we have when we wish to get the best present yield or return on money that we must hold safe and liquid? Here's the list:

- *Passbook savings accounts*—the good, old-fashioned accounts that many of us grew up with

- *Statement savings accounts*—the good, old-fashioned way without the passbook

- *Money market accounts*—created in 1982 as a competitive alternative to the now old-fashioned accounts. They earn you a slice more interest and allow you to write a few checks against them. Handy items.

- *Certificates of Deposit (CDs)*—created by banks to encourage you to leave your money in longer, in return for more interest

- *Non-bank sources for CDs, such as brokerage houses*—which often pay more interest

- *Credit union savings accounts*—managed by membership-only nonprofit "banks," they both pay you more for your money and charge you less to borrow.

- *The U.S. Government*—through U.S. Treasury securities

By now you may be wondering how to go about choosing among all these options. Let's begin with a checklist of the things that you should watch out for while shopping:

- Interest rates (before compounding) and yield (after compounding)
- Fees that you may have to pay
- Minimum balance requirements
- Tiered interest rates (higher rates for larger balances)
- Per-check fees on money market accounts
- Federal deposit insurance protection

In addition to these basic things, you should also read the fine print on special offers; many high interest rate offers these days are really only marketing "come-ons"; they "tease" you with a high rate—which can suddenly evaporate in three to six months. Once you have informed yourself of the pitfalls to shopping for returns on savings, try out the following *yield enhancers*. See which savings strategy suits your needs and comfort level.

TIP

Be careful of high yields. The higher the yield, the greater the risk. High yields are designed to attract investors, who may be better informed about the potential risks.

Yield Enhancer #1: Cutting the Umbilical Cord to Your Local Bank

A *yield enhancer* is a rational strategy for increasing the interest that you actually earn on your savings—without sacrificing the security and liquidity that you feel you need. The first strategy for enhancing your yields is cutting the umbilical cord to your local bank. Just as cutting the real umbilical cord frees us from total dependence upon our mothers at birth, cutting the emotional umbilical cord to the bank that you have come to feel comfortable with becomes your first step to financial gain through smart investing.

Here's a question for you: If it is a good thing for big banks to cross city and state lines to buy up other banks, presumably a good deal for the banks, why isn't it a good thing for you? Remember, the banking marketplace is not the same everywhere. In some states or cities there is more demand for the bank loans that your savings deposits help support. Banks in those areas will pay more to use your money—perhaps as much as 2.5 percent more. Why not let them? This is what I mean by cutting the umbilical cord.

You may be thinking right now, "Isn't putting my money in a bank in another state riskier than keeping it right next door?" If this is troubling to you, you should know about something called the *Bank Rate Monitor,* a publication that lists institutions accepting out-of-state deposits and whose accounts have Federal Deposit Insurance Corporation (FDIC) protection against loss. Call 800-3277-7717 to obtain a copy of the *Monitor.*

The first yield enhancer, then, involves cutting loose from your local bank and shopping for higher interest rates—throughout the country. Where do I shop for rates, you may wonder? Try the financial section of either the *Wall Street Journal* or your city newspaper for a start. Or call and obtain the *Bank Rate Monitor*.

Yield Enhancer #2: Serving Time

Can you afford to lock your money up for some time—let's say three to twelve months? In return for serving time, a certificate of deposit will yield you a significantly higher interest rate. A certificate of deposit is merely an old-fashioned time deposit dressed up in a defined time period and higher rate: You choose how long you commit your money for, and the bank gives you a corresponding rate; the longer the time, the higher the rate. How much higher? According to the *Monitor*, CDs yield from two to four percent more than passbook savings accounts, the precise amount varying with the time you tie your money up for. In percentage terms, that means that you receive a rate about 100 percent higher.

Did You Know?/¿Sabía Usted?

With banks, almost everything is negotiable. Depending on your balances and volume of transactions, the bank officer can waive or lower fees or get you special handling and free services. Before setting up an account (or pay one more month's activity fee), sit down with your bank officer and ask what he or she will do to keep—or get—your business. Remember, if one bank isn't flexible, the next might be. Smaller, hungrier banks are usually the most willing to deal, as are banks that make a practice of catering to "middle markets" and small businesses.

Understanding CDs

Many people avoid CDs because of the early withdrawal penalty: If you need the money you put in a CD before it matures, you lose some interest. That's too bad, because CDs offer us some very good short-term savings gains. Let's look at all the terms that you need to know to invest intelligently in CDs:

- *Principle*—the amount of money that you wish to deposit into a CD
- *Term*—the period of time that you will lock your money up
- *Rate*—the interest rate that the bank will pay you
- *Maturity*—the date on which the CD matures
- *Early withdrawal penalty*—the bank's penalty to you if you want your money before the maturity date

Helpful Hints for CD Shoppers

Shop till you drop. Compare rates for different maturities at five or six banks, not just one or two. You will probably find rates varying by as much as 2.5 percent. This is not small cheese; on a $10,000 CD, 2.5 percent means an extra $250 in earned interest to you *each year*.

Do some interstate shopping. Just as bank money market rates vary geographically, so do CD rates. The *Bank Rate Monitor* provides you with CD rates just as it does for money market accounts. *Hint:* some cities pay higher interest, based upon their overall economic activity and the aggressiveness of their financial institutions. Shop for cities that are hungry for cash.

Set your objectives first. How much money do you want to invest? For how long? How safe do you feel about shopping away from home? In other words, know exactly what you want to buy before you ever begin shopping.

Yield Enhancer #3: Join a Union

Remember that the financial services industry is a big money game with many players. One group of players that you should pay attention to are the credit unions. Because credit unions are not-for-profit extensions of various organizations, they can put more of your money to work for you. They don't pay huge salaries to executives or indulge in fancy headquarters. Because they are more efficient, their rates on both deposits and loans will favor you—not the shareholders. Let's compare:

Institution	6-Month CD	1-Year CD	5-Year CD
Bank	4.54%	5.61%	6.68%
Credit Union	5.42%	6.17%	7.04%

The first thing that may come to your mind is, "But are they safe?" Most credit unions are insured by the National Credit Union Share Insurance Fund, a federal agency that insures deposits in the same way as the FDIC. So, yes, they are safe.

TIP

Compared to many banks, credit unions pay higher rates on savings accounts, charge less for loans, have lower fees, and work harder to help their customers.

The next question is usually, how can I join one? This can sometimes involve a search. With a few exceptions, credit unions have restricted eligibility for membership. Nearly all of them are sponsored by an employer or an association, with membership restricted to employees or association members and their immediate families. Municipal employees usually have access to one, as do employees of major Fortune 500 companies. Some educational and religious organizations may also have access to credit unions. Search around to find out if you may be eligible to join one.

Yield Enhancer #4: Playing Advanced Strategies in the CD Market

You may have determined that you would like to play the CD game, but you feel uncertain as to:

- How long you can afford to lock your money up in a single CD, or

- How long you should lock your money up for, given interest rate changes

Notice that these are not the same concern. Some people worry that if they lock their money up too long, they may need some of it and have to pay a penalty. Other people worry that if they lock their money up too long, interest rates will go up, and they will lose out on bigger gains. Here's a simple strategy that will minimize your risks. It's called "laddering," and this is how you play the game.

TIP

Buy CDs through a stockbroker. Brokerage firms shop the nation's banks and get much higher rates than what individual banks offer.

Let's say that you have $10,000 in emergency funds that you wish to earn a decent return on. You are concerned both that you might need some of the money in the near future and that interest rates may be going up. Here's what you do:

Principle Amount	CD Length to Maturity
$2,500	3 months
$2,500	6 months
$2,500	1 year
$2,500	2 years

You buy four CDs with varying lengths to maturity, instead of a single CD with a "guestimate" for a best single maturity date. As your individual CD accounts mature, you can now either use $2,500 for some necessary expenditure or reinvest in a new three- or six-month CD—whatever length to maturity keeps your portfolio of maturity dates nicely spread out. What have you gained?

Flexibility. Now you are not locking up all of your money for a set time. You can move money to different accounts paying more interest when each CD comes due. You also have short-term access to some of your money should you need it.

Reduced interest rate risk. You reduce your likelihood of getting caught in a long-term CD when interest rates are moving up. You also reduce your interest rate losses when rates start to fall.

Few people know this simple strategy for avoiding losses while investing in CDs. With it, you can have the best of both worlds—fairly ready access to cash with no penalty and maximum secure returns.

Try this single strategy and you will generate a gain many times the cost of this book.

Yield Enhancer #5: Going beyond Banks

The Federal Government offers another set of options for savers. When most of us think about saving through the government, we think of the Savings Bonds we may have been given as a child or have gotten through payroll deductions at work. That's a bit unfortunate, because the government offers us many more choices than just Savings Bonds. Let's take a look at each, beginning with the one you probably know best—the Savings Bond.

Savings Bonds are special obligations of the U.S. Treasury; they have been developed to meet the needs of small savers. As it turns out, there is both good news and bad news about Savings Bonds. First, the good news. You can buy them in amounts as small as $25. That makes them a great way to get into the habit of saving. That is why many parents and relatives give them to young children. The bonds teach children about saving for the future. Unfortunately, Savings Bonds do not offer very good long-term savings results: They do not yield enough interest over time. I have had clients whose children have held as much as $20,000, $40,000, or even $50,000 in Savings Bonds. That's good news in that those amounts of money will certainly help with college costs; it's bad news in that the same amounts invested for better returns would have as much as doubled their children's savings for college. Many Americans buy Savings Bonds by payroll deduction at work. Again, they offer such savers convenience at the cost of poor long-term investment results.

TIP

Investing in EE Savings Bonds is safe. There is no fee to buy or redeem, and you'll never pay state or local taxes on the interest earned. Start with just $25 at your local bank or through payroll deduction.

What's the yield enhancer here? The Savings Bonds that children get for birthdays, Christmas, graduations, confirmations, first communions, and other wonderful occasions need to get reinvested and put to work to earn those children more money for the future.

Hints for Optimizing Investments

When the Producer Price Index moves up, interest rates will rise because the Federal Reserve will tighten money in order to keep inflation down. When this occurs, consider buying long-term CDs, bonds, and Treasuries.

When new business starts are up, the economy is healthy, so get out of money market funds and CDs and into growth stocks. When business failures are up, interest rates typically are high and the economy will trend down. Consider yields on CDs, Treasuries, and A-rated corporate bonds and move into recession-proof stocks such as food, beverages, and utilities.

When interest rates are high, lock in yields on long-term CDs, Treasuries, and bonds. Rates will eventually drop.

Now let's continue looking at government obligations. Besides Savings Bonds, you should also know something about *Treasury Bills, Treasury Notes,* and *Treasury Bonds.* Each of these government obligations gives you somewhat different benefits, but they all give you matchless security against nominal losses of your money.

Treasury Bills are very short-term investments that you can make. They mature in three months, six months, or one year. They have a big drawback for us, however. They come in $10,000 minimum amounts. They also work like Savings Bonds in that they pay interest at their maturity.

Treasury Notes, on the other hand, mature in longer periods—two, three, four, five, seven, or ten years. Here the minimum investment is much less—$5,000 for two- and three-year notes and $1,000 for longer terms. Notes of different maturities are actually auctioned off by the Treasury at different times, depending upon the government's needs for money and favorable interest rates to it.

When considering short- to medium-term investments, let's say up to five years, you really should compare the rates earned by these Treasury instruments to bank CD offerings. Which gives you better returns for your money, as well as better overall benefits? What other benefits should you compare, you may wonder? Government securities are the safest; holding them to maturity, you can never lose your principle or not receive all interest due you. If you wish to sell them prior to maturity, however, their price will vary with the prevailing interest rates: When interest rates go up, the market value of your government holdings go down—because nobody will pay you the same amount you bought in at, when they can now get a higher-interest-rate bond at the same price. This is called the inverse price-yield relationship, and it holds for all fixed-rate investments, including Treasury Bonds.

Treasury Bonds have the longest maturities of any government obligations—up to 30 years. The 30-year Treasury Bond is in fact the bellwether for long-term interest rates. News broadcasters frequently quote its latest interest rate as an indicator of the general direction for long-term rates. The minimum investment here is $1,000.

Treasury Bonds have some drawbacks as long-term investments. They suffer from having the same inverse price-yield relationship as do shorter-term treasury obligations—only worse. You see, the longer the maturity date for a bond, the greater its price will change when interest rates change. The time to maturity works like a magnifier. Time magnifies the price change from a given interest rate change. Of course, if you plan on holding your bonds to maturity, this isn't a problem. Like all government obligations, you do get all your money back upon redemption at maturity.

What's the yield enhancer here? Well, generally speaking, the longer you can commit your money for, the higher the interest rate you will earn. So if you wish to do some long-term savings, and you will not need the money until the maturity date, long-term government bonds provide absolute safety and decent guaranteed returns for savers. If you do not wish to take any chances with your long-term savings, government bonds can be ideal for you.

One last matter. You do not have to go to a Federal Reserve bank and buy these obligations. It may be much better, and more convenient for you, to shop for a mutual fund that holds only government debt. Now you are not limited by the minimum dollar requirements of individual bonds. Instead, you *buy a small share in a mix, or portfolio, of many bonds of differing maturities*. And you can do your shopping over the telephone, or on the Internet if you know how to do this. The value of your mutual fund investment can change over time with interest rates; but the change may be less dramatic than if you held, for instance, a single 30-year Treasury Bond.

RULES FOR DEALING WISELY WITH YOUR SAVINGS MONEY
....

- Cut the umbilical cord to your local bank. Instead search the market for good deals, anywhere.

- Consider putting some of your money out for longer time periods to get a higher interest rate.

- Join a credit union for higher savings rates—and lower loan rates.

- Ladder your CDs to reduce risk and maximize return.

- Talk to brokers about higher-yielding CDs.

- See what rates Uncle Sam will give you to lend him money.

Using Financial Elevators for Your Own Protection

In This Chapter

- See how insurance products not only protect your wealth but help you to maximize it as well.

- Finally understand how to make sense out of your auto and homeowners insurance policies.

- Understand the value of the greatest asset you possess, and how to protect it.

- Realize the cost to your family of not having a will.

- See how life insurance actually contributes to your wealth creation and to the good things in life *while you live*.

NEXT TO DEATH AND TAXES
....

Es peligroso estar vivo.

Next to death and taxes, the matter we're taking up next is the most unpleasant subject imaginable for many Latinos, and Americans generally. Just mention the word "insurance," and people's eyes glaze over. It's all captured in that classic expression: "Life insurance! What's in it for me? It's only good when you die!" It doesn't have to be this way. *Properly understood, insurance, of all types, can become one of the best friends you'll ever make.* Here's why.

The real villain in this story happens not to be insurance at all! Insurance is the *hero* of the story, the white knight in shining armor. What most of us really resent is not insurance and its cost, but rather the harms that sometimes befall us in life itself—job loss, painful illness, auto or home accidents, fires and thefts, and yes, death. We see all of these things as somehow cheating us. Then we perceive insurance *against* the financial losses from such catastrophes as being the message bearer of bad tidings, reminders that what we seek to insure ourselves against could in fact happen. When we become evasive about insurance coverage or angry about its cost, all we are doing is slaying the messenger.

TIP

Some life insurance companies, in an attempt to lure nervous travelers, sell special limited-term policies to cover airline travelers. Forget it. For one thing, you should already have enough life insurance, and this policy should cover you no matter when or how you die. If you still want additional protection, buy your ticket with a credit card. Many credit card companies provide free life insurance to cardholders who purchase their tickets with their card.

Let's look at insurance from another point of view, *bravely*. Some bad things in life will happen to us all; there's no getting around that. The only real choice that we have is whether we want to suffer in comfort, or suffer even worse because we have become financially broke. *Insurance can eliminate the only bad thing in life that we can protect ourselves against with near certainty*—the financial pain accompanying the physical and emotional pain of real loss. And insurance can protect us from financial pain more efficiently than we can possibly protect ourselves without it.

The reason is simple: Almost none of us are independently wealthy. We cannot afford to protect ourselves against such things as income loss, medical bills, lawsuits, and property losses arising from life's big harms. We simply do not have enough money. Here comes the white knight to the rescue: For as little as a few hundred dollars a year, you can buy several hundred thousand dollars of pure financial protection, for both you and your family, against any of life's ills. Just think about that for a moment! How little you pay, really, for so much. That's because the same financial elevators that can make you wealthy can also make so much insurance money available to you.

How can this be? The insurance companies know that in any one year, the odds are highly stacked against anything really bad happening to you or your family. So the few hundred dollars you pay them gets invested, *earning compound interest*. Everybody else doing business with the insurance company is just like you—unlikely to have anything bad happen to them. So thanks to the miracle of compound interest, everybody's combined premiums earn huge amounts of money for insurance companies. The financial elevator goes shooting up the wealth skyscraper. Yes, sometimes bad things happen to people, and then the company pays out hundreds of thousands of dollars on their behalf—maybe even millions. But don't you see what a blessing that is for people in deep difficulty—perhaps you someday.

Essential Information (**www.essential.org**) is a site that will link you to Nader-founded consumer groups, including the Center for Auto Safety and the Center for Insurance Research.

Insurance Corner (**www.insurance-corner.com**) is aimed primarily at insurance agents but provides consumers some useful tips on buying auto, property, and long-term care insurance.

Consider one more thing about insurance: When we purchase enough of it, we need *less of our own money tied up* in low-yielding savings accounts—money held against emergencies. That means that we have more money to pour into the growth sphere of our own financial lives. Then our money shoots up the financial elevators, too, and eventually makes us rich. In this way, insurance premiums actually *earn* us money in the long run!

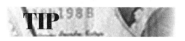

TIP

Bundle your insurance. If you get your homeowners and auto insurance from the same insurer, you'll save. Protect yourself. You'll save even more if you install a smoke detector and burglar alarm in your home, and a car alarm.

And They Lived Unhappily Ever After

Childhood fairy tales always end with the wonderful line, "and they lived happily ever after." That's only in fairy tales. Sadly, in life, the ending is sometimes: "And they lived *unhappily* ever after."

Once upon a time, Jesús and Marta were driving along a pretty road after having had dinner with some friends. The night was lovely, and they felt very happy and very much in love. As Jesús drove through the nasty intersection on the way home, a driver in a big, black car shot through the red light, and smashed into their little white car. It was just a flash of lights, a shriek of tortured steel—and everything went black for both Jesús and Marta. When they awoke from this nightmare, each one found himself or herself alone and in pain in a hospital bed. Neither one even knew if the other were still alive.

Both Jesús and Marta went through months of painful rehabilitation from this terrible accident. One year later, Marta still cannot completely care for her two young children at home, due to her lingering disability. Jesús's employer fortunately kept his job for him, and now he is able to work once more. But neither he nor his employer kept long-term disability insurance for him, so the family lost over six months' earned income. Their health insurance policy through the company ended up not covering total medical expenses.

When the full extent of their losses became apparent to them, they sought out the help of an accident claims lawyer, who assured them that they could sue the other party's insurance company for $250,000, based upon their lost income, medical bills, and stress upon their family. Unfortunately for them, the lawyer was wrong. The other party had been driving a twelve-year-old car and carried only the state-mandated minimum liability protection. Jesús and Marta could sue, but the most they could collect would be $25,000 each. In fact, the other driver's insurance company did pay them $50,000, but that still left them out a lot of money. Jesús and Marta had never before studied their auto insurance policy, but now they got it out and dug into its contents to find out if maybe they might have some options that would help them out. They found that they did—and so do you.

This story about Jesús and Marta is hypothetical, of course—but it happens to be very close to several experiences that friends of mine have had over the years. Similar stories happen to people every day. Tell me something, what would you find out if you were in their situation, and you just opened your auto policy and looked at the details for the first time?

Go ahead. Right now, get out your automobile insurance policy and look carefully at its declaration, or "dec," page, as we go ahead with this story. In the box below, you'll find out what each one of the items on your "dec" sheet means.

Bodily injury liability protects other persons against losses from any bodily harm you may cause them by driving negligently. Think for a moment what might happen to you if you *were* the driver of a car causing an accident. Without this protection, you could be *forced to sell most of your personal assets* to pay for the financial harms done to them. *What kind of coverage should you have to adequately protect yourself from this sort of personal financial disaster?* If you are married and own a home, the *absolute minimum* bodily injury liability protection that you should have is $300,000. Your ability to purchase higher amounts of protection depends upon your driving record, age, and the particular kind of risks each insurance company will assume. The cost for increasing your liability coverage will also depend upon your driving record, as well as your geographic location and each company's policy toward higher liability limits.

Property damage liability will pay for any property damage that you may cause related to an accident. Obviously, it will apply to the other driver's car—but also to such objects as buildings, fences, and utility poles that you may have the misfortune to contact. With the average price of a new automobile now over $22,000, and an increasing number of cars in the $30,000–$50,000 range, you really need quite a bit more coverage than the minimum. How much more? I would say at least $50,000, if not $100,000 as a minimum.

Medical payments covers the occupants of your own car. It will pay medical expenses resulting from an automobile accident regardless of which driver was at fault. In states with no-fault insurance provisions, drivers are required to purchase what is called personal injury protection (PIP) insurance, which covers not only medical bills but also lost wages, replacement services such as child care costs, and even some funeral expenses. Most states mandate a PIP of $10,000—but you can, and probably should, purchase additional PIP coverage of up to $50,000 or $100,000.

Uninsured motorists protection. If you get involved in an accident with an uninsured driver, the only source for recovery of your losses is the other driver's assets. But if he is driving without insurance, how likely do you think it is that he will have any assets that even come near the total of your losses? And you have the costs of suing to get those assets. That is a losing game. You must have this protection.

Back to Jesús and Marta

There is a form of protection closely related to uninsured motorist protection. It is called *underinsured* motorist protection. Now let's go back to the story about Jesús and Marta. They were involved in a serious accident in which the other driver carried only a $50,000 bodily injury liability limit. He was very underinsured compared to Jesús's and Marta's needs. When the two of them looked over their policy carefully, they discovered that their policy actually did provide under-insured motorist protection. They simply never knew it. In fact, they had this coverage up to the same maximum as their base bodily injury liability coverage—a $300,000 single limit.

Whoever sold them this auto insurance policy turned out to be one of the best friends they ever had. So the ending to this story is not all sad. Jesús and Marta found that their own insurance company willingly paid them for the difference between their actual losses and the other driver's bare-bones policy coverage.

You know, all fairy tales end with a lesson, or a moral. So does this story. *The moral is that your auto insurance policy in modern America is your first line of defense around your house and lifetime savings.* Too many of us fall into the trap of thinking that our auto insurance covers little more than the loss of a rapidly depreciating asset—the car itself. Wrong! That's small cheese. Your auto policy actually protects not so much your car as all of your largest, *appreciating* assets—home, saving accounts, retirement accounts, other investments, jewelry, and business assets. The next time that you write a check paying your auto policy premiums, think about this for a moment. You should feel far better about paying that premium.

Home, Sweet Home

The old song tells us that there is no place like home. Unfortunately, for some of us some day, there may be no home. It may burn down or be struck by a so-called "act of God"—a natural disaster. Or we may come home to find the house broken into and many things stolen. Nothing can prevent these nasty things from happening. Once more, all that we can do is protect ourselves against the financial losses from these harms. If you own a home with a mortgage upon it, the bank requires you to purchase homeowner's insurance—because in the event of a harm done to your house, the bank does not want to lose financially. By pushing you to have homeowner's insurance, the bank has done you a favor. Bankers are not bad people by any means—they are simply interested first in the well-being of the bank, just as we are interested in our family's well-being.

TIP

> To ensure a full settlement from your insurance company when you have a loss from fire, flood, earthquake, or theft, you should videotape your home and its contents, reciting on the tape the purchase price of major objects. Put the tape in a safe-deposit box. It can make up for lost records.

Did You Know?/¿Sabía Usted?

...how you can pay for higher liability limits if you're on a tight budget? Look at your policy deductibles—those relatively small sums that you will have to pay in an accident before your insurance company begins to pick up the tab. The truth of the matter is that insurance companies love you when you take a small deductible; the premiums that we pay for low deductibles are so profitable to them. Think about raising your collision and comprehensive deductibles to $500. Then take those big premium savings and invest them in higher liability limits. In return for your exposure to $500, you then receive several hundred thousand dollars of additional protection. That way, you get off a big hook and put your insurance company on the hook for all that additional protection.

The amount of homeowner's insurance that will satisfy the bank—protecting the bank's money—will not be enough to protect your money in your house. So every one of us needs to consider carefully just how much home protection we need. A homeowner's policy contains *five key components*, each protecting a different aspect of your wealth. Let's take a look at them, one at a time:

Coverage A applies to the actual structure of your house. It specifies the maximum amount of money the insurance company will pay you to rebuild your house, in the event of a major harm befalling it. Otherwise, you will be out a lot of money. This is why it is important to have something called *replacement cost coverage* in addition to your regular Coverage A. The replacement cost coverage will ensure that your insurance company pays those additional costs you incur due to the rising costs of rebuilding. This coverage works as a sort of cost of living adjustment on your policy.

TIP

How big should my Coverage A maximum be?
A good rule of thumb is a minimum of 80 percent of the current replacement value of your house!

Coverage B applies to the other structures on your property, such things as detached garages, swimming pools, storage sheds, and such. Usually Coverage B maximum protection amounts get stated on your policy as a percentage (usually ten percent) of the Coverage A maximum that you choose.

Coverage C protects you against losses of your personal property that you keep in your home and other structures on your property. This coverage also gets stated as a percentage of your Coverage A—usually either 40 percent, 50 percent, or 60 percent. This coverage will reimburse you for the actual *cash value* of personal property that you lose—*not what it would cost you to go out and buy a new item*. This is why it is so important to have your Coverage C be of the type that guarantees that you will be made whole in your losses—*replacement value coverage*.

Coverage E pays for medical bills that result from someone not in your own family getting injured on your property—up to a specified limit of from $1,000 to $5,000 depending upon the policy.

Coverage F applies to your personal responsibility for bodily injuries and property damage that you may cause to others. It includes coverage for any legal bills that you may run up if someone sues you for such injury or loss. The liability limits for this kind of coverage usually begin at $100,000; and go much higher. You may think that you do not need this coverage—after all, you have never harmed anyone or damaged anyone else's property. Sadly, today in America people very frequently sue other people for the most trivial things—or for things that we really are not responsible for at all. Because of this sad fact, I tell my homeowning clients that they should have at least $300,000 in personal liability coverage—better yet, $500,000.

Keeping Dry under an Umbrella

In America, it is sometimes said that when bad things happen, they "rain down" on us. Rather than getting rained on, we can stand under an umbrella—a financial protection umbrella. What is it? An insurance umbrella is something that spreads a huge cover of additional protection over all of your assets. You see, your automobile and homeowner's policies are only *first lines* of defense—adequate for normal bad circumstances, for keeping predators away. These policies themselves will not suffice when a really big financial threat comes your way. For these once-in-a-lifetime threats to our total financial well-being, we need excess liability insurance, in the form of what is called an umbrella policy. An umbrella policy creates an "El Morro"–like barrier between our assets and an otherwise fatally harmful lawsuit.

Umbrella liability coverage does this by increasing the normal coverage limits on our auto and homeowner's policies. Because this is serious protection money, umbrella policies *begin* with a $1 million maximum coverage amount—and then go up from there. If you need it, you can buy $2 million and $5 million umbrella policies. The same company that provides you—or "writes"—your auto policy usually will be willing to also "write" this policy for you. Why your auto policy? Well, you are far more likely to accidentally cause someone else a serious personal injury with your car than in your own home.

Umbrella policies cover only *personal* liability—that is, personal injury and damages to property caused by you, whether you meant to cause them or not. It may surprise you to learn that personal injury does not get limited to *physical* harms. Your umbrella policy covers you for such other personal harms as slander, libel, and the legal costs of defending yourself in a lawsuit.

Umbrella polices, as you can see, are a very good thing to have, once your personal financial planning efforts begin to pay off even modestly in the form of growing financial assets. The umbrella can keep you from losing all that you have struggled so hard to earn. And the amazing thing about an umbrella policy is that it often costs you very little.

How do you know whether you need an umbrella policy? As a general rule of thumb, if you own a home and have children, you should take a serious look at buying such a policy—especially if you have a child who is, or will be starting to, drive soon!

TIP

> If you own a house, have major assets, or serve on a nonprofit board, get an umbrella liability policy. You'll be protected from financial loss above your property/casualty coverage in case you're sued for damages. About $300 should buy you $1,000,000 in coverage.

AN ACTION PLAN FOR PERSONAL LIABILITY PROTECTION

Let's pull together everything that you've learned so far. Here's what you should do—a general action plan for your personal liability–related insurance protection:

- Review your existing auto policy for liability limits and for uninsured and underinsured motorist protection.

- Consider buying as much personal liability protection as you can under your existing auto policy, and offset the cost if you must by increasing your deductibles for comprehensive and collision coverages.

- Review your homeowner's policy. Make sure that the Coverage A maximum amount on your basic dwelling has kept up over the years with inflation. Remember, your Coverage A should equal *at least* 80 percent of the current replacement cost of your house itself. (If you are uncertain as to what the replacement cost would be, a good real estate agent may be able to help you, or you can contact a real estate appraisal specialist.) Make sure that your policy contains replacement cost guarantees on both your dwelling and your personal property! Also make sure that your liability protection is at least $300,000.

• Talk to your broker or auto insurance company sales representative about how much an umbrella policy would cost you. Have this person help you compare the costs of increasing your current policy limits to the cost of adding the additional protection of the umbrella policy.

Congratulations! You have now taken the steps necessary to protect yourself and your family from the risks of being sued. You're now ready to move on to the next big area of family wealth protection—the property right that you possess in the fruits of your own labor.

THE FRUITS OF OUR OWN LABOR

For the great majority of us, our greatest asset is our ability to get up each morning and head off to work. We are a people who work diligently; we do not rely upon the government to help us with either our expenses or a job. That means, in turn, that the loss of our power to earn money by working will hurt us even more than the average American. Yet most Latinos have only the most minimal protection in place for this most precious asset.

For a moment, think of yourself as a human money machine—a machine that spits out dollars for your personal financial system. You are like the heart of your financial system: All of the money you and your family earn and spend depends upon that heart keeping up its beat. How much money does your financial heart pump in a year, a lifetime? Well, a 30 year old with a college education or a good trade will easily earn an average of $50,000 over the next 35 years of work—or $1,750,000. That's a lot of money.

In fact, if you had a machine in your basement turning out $1 bills at the rate of 50,000 per year, you would probably want to make sure that it was well maintained and in good working order. You probably would insure it against loss and damage, just as you do your automobile. You might even buy a protection plan that would keep paying you the dollars your machine makes in the event that the machine should break down; that would be like the sort of business interruption insurance that pays you for lost income if your location floods or burns to the ground. Isn't it funny that so many of us would carefully protect that money machine in our basement, and worry so much about it, and still do nothing to protect the one real money machine that we all have—ourselves?

So you see, we have entered into another, even more important role for financial protection in each of our lives. Think about this. If you had no liability insurance at all and got sued for something, and then you lost all your assets, you could still go out and earn back everything you lost, by your own hard work. But if you lose your ability to go out and work, you can never recover from that loss—without some kind of personal "business interruption" insurance. Providing an income for yourself and your family in the event of an illness or injury that prevents you from working is the purpose of disability income insurance.

The Most Important Protection Anyone Can Own

Income disability insurance is the *most important* protection *anyone* can own, and also the form of protection that *most* people *do not have*. We

Latinos are even more exposed to this risk than the average adult American. Why? For a start, we are younger, have fewer assets to support us independently of our work, and lack access to the types of protection against earnings losses that most middle-class Americans take for granted. Remember, when we are young, we tend to think that we are immortal—that we will live forever, and nothing bad will happen to disable us. But that's a lie.

Ask yourself the following question: *If I could no longer go to work, starting tomorrow, how long could I afford to stay at home—and still maintain my present standard of living?* For many American families, life is lived *three months away from disaster.* That is because these families do not have adequate savings or income disability protection. The federal government reports that 48 percent of all bank foreclosures on homes come from disabilities that cause income loss. How about you? How well protected are you from income loss devastation?

Let's look at the sources of protection.

Worker's compensation protects you against financial loss coming from injuries that you sustain while on the job. Good news! If you work for someone else, your employer must pay for this coverage. If you work for yourself, however, you must pay for such coverage—and many self-employed people do not do so, so they do not have a primary shield against income loss. While worker's compensation programs vary from state to state, disability payments do go as high as two-thirds of your gross pay, up to a maximum.

Social Security disability. The federal retirement system includes a disability benefit plan, although it is small and usually so hard to qualify for that it offers very little real protection against income loss. In order to qualify, you need to be out of work for five months and so disabled that you cannot find any job. In addition, your doctor has to certify that your disability will last for at least one year or lead to your eventual death. As a result, two-thirds of applicants get turned down.

State disability funds. Certain states—including California, Hawaii, New Jersey, and Rhode Island, plus Puerto Rico—have their own state-run disability programs. These programs pay a very limited amount (New York, for instance has a $172 maximum per week) for up to 26 weeks.

Employer-paid group coverage. If you work for a large or medium-sized corporation, you may be provided with what is called group LTD— long-term disability coverage. Under most LTD plans, after a six-month waiting period, the insurance company will pay you about 60 percent of your base salary. LTD plans have a monthly maximum benefit, usually somewhere between $2,000 and $5,000. These plans, if you are fortunate to be covered by one of them, offer some clear benefits: You have coverage against income loss from long-term injury and illness, and you do not directly have to pay for it. Drawbacks? Any benefits you receive are taxable, so that the 60 percent of your salary that you receive gets reduced even more. Also, it is not portable: You do not own the coverage yourself, there is no conversion privilege, and you cannot take it with you if you should leave the company.

The Ins and Outs of Individual Disability Insurance

When you start to examine individual disability insurance, you discover something new immediately: Unlike the other types of policies that we've looked at so far, this one gets priced out on an *occupational* basis. *What you do for a living determines how much you pay.* Actually, a whole range of factors goes into pricing disability insurance, but occupation matters the most. The other factors include your age, your medical history, and the benefits you apply for.

What kinds of benefits do these individual insurance policies offer us?

- Premiums are level until age 65 (the rates will not change with age; they may, however, go up for everyone at renewal time, if the company's claims history warrants a general rate increase).

- Definitions of disability favor you, not the company.

- Portability: The policy goes with you no matter where you work.

- Renewal guarantees: The insurance company cannot simply cancel you when your policy comes due for renewal.

- Residual or partial disability protection: You do not have to be totally incapable of work to receive payments from your policy; you merely have to be unable to perform your current occupation or earn your current rate of pay.

- Benefits that you receive come to you tax free.

Clearly, these policies work in your favor when you need to claim benefits from them; of course, they should, because you pay for them.

Once More: How Much Is Enough?

The cruel reality is that once we become disabled and cannot earn income, our expenses still continue—except for some commuting costs. Not only that, we often find that we have totally new expenses hitting us—such as nonreimbursed medical care, medical equipment and rehabilitation, personal services such as housekeeping and child care, special transportation, nursing home care, and therapists. What's this simple answer, then, to how much coverage to buy? *As much as I can get.* Personally, I want as much as I can get, so that if I ever do become disabled, nothing will worry me except getting better and back to work. How do *you* feel about this?

Actually, it turns out that we can't just get any amount of coverage that we want. Our coverage will be limited by the insurance company to about 55–60 percent of our gross income. Some companies will take into account the commissions, bonuses, and overtime that you regularly earn, but 60 percent is still 60 percent. (Note that if you work for yourself and you file a Schedule C tax form, the most you can get becomes your net income after business expenses.) Even the most that you can get will not make you completely financially whole should you become disabled.

TIP

> Get COBRA. The Congressional Omnibus Budget Reconciliation Act (COBRA) permits you to keep your health insurance after you lose or leave your job. You need to fill out the form. If you leave, coverage runs for 18 months. If you are disabled, it runs for 29 months. It continues for 36 months in the event you become a widow or are divorced or if the company becomes bankrupt.

Going Ahead with Disability Protection

As you have probably realized by now, purchasing disability coverage has quite a few complexities. You may even wonder where to buy such a thing. We can now take up these two things: *where to buy*, and *what things to look out for?*

Individual disability income policies are sold by insurance agents and brokers. When it comes to such a complicated policy, however, not all salespeople are the same. Make sure that you deal with someone who has experience specifically with disability policies and who can recommend the most appropriate and *cost effective* policy for you. An expert in this field will know the ins and outs of these policies, including some pretty detailed terminology.

"Non-cancelable" means that the insurance company cannot make changes in your policy's benefits in the future, cannot raise the premium, and cannot cancel your coverage so long as you pay the premiums. The policy is guaranteed renewable each year, at the same level premium rate.

Own occupation versus income replacement. "Own-occ" policies insure you in your own occupation; if you cannot return to work in that occupation, you get paid even if you can work in another occupation. Income replacement policies will only pay for any loss in income.

Benefit period. The benefit period is the amount of time that you will receive benefits, after which the payments stop. Benefit periods usually run for two or five years, until age 65, or for life.

Elimination period. This period is the amount of time you need to wait before your benefits begin. These waiting periods include 30, 60, 90, 180, and 360 days. *The longer you can wait, the lower the rate.*

Residual/partial disability. Suppose you become only partially disabled, but you can still work half time? If you have a total disability policy, you will not receive any benefits. On the other hand, if you have a residual/partial disability policy, you will receive a benefit equal to your lost income from having to accept part-time work.

Waiver of premium benefit. If you become disabled, would you want to be able to stop paying premiums on your policy—and still collect the benefit to full term? Of course you would. Remember, your benefits after your disability will pay you only 60 percent of your income.

Inflation protection. This provision will index your benefit to a specific rate of inflation—usually three to five percent—or to the Consumer Price Index (CPI). It protects you from *long-term erosion* of your spending power while you are disabled. It appears as a very expensive rider to a policy—increasing your premium by 20–30%.

Future increase option. This rider gives you the right to purchase additional coverage in the future regardless of your health, as long as your income justifies it.

The following set of actions gives you the five essential steps to take to protect your income—which is, after all, your most important asset.

Steps to Protecting Your Income

- Find out how much coverage you can obtain, based upon your income and occupation.

- Review your other sources for income should you become disabled (Social Security, company-paid, and association-paid plans).

- Consult an experienced disability agent/broker about your particular needs.

- Compare benefit periods, waiting periods, own-occ definition versus income protection, waiver of premium, inflation protection, and future purchase options.

- Purchase the most base coverage that you can get, and focus on these most important riders: waiver of premium, residual benefits, future purchase options, and automatic increase options.

TIP

Get a disability policy that can't be canceled, has a residual benefit rider that lets you work part time or in a lower-paying job, and provides "own occupation" coverage. Get coverage for 70 percent of your income. You are much more likely to need disability insurance than life insurance.

TAKING A BIG STEP BEYOND DISABILITY

Now that we've gone through the complexities of disability insurance, we come to the last major area of protection for your family: what happens to family members should you suddenly die. This gets a little unpleasant, but remember, we agreed back some twenty pages ago to deal with these matter *bravely*. What I mean here is very simple: what will happen to *your* family should you die tomorrow? Or if you are married, what if both you and your spouse die tomorrow, leaving behind children? What would you want for them, should this tragedy occur?

Here's the place to begin—with a *will*. In my work over the years advising Latino clients, the single most glaring omission in their personal financial plans is a will—a "testamento" that becomes your instruction sheet to those you leave behind. Your will or testamento makes sure that your wishes are carried out and eliminates confusion, doubt, and delay.

TIP

Prepare a will. Update it every few years. Retirement, marriage, buying or selling a house, the birth of a child or grandchild, the death of a loved one, a move to a new state, divorce, or a change in health mean it's time to revise.

Think about it this way: *Everybody has a will!* Your will—what you desire for your family—may simply not be written down, but you know in your heart what you would wish for them. Then why not write it down? You see, without a written will, you have in effect given over the decision-making power in your family's life to the state. Literally, when you die "intestate" (without a will), you turn over your assets to the state's representative, usually a judge, to allocate as he or she deems appropriate. Parents have the added dimension of knowing that the state will determine your children's future as well. Do you want this?

Worse Luck for Jesús and Marta

What if Jesús and Marta both got killed driving home that night, instead of being severely injured? Their children happened to be with their abuelita when their car was struck by another vehicle driven by a drunk driver. Now what? As it turns out, Jesús and Marta have left no will. They had thought about having a will drawn up for years but somehow just never got around to it. Now, it is too late. They left behind two children ages 4 and 8, a large home (with a big mortgage), two cars, personal property, jewelry, retirement plan assets, bank accounts, some investments, family treasures, and a lot of memories for their children.

Without a will, look at what happens:

- A judge will decide who will be their children's guardian.

- Family conflicts may arise over who cares for the children and gets the assets to provide that care.

- There will be no guarantee that those assets will be properly managed for the children.

- Jewelry and family treasures may be given to the wrong people.

- There is little likelihood that any money will go to Marta's favorite charity, where she had spent many hours doing volunteer work.

- No one will think that the process is fair and just, and all their relatives and friends will wonder why Jesús and Marta did not plan ahead so as to avoid all these heartaches.

As we Latinos become more and more wealthy, *we simply must* take responsibility for ensuring that we *take control of the wealth we create.* That means control both while we live and after we die. A will empowers each one of us to determine what happens to our assets and prevents the state from assuming control of all that we have worked so hard to create. Consult an attorney for specific recommendations regarding your will.

TIP

Get a durable power of attorney that directs someone to run your finances if you become incapacitated. If you don't, a judge will decide who will.

One last thing. In Chapter 12, I will suggest to you that an important part of our personal wealth creation plan should be the activity of giving back something to our own community. Marta, for instance, in this story that I have just told you, very much wanted to do something for the local charity that she loved. Now it is too late, and that desire will die with her. A well-thought-out personal financial plan, updated regularly, can in this way become a future financial support for Latino organizations. We need this ongoing support within each local Latino community, and it can only come if we take the specific steps involved in putting these things into our legal wills. That way, we strengthen the bigger Latino family as well as secure our family's well-being.

Steps to Having a Working Will

If you do not yet have a will, contact a local lawyer to draw one up, or purchase legal software that will let you prepare one. Work through the following steps first. If, on the other hand, you have a will and it is more than *three years old,* review it for accuracy and consider carefully how well it still meets your current situation.

If you have children, have a serious discussion with your spouse about choosing a guardian for them in the event that both of you die. This will be emotionally draining for both of you, but you simply must do it if you wish to fully protect your family's future.

Decide who will get what you own. For instance, if one of you dies, does everything pass to the surviving spouse?

Now go see a lawyer. For the $200–$500 that a qualified attorney will charge you for a simple will, look what you get:

- A will that directs your assets exactly as you wish

- A better understanding of the different ways that you and your spouse may own property

- The assurance that your will matches up with how you actually hold your property

- Reduced inheritance taxes

- Finally, the good feeling when you know that you have done something hard that needs to get done

ENTERING THE BLACK HOLE
OF PERSONAL FINANCE
....

Obtaining a will, of course, only begins the financial planning process that has to do with what happens when you die. Now we enter into what often seems like the "black hole" of personal finance—life insurance. We have more trouble understanding life insurance than any other financial product—perhaps because we do not want to. Life insurance has been in existence for some 200 years now, yet the product itself and the industry that sells it remains a source of darkness rather than light. If anything, the confusion over the product has grown to gigantic proportions—right along with the industry that supplies it.

Why do things remain so confusing? Partly it has to do with the self-proclaimed experts who write for personal finance magazines. They frequently condemn the life insurance industry while they themselves make simplistic arguments for why the one product they like fits everybody's needs. And the industry itself continually shoots itself in the foot by failing to teach us the real benefits of its own product! That leaves most consumers focused upon just one thing—that they really should have this protection because they love someone or have an obligation to someone. Notice, this is *death focused*. Every so-called expert that writes about life insurance will say the following about it:

- It is for the people you leave behind.

- You only need it for a specific amount of time.

- You should focus entirely upon buying it cheaply.

This represents the conventional wisdom about life insurance, and it really does a big disservice to all Americans interested in buying it.

I am going to advise you very differently. The conventional wisdom has a big bias in it, toward death, and it fails to serve the goal of Latino family wealth creation. Fundamentally, the conventional wisdom fails to see these things about life insurance:

- It is for you while you are living.

- It is for the rest of your life.

- You get what you pay for.

Needs versus Wants Once More

Every conventional discussion about life insurance begins with an analysis of *how much insurance you need*. Opinions about this differ. Some experts point to rules of thumb, such as: You "should" have four, or five, or even ten times your annual income in life insurance protection. (The Consumer Federation of America, for example, recommends six to eight times annual income for a married couple with two small children.) Many books on insurance include "calculators"— charts detailing how much life insurance you "need" based upon your circumstances. These calculators ask you to look at the following:

- Current family cost of living

- Surviving (with you taken out of the picture) family income sources

- Investment assets and rates of return

- The likely income gap in the event of your death (the second two items subtracted from the first)

- Life insurance needs, based upon covering the income gap

The whole point of such a conventional analysis leads toward a consideration of your minimum *needs*. This becomes the *mantra* for most of the financial planning press and industry: Put as small an amount of your money as you can into life insurance—because it takes your money away from real wealth-creating uses.

As I see it, the belief that life insurance only exists to meet *minimum* income replacement needs in the event of your untimely death leads to the heart of the black hole of confusion. How about looking at life insurance, instead, as very important way for providing financial security—for your whole family, including you? Remember, *¡Sí!, Se Puede* is all about creating *maximum* wealth potential for our families, not meeting minimal needs. The proper question does not have to do with *needs,* but rather with *wants.* Think about *what you want your life insurance to do for you.*

In order to answer that question, each one of us needs to name the basic objective that we have that life insurance will allow us to reach, such as:

- Providing for my family the minimum level of income based upon my current earnings situation should I die, or

- Providing as much future wealth now as I can for my family, in any circumstances

Put another way, the second objective answers this question: *Do my dreams for my family have to die with me?* Now if you feel that the first objective meets your needs, you may go the appendix in this book, and you will find an easy-to-understand calculator that will help you determine these minimal needs. Just follow the instructions, write in your particular details, and your specific minimum needs for coverage will pop out. But if you would like to pursue the second objective, read on.

In order to follow this discussion, you really must work at answering this question: *How much life insurance would you like to have?* If you find that you do not know quite how to answer this question, here's a little help: If you were killed in some sort of an accident tomorrow, an accident in which someone else carelessly deprived you of your life, how much would you want your spouse to sue for? $500,000? $2 million? $10 million? What would be your answer? A lawyer, of course, would advise, and a jury would award, an amount based upon your age, occupation, education, salary, future prospects, and family situation. But do you see that this resembles dying without a will—somebody else determines what happens to your family's well-being? I think that your spouse would want as much as she or he could get! I think you would too.

TIP

Buy enough life insurance to cover at least ten times your annual spending (not your annual income). If you have young children, add enough to pay off the mortgage and their educations.

Here's another question: If your spouse would want as much as she or he could get, what difference does it really make whether your death happened to be accidental, or not? Does it make any difference whether the payout would come from a lawsuit or an insurance policy that you own? Wouldn't she or he still want as much as possible?

Now if we would all like as much as possible, can we in fact get it? *No!* Believe it or not, insurance companies will actually limit the amount of life insurance that they will sell you. Usually that limit will get tied to your income—anywhere from 15 to 20 times your income, as a general rule. And this does not mean the total amount that you can buy *per company,* it means the total amount of life insurance that you can have in force from all sources and all companies. This means, for instance, that Jesús's $60,000 salary would qualify him for between $900,000 and $1,200,000 in total protection. Should he die tomorrow, that would mean that the lump-sum payout from the insurance company, invested at six percent, would produce between $54,000 and $72,000 in earnings each year.

Now, $1,200,000 sounds like a very big amount of protection, but let's break it down and see how it might actually be used:

Pay the balance of the mortgage	175,000
Pay final expenses related to your death (burial and administrative costs)	30,000
Set up a college fund for the children	100,000
Total	**$305,000**

Now the $1,200,000 has been reduced to just about $900,000— which would earn your family $54,000 each year when invested at six percent. That amounts to less than Jesús's income while alive, and it makes no allowance for inflation over the years. So it is not so great an amount after all.

What we have learned so far is this: The maximum amount of life insurance that most of us would be permitted to buy would only barely keep our families at their current standard of living. Sadly, most Latino families have nowhere near the maximum life insurance coverage: Many have none at all, or an amount that will not pay much more than burial and administrative expenses. This needs to change— for our families' sakes.

What if you really want this much protection, but the current cost seems too high for you? We should now take a look at the other sources of family income that may allow you to reduce your life insurance wants somewhat:

Social Security provides family survivor income payments to dependent family members. The amount of those future benefits depends upon your current status with the Social Security Administration. You can call 800-772-1213 and ask for a Personal Earnings and Benefits Statement—Form SSA-7004. This form will tell you exactly what your family would receive in the event of your death.

Surviving spouse's wages. Should the surviving spouse either continue working or choose to go back to work, the income that this work produces reduces the monthly amount needed to sustain the family at the present standard of living. If the surviving spouse had not worked for child care reasons, that raises the issue of whether he or she can go to work and still find care for the children.

Clearly the issue of a surviving spouse working can be a complex one for you in your financial planning. It becomes another sensitive thing for each family to resolve. It does impact upon life insurance choices when you feel you cannot afford all the coverage you could get.

What Kind of Life Insurance Is Best?

Once you have decided to buy life insurance, you will find that you run right into one of the most confusing financial decisions of modern life: what *kind* of life insurance to buy. You will quickly find that there are a number of types of life insurance. You will also find some of the so-called "experts" telling you that one particular type must be best for everybody. This last thing cannot be true: The reason why so many types of life insurance exist is simply that people in different circumstances desire different types of protection. Let's take a look at the confusing mass of life insurance products and make some sense out of them—for you.

At the simplest level, you can only buy two kinds of life insurance; everything else falls under one of these two categories: *term insurance* and *permanent insurance*.

TIP

> The *premium cost principle* behind life insurance: The older you are, the higher your life insurance premium cost—because you become more likely to die.

Term Insurance

Term insurance is pure protection. The only thing it will ever do for you will be to pay out a death benefit to your beneficiary if you die *during the time period,* or *"term,"* that the policy is in force. After the term runs out, your coverage is "terminated," so to speak! It will never help you increase your family's assets while you live: "It's only good when you die." For that reason, term insurance is cheap; it costs you far less than "permanent" coverage, because term insurance premiums only have to cover the cost of insuring you against death for a given time period.

Term insurance includes annual renewable (where the premium increases each year) and extended term products (that allow you to purchase a fixed rate for a specified number of years). Term policies give you choices among these key features: term period, guarantee period, renewal privilege and conditions, projected renewal costs, and conversion privileges. Let's summarize the valuable features that term insurance can provide you:

TIP

> The *health principle* behind life insurance: You can buy life insurance more easily when you are healthy than when you are sick—and at much lower cost. In other words, the people who most need insurance protection will have the hardest time getting it—and it will be expensive.

Term insurance allows you to match your annual premiums to your ability to pay.

At the same time, term insurance allows you to buy the greatest amount of coverage for the lowest cost—when you are younger and not making much money yet.

Most term policies allow you to convert to permanent policies on a guaranteed basis.

Now let's look at permanent life insurance.

Permanent Insurance

Whereas term insurance only considers the death part of your coverage, *permanent insurance* considers the "life" part as well. Let me explain. Permanent policies do not only cover you for some term of your life, they apply to your whole life—until you die, provided you keep them in force by paying necessary premiums. In addition, permanent policies add to your personal wealth as well as provide your family with pure death protection should you die. I'll add one more factor to this standard list: As you grow older, you will face a number of difficult financial decisions. Some you will view as obstacles to overcome; others, as opportunities to seize and take advantage of. If you have permanent life insurance later in life, you will have more freedom to make those decisions than you would without such insurance. Permanent life insurance provides its owner with permission to take action in the future that can result in increased income, reduced taxes, and greater comfort and dignity in life. For instance, what if once the children grow up, you and your spouse wish to start that business together that you have always dreamed of. Without permanent life insurance, you might not risk your savings in such a venture—for fear that if one of you died, the other would not have the money to carry on alone. So you see, permanent life insurance really can put the "life" back into death.

Looking closely at permanent life polices, you'll find that three basic types exist:

- Participating whole life
- Universal life
- Variable life

Let's look at each type.

Whole Life

Whole life policies guarantee a specific and level (same) premium for the life of the contract—your life. The pure protection part of the premium cost to you each year will be higher in the earlier years than term insurance would be, but lower in the later years—because it does not increase with time as term life does. Held long enough, your term insurance would eventually cost more—perhaps much more—than your whole life policy's protection feature. In other words, the whole life policy *averages* the costs of one-year term premiums that extend to your likely or expected age at death when you buy the policy now.

In addition to pure protection, a portion of your premium in a whole life policy gets invested for you, so that your family assets grow, and you have access to cash should you need it. In the basics, then, every whole life policy looks like a lifetime, guaranteed level term policy with a savings account added on. A whole life policy in fact gives you these three guarantees:

- A guaranteed level premium—for life
- A guaranteed death benefit—for life
- A guaranteed cash value

In contrast, term insurance only gives you a guaranteed death benefit for a specific term.

Besides cash values, a permanent whole life policy provides you, the policyholder, with several other living benefits, as opposed to death benefits. You get increased wealth protection against the risks of disability and lawsuits. The premium benefit guarantees that the insurance company will continue to make full premium payments on your behalf should you become disabled and unable to work, according to the policy's definitions. Unlike contributions to qualified pension plans and other retirement accumulation vehicles, whole life insurance provides a self-completion guarantee to the policy holder for the cash values at retirement.

Did You Know?/¿Sabía Usted?

If you are faced with a legal confrontation, consider resolving the matter through arbitration. The legal and business communities are increasingly using mediation, arbitration, negotiation, and other dispute settlement techniques as a way to resolve disputes.

American Arbitration Association
140 West 51st Street, New York, NY 10020-1203
800-778-7879, **www.adr.org**

National Arbitration & Mediation
1010 Northern Blvd., Suite 376
Great Neck, NY 11021
800-358-2550, **www.namadr.com**

Lawsuit protection is also a great thing to have, given our litigious society. We all face the potential threat of lawsuits, for any reason—accidents, workplace issues, personal relationships. If we are sued, any and all assets that we own or have an interest in become subject to loss. This includes bank accounts, personal property, homes, and investments. Any extra protection over liquid assets that we can get adds an extra layer of protection for us. Permanent life insurance provides such an extra layer—because in most states creditors (except the IRS) cannot touch its values.

Universal Life Insurance

The second major form of permanent life insurance, *universal* policies were created in the 1970s in response to the interest rate upheavals of that time. Universal policies "unbundle" a number of policy features, allowing policyholders to specify just what they would like for these features. Universal policies become flexible contracts that put the investment risks in the policyholder's hands. The basic idea is that policy savings will grow faster than your increasing insurance costs as you age, thereby providing you with both lifetime insurance protection at modest premiums and growing cash values. But it all depends upon how well the financial markets perform.

Universal life can be a good choice if:

- You are young (25–40) and have many years to build up cash value.

- You want greater flexibility in the premium amount that you want to pay.

- You can pay the so-called "target" premiums that the insurance company stipulates will guarantee coverage for life.

However, *do not:*

- Listen to an agent or broker who tells you to put in less than the "target" premium because it is "cheaper."
  Why, if your cash value later in life proves to be too small to cover your insurance costs, your policy could "blow up," as so many of them written in the 1970s and 1980s did. If you want the coverage and cannot put in the target, consider term insurance until you can afford higher premiums.

- Believe that you will only pay a few years' premiums and then be able to stop because of your great interest earnings.

● Assume that every component of a universal policy will remain the same as whole life. Remember, with a universal policy you get only these two guarantees: minimum interest rate and guaranteed cost of coverage.

Variable Life

This third and last form of permanent life insurance also "unbundles" an ordinary whole life policy. Now, you get life insurance itself plus a side fund that can be placed into mutual fund–like investments. You can have your premiums work as they do in whole life, where you must pay a set premium amount each year. Or you can choose the more popular universal form, in which premium levels and payments become flexible. We'll be focusing on the variable universal form here.

Variable universal policies offer you the opportunity to have your life insurance cash values generate the higher-than-average growth rates available in equity mutual funds. You are offered a range of investment choices—growth, balanced, income, as well as money market, and guaranteed interest rate funds. Variable universal life has become one of the most popular policy types recently, due to the spectacular performance of equity markets. Boring old whole life insurance becomes downright jazzy. Variable universal becomes seen as the perfect solution to such needs as saving for college expenses, retirement, and other long-term goals. While returns are usually not projected above a 12 percent gross rate, many people buy these policies believing that higher returns will come their way, just as in 401(k) plans.

Keep in mind these key points when you consider a variable life insurance purchase.

Variable universal life may be presented to you as a best-of-both-worlds choice. Be careful; these policies contain even more fees and charges than regular universal life does—that can reduce your return by up to 2 points per year. That means that a gross rate of 12 percent could really net you 10½ percent. Big difference.

As in the case of universal life, the insurance company can increase the costs for mortality (pure insurance) and other fees over time.

These policies contain few guarantees—the death benefit may not be guaranteed even if you pay the premiums, because of the risk that the cash value may evaporate due to stock market losses.

So consider variable universal life insurance if you:

- Have a medium- to long-term desire for life insurance protection.

- Want to assume the increased risks of equity investing with your life insurance premiums.

- Are able and willing to fully fund the policy.

- Will put the premium into the stock fund portion of the investment accounts. Putting your money into "safer" accounts such as money market or bond funds will not produce the gross rates of return necessary to balance out the increased variable universal fees.

A Final Word on Permanent Life Insurance

Whatever type of permanent life insurance you buy, the value of having protection that continues for your entire life lies in the options that having such coverage gives you, versus not having that protection. The argument for term insurance gets based on the idea that we need life insurance only for a limited time. I take the position that need is a flawed basis for making life insurance decisions. The case for term insurance rests upon the argument that limiting insurance expenses allows for the pursuit of more "productive" employments of our money in such things as stock mutual funds and other growth investments. This case ignores the critically valuable roles of life insurance in your wealth creation process. It is not an expense but rather an important tool in the overall wealth creation model that we should use. It provides important tax benefits that counterbalance the erosive impact of taxes upon our savings and growth investments. It provides critical disability and liability protections that create or expand the wealth preservation components we already have in place, assuring that the wealth that we have built will be there when we want to use it.

Having life insurance in force later in life affords us the right to make financial decisions that others without this protection cannot, or would not, make—in order to maximize our incomes and our quality of life. For example, we can spend down our other assets in order to maximize our retirement incomes, taking the highest pension benefits while knowing that our spouse will be protected. Or we can use a reverse mortgage as part of a coordinated retirement plan, not out of a desperate need for increased living money. In the same way, we can take advantage of the income and estate tax benefits of charitable giving strategies if we are so inclined. Notice something very important here: *None of these things have any relation to the need for life insurance in the conventional sense!* But then, the Latino community's absolute need to accelerate its wealth creation is not a conventional topic. It is urgent and critically important. Traditional approaches will simply not do the job as quickly as we need it done. This is a twenty-first century approach to wealth creation, and permanent life insurance can work as a catalyst.

STEPS FOR MAXIMIZING WEALTH PROTECTION
....

- Review your automobile and homeowners policies carefully, paying particular attention to the liability coverage that protects your wealth. Make sure you have $300,000 as a *minimum* level of protection.

- Review your disability coverage, whether through work, an association, or your individual plan. How long can you afford to live with no income coming in? Make sure that it covers your income to age 65, contains a residual benefit, and is noncancelable.

- If you do not have an umbrella policy for at least $1 million, ask your broker about getting one.

- If you have a will, have it updated; if you do not have a will, and especially if you have children, get it done. *Now!*

- Review your life insurance portfolio. How much do you want, and how much do you now have? If you do not have a personal life insurance advisor to help you, find one who can. A good source is the Society of CLU and ChFC (Chartered Life Underwriters and Chartered Financial Consultants), which has chapters in many cities and towns across the country.

- Keep your life insurance as healthy as possible. Cheaper is not better. Do not underfund universal or variable life policies just because someone says you can get away with this. This approach will not work in the long run, and it will likely rob you of wealth.

Making Your Financial Elevators Run Fast: Life in the Growth Sphere

In This Chapter

- Learn eight key rules for investing successfully.

- Learn how badly taxes and inflation erode your real wealth, and what to do about it.

- Take a new look at risk in investing, and learn how to avoid the *certainty* of loss.

- Learn about the basics of stock, bond, and mutual fund investing.

- Learn strategies for maximizing wealth growth using mutual funds.

STOCKING UP FOR THE FUTURE
·····································

El que no arriesga, no pasa el charco.

Traditionally, most American families did the same thing that we Latinos like to do—they bought a house, with the help of the bank, as soon as they could in life. For many years, the typical American's most valuable asset remained the family home. Real estate formed the financial security base for most of the American generations growing up after the Great Depression. If you had a little extra cash, you "invested" in some form of home improvement. Recently, all of that has been changing. While we Latinos still think that real estate will bring us wealth in the United States, many other Americans have moved on to something different—stocks in American corporations.

In 1997, for the first time in over forty years, the biggest share of American household wealth (over 50 percent) was held in equity investments—stocks. This new trend began with the 1982 bull market on Wall Street and has continued ever since. According to the Investment Company Institute, by 1997 *four* out of ten American households owned at least one mutual fund, with the percentage of households growing each year. The American household's average mutual fund holdings reached $25,000 that year, and the top 1 percent of all households had average mutual fund holdings of $100,000. *Mutual fund assets now total over $5 trillion—up from only $500 billion in 1985.* Half of that total—or $2.5 trillion—took the form of equity-based accounts invested in stocks for the long term. In fact, the annual flow of new deposits into equity funds increased from $8 billion in 1985 to over $270 billion in 1997!

TIP

Listen to your kids. They can tell you what companies to invest in. What do they like? Pepsi-Cola? Taco Bell? Both are owned by PepsiCo, which has traditionally been a high-performing stock. Disney? Nike? Also good companies to invest in. You get the picture.

What does this tell us? Americans now pursue personal asset growth largely through equities, in order to make the most money they can from their investment portfolios. Just look at another statistic: The number of mutual fund accounts in America has exploded, going from 34 million in 1985 to over 150 million in 1996. The expansion in American household wealth during this period, as a result, has been unprecedented and has resulted in a dramatic change in how Americans, especially younger ones, view their financial lives and responsibilities.

To give you a vivid idea of just how great this change in outlook has become, many Americans now view Social Security—the retirement program that provided much of the previous generation's financial security—as a source of real *wealth erosion* now, not wealth creation. Today we contribute payroll taxes into Social Security, not to see our wealth shoot up rapidly, but to guarantee benefits to people currently receiving them—a "pay as you go" system. If we could pay directly into our own plans invested in equities, we could be much better off.

Meanwhile, the explosion in investment activity, together with the realization that the Social Security net is more like a prison of financial dependence, has led to an extraordinary increase in information about investing available to consumers. The new *cult of investing* has led to a never-ending stream of financial magazines, how-to books (including this one), news shows, investing clubs, college courses, Internet sites, and other products. It has produced expert after expert, celebrity advisors, get-rich-quick schemes, get-rich-slow programs, and such a deluge of information that many Americans end up more confused than enlightened—and more aware of what they should be doing than what they are actually doing.

Where are we Latinos in all of this?

THE SECOND KIND OF POOR

If it seems to you that we have been left out of this discussion so far, you are right. *That's the problem!* While 40 percent of all Americans have invested in mutual funds and benefited from their rapid rise in value, *only 4 percent of Latinos own mutual funds.* Some people in the investment industry may perhaps think that this is because of low incomes—that most Latinos do not have the money to make these investments. In other words, *financial* poverty keeps us out of these markets.

But this simply cannot be. Remember, nearly 50 percent of all Latino households have reached middle-class income levels, and another 20 percent have become truly affluent, with annual household incomes exceeding $50,000. A large proportion of our people in America have become successful, earning more money and feeling more confident about the future. Now, as a people, we need to put all that money to work, converting our emerging wealth into real, lasting wealth— money that will help our children and our communities. The challenge we face has to do with getting onto the financial elevators of life, so that our wealth begins to rise as rapidly as the average American's.

Do you know what kind of poverty we really face? *We suffer not from cash poverty, but from information poverty.*

How has this come about? Partly we have ourselves to blame; we have not as a people cast aside the old attitude that wealth is created only from owning real estate. But partly this situation has to do with the financial services industry. This industry that tries so hard to sell anything it can to anyone with money has simply ignored us. The major financial services firms of the world have long focused their out-reach efforts on wealthy areas and potential customers, in order to gather in large amounts of assets from them. Their feeling has long been, why waste time and money on an ethnic group that does not have much money to invest anyway? Again, that perception that we are all poor hurts us.

Fortunately, this perception has begun to change, as financial ser-vices companies finally read the same census and demographic findings that other marketers have for years. In the March 1998 issue of *Hispanic Business* magazine, for instance, a special report on money manage-ment highlighted the financial services firms' growing awareness of the rising Latino middle classes' customer potential. A Charles Schwab executive is quoted as saying that Schwab management thinks Latino households in America hold $30 billion worth of savings and invest-ment assets. Sadly, most of this wealth appears underinvested—riding up slow freight elevators when it could be shooting up the high-speed elevators of the American financial growth sphere.

What does this mean for us? It means we better become equipped to make good financial decisions and learn to ask the right questions of any salesperson trying to sell us anything. The rest of this chapter seeks to be your primer or introduction to the world of fast-growth investments.

Let's start at the very beginning—with the minimum things you need to know:

- Lessons about what has worked in the past

- Why focus on growth? An understanding of taxes and inflation

- What the past has to say about the future—an understanding of risk

- An understanding of stocks, bonds, and mutual funds

- Strategies for maximizing growth, including asset allocation and dollar cost averaging.

Lessons Learned from the Past

The past can teach us eight key rules for investing in the future:

Invest for the long term in stocks. Over almost any 10-year period, stocks have outperformed—made more money—than any other investment choice. Since 1946, the annual return for the Standard and Poors 500 Index, the best barometer of the general United States equity markets, has averaged 11 percent. No other investment has done so well.

Diversification is the key to healthy investing. Putting all your proverbial eggs in one basket works just fine—unless the bottom falls out of the basket. Why take the chance of trusting everything to just one container? Putting all of your money into just one stock is doing just this. Instead, own more than one stock; better yet, own many more companies than just one. That way, you can decrease the risk that the performance of a single company could sink your whole financial plan. Even better yet, spread out, or diversify, your risks among whole classes of assets—such as bonds as well as stocks—to provide even better protection against too much rapid change, or volatility, in your portfolio.

Consider buying stock mutual funds instead of individual stocks. We will discuss mutual funds in more detail later, but for right now just recognize that by investing in a mutual fund you get important instant benefits: diversification, professional investment management, and clear investment objectives.

Stick to a buy-and-hold strategy. Unless you wish to spend the 40 to 60 hours each week that professional investment managers devote to their jobs, trying to gauge the market for the optimal buy and sell times will be a no-win strategy for you. And remember, short-term buying and selling cost you trading commissions. To show you just how difficult short-term buying and selling for maximum profit can be, if you had sold out of the market for the best 20 days between 1987 and 1997— that's over a period of ten long years—you would have missed 173 percent of the market's overall performance!

TIP

Don't panic. Losses in the 1987 stock market collapse were recovered within 12 months.

Reinvest your dividends. Remember how the compound interest elevator works? Well, stock dividends perform the same way. If you do own individual companies' stocks, you must reinvest any dividends you receive in order to have compounding work for you. *Over the 70-year period between 1925 and 1995, reinvesting dividends from an initial $100 purchase of the S & P 500 would have meant more than $130,000 in greater total wealth accumulation than taking dividends out in cash and spending them!*

Keep the money flowing into your investments. By investing on a regular basis, even if only small amounts, you avoid the temptation of market timing—and that allows you to make investments in both up markets and down markets. Remember, if you are investing for the long term, short-term declines are irrelevant to your overall goals.

If you need advice, get the best you can. Find a financial advisor you can trust and whose investing philosophy matches your goals. Be wary of listening to your brother, cousin, brother-in-law, uncles, or any other well-intentioned "advisor" about what you should or should not do. Watch out for "hot tips" or "can't miss" investment situations: Most can't misses do. If it sounds too good to be true, it probably is.

Patience, patience, patience. You do not invest for the short term. Before you invest, figure out what your goals are, chart a course, and stick to it.

An Investor Personality Profile

Recognizing your investment personality will help you build an investment portfolio that suits your needs. The following questionnaire will help you determine if you are aggressive, moderate, or conservative.

Determine your score by assigning points with the following values:

The first answers = 1 point each
The second answers = 2 points each
The third answers = 3 points each

To see where your total points rank you, see the answers on page 268.

1   I believe in luck.
     Definitely
     Sometimes
     Not at all

An Investor Personality Profile (Cont.)

2   I am at ease making investment decisions by myself.
Sometimes
Always
Never

3   If I were one of five finalists in a $100,000 raffle, I would keep my ticket
and take my chance rather than sell it for $15,000.
Yes
Maybe
No

4   I think people who carefully plan out their investments will always succeed.
No
Sometimes
Yes

5   Inflation is rising faster than my salary, and I need extra income. I would
consider cashing in my bank-guaranteed CD for a higher-yielding long-
term bond.
Yes
Maybe
No

6   If I invested in a stock that rose 50 percent the year after I purchased it,
I would:
Buy more shares
Sell some shares
Sell all my shares

An Investor Personality Profile (Cont.)

7 I like spending money at casinos, gambling on professional sports, or betting with friends.
Always
Sometimes
Never

8 I would go into debt to make an investment that might double my money.
Yes
Maybe
No

TIP

Know your rate of return. Take the current value of your investment (the price of a stock or net value of a mutual fund), subtract its value from a year ago, and divide the result by the value of a year ago. That's your return for the year. For example: if your mutual fund was worth $10,000 a year and today it's worth $15,000, your return is 50 percent ($15,000 minus $10,000, divided by $10,000). Compare your return with the S&P 500.

Why Focus on Growth?

Remember that in an earlier chapter, we looked at the reasons why you need to increase your yield on your savings accounts: Inflation and taxes will otherwise eat up your savings. You learned to see that what your savings accounts actually earns comes from your interest less your costs of saving—again, interest and taxes. It turns out that the same principle holds when looking at all financial investments. We need to consider the net result after costs for each investment in order to know which ones make us the most. The net gain, after all, becomes the money that we can actually use to live on some day.

The Bureau of Labor Statistics in Washington, D.C., tracks the increase in prices for the everyday goods and services that we all buy. They issue the Consumer Price Index (CPI) every month; this for most Americans defines the inflation rate. For most of the 1990s, the CPI has been in the two to four percent range—small cheese apparently. For those of us who remember the 13 percent inflation of the oil-shock 1970s, I know that three percent does not sound like much. But just look at how much prices for common products have changed between 1986 and 1996, a time of "small cheese" inflation.

Product/Service	Price Change
Sofas	+ 38%
Steak	+ 39%
Housing rent	+ 42%
Eggs	+ 60%
Apples	+ 66%
Auto insurance	+ 94%
Tobacco products	+ 94%
Prescription drugs	+ 97%
College tuition	+ 128%

In ten short years, during a period of relatively low inflation, just look at what has happened to the prices of these common goods and services that we all want to buy. Even those that have only gone up at the rate of inflation have become much more expensive for us—in 1986 dollars.

Others will have become prohibitively expensive if we tried to buy them with 1986 dollars. Let me ask you just one simple question, and then you decide for yourself how much it matters whether your savings and investments do better than inflation: *How would you like to buy these products at 1996 prices with the money you had in 1986?*

In order to create for ourselves enough net usable wealth for the future, we must overcome the downward drag that inflation has upon our purchasing power. And we must tackle head on the wealth-eroding power of taxes. Taxes are nothing more than a price—the price that we pay for the privilege of living in a democracy and sharing in the benefits that a strong government provides us—such as the protection of our own private wealth. Taxes nevertheless can eat up much of the gains we would otherwise make on low-yield investments. For instance, if Jesús and Marta invest their money at an 8 percent fixed rate, and if they are in a 28 percent tax bracket, they will only see 5.76 percent after taxes—and 2.76 percent after adding in the silent tax, inflation.

The question for Jesús and Marta is whether a real growth rate in wealth of 2.76 percent annually will produce the kind of long-term gain that will allow them the quality of life they desire. And what about you? The answer in all cases? Probably not.

So what's the alternative? Stocks. The tremendous growth in Americans' wealth over the past ten years has been driven by an unprecedented boom in the stock market. Let me give you a context for looking at this growth. In his 1993 book *The Coming Boom*, Harry Dent predicted that the Dow Jones average could reach the 8,500 level by the year 2003—in ten years. In April 1998, the Dow Jones average of thirty industrial stocks actually climbed over the 9,000 mark for the first time. Stock market growth has outrun even the most optimistic experts' predictions of only five years ago.

Because the growth in stock values has been so unprecedented recently, it has also been frightening to some people. Many people have invested in stocks for the first time in their lives over the last few years; many experts wonder what these people will do when the growth slows, or the market declines. Will people panic? Clearly, we should take a look at how the stock market has performed over the long term, and rethink the whole concept of risk.

What the Past Has to Say about the Future— an Understanding of Risk

People put money into FDIC-insured bank accounts for one big reason: Their money is assumed to be "safe." But what do we mean when we say "safe" or "guaranteed"? Here it means that if the bank cannot give you your money, the Federal Deposit Insurance Corporation will. You will never lose the face value of the money that you put in, plus interest—if you have patience. Why patience? We all recently witnessed during the S&L debacle what FDIC insurance can really mean for us; hundreds of savings banks went broke, trapping their customers with frozen deposits. The FDIC and the Resolution Trust Corporation worked for several years to restore the savings bank industry. Every affected customer got his or her money back, eventually. The rescue cost the American taxpayers hundreds of billions of dollars by the time it was finished.

What did this crisis demonstrate? It showed that while the insurance guarantee system does work, it works very differently than most Americans thought it would. Many people experienced a lack of access to their own money and had to wait for full payment, some people for an extended time. FDIC insurance turned out not to be insurance as we commonly understand it—something that gets you get a check in the mail in days after something happens to you. People did not, by any means, receive payment upon presentation of a claim.

What then do we get from our guaranteed bank accounts? We get the promise that if our bank goes under, an agency of the federal government will get our money back to us—sometime in the future. For that "protection" we assume the *much greater risk* of losing our purchasing power to inflation in these accounts. Doesn't this seem like rather a poor trade?

Look at the higher-risk stock market. Here, no guarantees exist. A stockholder actually owns a portion of the corporation and therefore shares in the gains and losses of the company. No guarantees. What risk does the stockholder take on? The risk is the chance that the market will not value the company's shares as highly as expected, lowering the share's value to the stockholder. The hope is that the stocks we buy will give us a higher rate of return than supposedly "safe" investments will, to make up for the greater "risk."

But remember, we must face the reality of *two kinds* of risk—risk of capital loss if our investments go down in value, and risk of purchasing power loss if our savings returns do not keep up with the unholy couple—taxes and inflation. What about the first kind of risk—that of capital loss? Well, we have already seen that since World War Two stocks have gained an average of 11 percent per year. If you place your capital in a mutual fund that performs the same as this average, then over the long term you will most likely not see your capital fall in value but rather double every six and one-half years. All of this only holds, of course, if you follow the lessons from the past that I have given you. On the other hand, as we've already seen in Chapter Nine, when you put your money into a traditional savings account, you receive the guarantee that you *will* lose purchasing power every year! Compare that to a likely 11 percent gain. Which risk is the bigger and the more likely to give you a loss?

TIP

Bulls make money and bears make money, but pigs get slaughtered. When a stock or mutual fund is up 30 percent, consider selling one-fourth of your position.

How can we summarize the lessons we have just learned? Very clearly, your ability to create real, usable wealth for your family's future comes through investing in stocks. On the other hand, putting most of your money in "safe," guaranteed investments only gives you one certain form of security—the guarantee that your money will become worth less each year! How do you feel, now, about having held money in savings accounts for so long?

Now we can go ahead to think more clearly about risk. Remember the two kinds of risk: so-called "normal" risk from investing in non-"guaranteed" stocks, and the very real risk that comes from not having enough purchasing power to live on in the future. (You may wish, right now, to turn to the Investor Personality Profile on page 228—to determine your *real* risk tolerance level.) Hopefully, this new perspective on risk will carry you forward to new realms of wealth: You have become more willing to take the risks of investing in order to offset the certainty of purchasing power loss. Now we can give more certain answers to these fundamental questions:

● What is the real risk that we face in investment markets?

- How have these markets behaved over time—what's their track record?

- What should our strategy be for maximizing our wealth-creating momentum?

Let's begin with a basic truth about the stock market: *market declines are natural occurrences*. Because they have this nature, you do not have to become alarmed at the prospect of declines happening every so often—so long as you remain steadfastly a long-term investor. Then you will ride out the occasional stumbles in the market without coming to any real harm. On the other hand, when you panic and sell out at the bottom of a decline, you lose twice: You've sold out at a loss, and chances are you will not buy back in again until the market has gone up, thereby losing the gain that could have been yours. Too bad. Remember, nobody can predict the peaks and valleys in the market: Wall Street is a random walk. The best way to lose is to try to do what nobody can do: call the ups and downs of the market.

Here's a little history lesson: Over the past 97 years of its records, the stock market has gone through 322 routine declines of 5–9 percent, 107 moderate declines of 10–14 percent, 50 more severe corrections of 15–19 percent, and 29 actual "bear markets" in which values declined 20 percent or more. What can we conclude from this quick walk down Wall Street? Well, first of all, investing in stocks *is* risky. If you sell out at the wrong time, you could lose substantial sums of money. But second, *you only lose money in the stock market when you sell!* This is something that novice investors often fail to understand. Let's say that you buy a stock at $10 per share, and the stock price declines to $5 per share. How much money have you lost? $5 per share? *No!* You have lost nothing—unless you sell at $5 per share. Now if that stock happens to be part of your long-term investment portfolio, and you hold onto the stock through a decline, nothing has happened to you at all.

What if the stock that you bought at $10 per share increases to $20 per share? Again, you do not sell it. Have you gained anything? *No!* The same rule applies: any gain or loss on that stock remains *unrealized* so long as you hold rather than sell. You just *feel better* when your stock shares go up in value. If your shares go down from $20 to $15, you then feel poorer. Market movements such as these happen all the time in equity markets; they become part of everyday life. *Let go. Don't worry about this.* Remember, you have a powerful ally on your side: that ally is named *time.* The history of stock markets has shown that the longer you hold an investment, the less likely you are to realize a loss.

UNDERSTANDING STOCKS, BONDS, AND MUTUAL FUNDS

Stocks, bonds, and mutual funds each represent distinct approaches to investing, and each has its own potential benefits and weaknesses or risks.

Did You Know?/¿Sabía Usted?

The Investor Protection Trust, a nonprofit unit that offers tips to consumers, has launched a Web site (**www.investorprotection.org**). It features basic investment information, such as "101 Questions to Ask Before Investing"; how to check out your broker or financial planner; where to turn for help with problems; warnings about the latest financial scams, including "Practical Tips for Older Americans"; and a market-knowledge quiz.

Owning a Piece of the Pie: Buying into the Stock Market

Let's begin with stocks. What if you owned a very big, delicious fruit pie, and you agreed to sell me half of it? We would then each have a one-half share in the pie. Or rather, the whole pie would now consist of two equal shares— each of us owning one of them. Ownership of corporations is just like that. The total pie—the stock of value of the entire company—is divided into equal pieces or shares. We call these equal shares equity stocks—because they represent shares of the company's stock value above all of its debts. How much of the company do I own when I buy, say, 1,000 shares in it? That depends upon how many shares other people also own. If the company has 1,000,000 shares outstanding, held by other people, then you own 1/1,000 or 0.1 percent of the company.

As a shareholder, then, you own a piece of the business. As the owner of even one share—because all shares are created equal—you receive certain ownership, or property, rights and benefits:

- The right to vote for the company's board of directors and on certain company decisions

- The right to receive your fair share of dividends if the company decides to pay out any earnings

- The right to sell your shares at the current market price

- The benefit of receiving your share of any capital gains that come through share price appreciation when you do decide to sell

- The right to participate in the liquidation of the company's value should the need arise, only after all the creditors owed money by the company get paid

Of course, like any property holder, you also face certain risks of ownership. In the case of corporate stocks, your risks include things such as these:

- Dividends and dividend amounts are not guaranteed.

- The market price of your shares fluctuates unpredictably.

- You are last in line after all creditors to receive any money back should the company go bust.

Given risks and benefits, why do people buy stock? Stocks tend to increase in value over time, and when we sell them we *realize gains*. Through dividends, some corporations do pay us some of their earnings, which we can then choose to spend if we like.

TIP

Remember KISS (keep it simple, stupid.) Don't own so many investments that you can't keep track of them. Five to ten stocks are plenty. If you're wealthy enough to own more, hire someone to manage your investments for you, and tell them to KISS.

Stocks can be divided into four categories for our investment purposes, and we need to be very careful to understand what category of stock fits our overall financial plan *before* we buy. Each of these stock categories offers advantages to investors, but which type you buy depends upon your investment goals. If you wish to achieve rapid growth and are willing to assume greater risk, you will buy growth and emerging shares; if you desire less volatile long-term returns, you will tend to invest in total return and value stocks.

The Four Categories of Stocks for Investment

Growth stocks. Growth companies will usually appear in attractive industries that expand rapidly—technology, information, the Internet, specialty retail, pharmaceuticals, and health care are examples from the recent past. These stocks show a steady pattern of increasing sales and profits.

Total return stocks. Companies that offer higher-than-average total returns have some growth potential and also pay out dividends with higher-than-average yields.

Value stocks. These are companies whose shares have fallen out of favor with investors, hopefully only temporarily. Something within the industry or the company has caused them to decline in value relative to other companies' shares in the industry.

Emerging or small-cap shares. These are shares in very young companies that have an exciting story, possibly a strong revenue-growth track record, and great perceived potential for continued growth in the future. They may, or may not, become the growth star shares of the future.

When you find listings for stocks that interest you, how do you know how well they are doing in the market? One basic way is follow a stock market *benchmark*. One such benchmark we all know about is the *Dow Jones Industrial Average*. A benchmark, then, is an average of the results achieved by many stocks. Stock market benchmarks give us some idea of how stocks have done recently in general. A particular stock can then be compared to the benchmark to judge whether it has done better, about the same, or poorer than the benchmarked average stock.

The same principle applies when you wish to compare mutual funds: You may determine how well a mutual fund has done against a benchmark index.

Major Stock Market Benchmarks

Standard & Poors 500 Index. This benchmark averages the performance of 500 of the largest U.S. corporations. Because the S&P 500 can stand in for the whole U.S. stock market, it often gets used as the model for something called a "stock index" mutual fund. These mutual funds aim to achieve the same performance as the S&P 500 by owning a somewhat similar mix of individual company stocks.

The Dow Jones Industrial Average. This benchmark is the granddaddy of all stock averages. It is the most widely known stock index, and the one you hear about most often in the news. Whereas the S&P 500 gets based upon a large number of companies' results, the Dow Jones comes from only 30 selected large industrial "blue-chip" stocks.

Of the 12 stocks that reflected the industries of the day when the Dow Jones was instituted over a century ago, only one listed back then still remains today, General Electric. The DJIA has evolved, as has the United States.

The original 12 companies that made up the DJIA

American Cotton Oil	Laclede Gas
American Sugar	National Lead
American Tobacco	North American
Chicago Gas	Tennessee Coal & Iron
Dist. Cattle Feeding	U.S. Leather
General Electric	U.S. Rubber

Major Stock Market Benchmarks (Cont.)

The current 30 companies that make up the DJIA

Allied Signal	Coca-Cola	Goodyear	J.P. Morgan
Alcoa	Disney	Hewlett-Packard	Philip Morris
American Express	Du Pont	IBM	Procter & Gamble
AT&T	Eastman Kodak	Johnson & Johnson	Sears
Boeing	Exxon	McDonald's	Travelers Group
Catepillar	General Electric	Merck	Union Carbide
Chevron	General Motors	3M	United Technologies

NASDAQ 100 Index. This benchmark indexes the 100 largest stocks that trade over the counter in the NASDAQ exchange. It includes both the smallest of publicly owned companies and some of the fastest growing, such as Microsoft, Intel, and Oracle.

Russell 2000. This index specifically excludes large companies and consists of 2,000 companies with market capitalizations (or total values) of less than $600 million. This index works well for many small companies and mutual funds made up of recently started high-technology ventures.

Morgan Stanley EAFE. Made up of 1,000 large companies outside North America and mainly in Europe and Asia, this index applies to international stock investments.

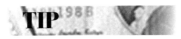
TIP

When orders for durable goods are up several months in a row, buy stock in durable goods companies. A durable good is a product with a long shelf life, such as furniture and cars. When orders are down or flat, buy recession-proof companies (such as manufacturers of food and beverages).

Joining the Creditors: Buying Bonds

Next, we can take a look at bonds. Owning a piece of the equity pie is not the only way to gain ownership into corporate America. We can also buy bonds—which are shares of a company's *debt*. So you can choose to own either equity or debt in a company. You do need to know just how different these two choices are.

When you buy a bond, you *lend* money to a corporation. You do not own a piece of the pie, you become one of the company's *creditors*. Usually, such lending gets done in $1,000 amounts or denominations; you buy bonds in multiples of $1,000—just as shares are usually bought in multiples of 100. When you buy a bond, you actually purchase two things:

- The company's promise to repay your principle at the end of a specified time period called the *maturity date*

- The company's promise to pay you a specified rate of interest (called the *coupon rate*) on the principle each quarter of a year until the bond matures and the principle is paid back to you

Notice that this investment differs significantly from stocks: A stock has an indefinite lifetime—a life as long as the company exists. A stock carries with it no promise to pay a dividend.

You might now leap to the conclusion that the value of the bond is guaranteed to you, whereas that of the stock is not. But that would be too hasty a conclusion. Why? Until the maturity date, the value of the bond that you buy is determined in the bond market. The bond market, however, values bonds in a very different way than the stock market values stocks. Bond markets value bonds on something much more certain—the *yield* that the bond offers.

A bond's yield is a similar idea to its interest rate—except that yield is based upon the bond's *current market price*, not its principle value at maturity. The longer the time to maturity, the greater the potential losses, or gains, in annual interest payments should the market interest rate trend go up some more, or go down. As a result, the longer the time to maturity, the greater the bond price's *volatility*.

For example, if the market interest rate goes up, and you hold a bond with 29 years remaining to maturity, you may lose the difference in interest rates between the current rate and the coupon rate for a long time period. Of course, the market interest rate may go back down again in a few years. Nobody knows, but the potential interest rate losses, or gains, impact the bond holder more when the maturity date is farther off—a greater number of years for losses or gains to accumulate. So the price gains and losses for longer-term bonds will be greater than for bonds close to their maturity date. What is the overall lesson? If you buy bonds, try to match the time remaining to maturity to the time in which you think you will need the principle paid back to you.

TIP

> To know if a tax-free bond is worth buying, divide its yield by one, minus your tax bracket. This figure shows how much you need to earn from a taxable investment to get the same return. For example, a tax-free municipal bond yields 4 percent. You're in a 31 percent tax bracket. Divide 4 percent by 0.69 (1 minus 0.31). The result is 5.79 percent. In this case, a taxable investment would have to yield over 5.79 percent to give you more income.

What if the company that you lent money to gets into trouble? The law says that the company must first pay off all of its creditors, before the shareholders get a thing. This means that you as a bondholder receive much more security than you would as a shareholder *in the same company*. On the other hand, bondholders never gain more interest or principle when a company does very well—and shareholders do. So again, it is a risk-reward trade-off that we face between stocks and bonds.

Notice, however, that the risks are *of a different kind*. Shareholders face losses and gains in the value of their shares and in dividend payouts as a normal, everyday risk. In a catastrophic situation, they stand to lose everything. Bondholders, on the other hand, face normal risks from changes in interest rates in the economy (*interest rate risk*). In the event that the company faces a catastrophe, bondholders face a *credit risk*—the risk that they will not receive full interest and principle payments. But their credit risk is far less than the shareholder's risk. Bondholders get paid off before stockholders get anything.

Many different kinds of organizations offer bonds; unlike stocks, bonds are not issued only by for-profit corporations. As we've already seen in Chapter 9, the U.S. Government issues bonds—rather low yielding, but of course very secure for the long term. States and cities also issue bonds, as do other governmental agencies. Some of these bonds pay interest that does not get taxed—if owned by the residents of the cities or municipalities that issue them. Of course, the interest rate that they pay is lower when they have this tax-free feature. The bonds issued by corporations generally pay higher interest rates than government and other nonprofit organization bonds do, largely because government bonds have the taxing power of a government to back them up. That makes them more secure, so they sell at lower interest rates.

TIP

> To determine how much you should have in bonds, multiply your age by 75 percent. If you're 40, it will be about 30 percent. Divide that among corporate, Treasury, and municipal bonds. The rest should be in stocks.

At this point, you understand the basic differences between the investment world of stocks and the investment world of bonds. Now we can go on to describe the *third world* of investments—the "hybrid" world of mutual funds.

Investing the Easy Way: Mutual Funds

In a very real sense, mutual funds are to the *investment kingdom* as hybrids are to the plant kingdom. Hybrid plants are crosses between many different varieties of the same basic plant. Hybrid corn, for instance, comes from breeding many different kinds of corn. Hybrids get created by plant breeders because they offer certain unique advantages—such as resistance to crop losses from disease and from destructive insects. Like individual plants, stocks and bonds have "lives"—they live and grow in value. Individually, some of them may die off, falling victim to time itself or to outside predators, but others like them carry on.

Similarly, mutual funds are collections of many similar investment instruments—such as stocks, or bonds, or other things. When you buy a mutual fund, you buy a share in this total collection of investments. The collection gets called a *portfolio*. Just as hybrid plants resist destructive disease, because they carry the genes of many different individual types of plant, hybrid mutual funds resist loss of your principal, because they carry many different companies with different exposures to financial risk. Both hybrid plants and hybrid mutual funds, then, resist loss. They have both been *engineered* to do so, by plant engineers called biologists or by investment engineers called financial managers.

Hybrid plants also resist some destructive insects, because these plants have been engineered to produce certain insect-killing substances. Similarly, the hybrids of the financial world get engineered to resist the most nasty insects that threaten your own investments—inflation and catastrophes that can strike individual organizations. These things are like giant bugs that can eat up your investments. Maybe now you can better understand why mutual fund growth has been so spectacular in the United States. Who wouldn't want these sorts of resistance to financial disease?

Let's dig into a little more detail about how these hybrid mutual funds actually work. We might call them "user-friendly" organisms. They provide a simple way to pool together the relatively small amounts of money each of us has to invest. That way, a common pool of money gets created, big enough to buy many, many different stocks, or bonds— far more variety than any one of us could afford to buy as individuals. And the financial managers at the mutual funds can buy these many stocks, or bonds, at a much lower cost to us than if we could buy them ourselves. Joining into a common investment pool, then, turns out to be much cheaper and more efficient than if we were to act on our own. When we buy into a mutual fund, each of us buys a number of *shares* in the total portfolio owned by the common fund. These shares have many of the same features as shares of individual common stock in a company—except the risks of ownership now get spread out among many companies. One share in a mutual fund, then, makes you a joint, indirect owner in, or lender to, hundreds or even thousands of individual companies.

Did You Know?/¿Sabía Usted?

Plain English is the official language of the mutual fund industry. The SEC wants to make sure investors can understand the information funds are required to give, and among the new rules it has enacted the following:

Plain talk. The SEC has banned legalese from key parts of mutual fund prospectuses and variable life insurance policies.

Less clutter. Technical matters are moved to a fund's Statement of Additional Information.

More disclosure. Funds will have to run a risk/return summary at the front of the prospectus, spelling out their risks. They also will have to show year-by-year returns for the past 10 years.

There will also be a slimmed-down prospectus, called a profile prospectus, effective June 1, 1998. Its 12 sections will detail a fund's objectives, risks, and costs.

Just as there are many different hybrid plants, there are many different mutual funds. Just as hybrid plants fall into a few basic types, so it is in the world of mutual funds. One basic way to type mutual funds is by the nature of the shares that you buy in them. Some mutual funds get called "open-ended" funds—because they place no limit on the number of shares that they sell to investors. Obviously, the other basic type gets called a "closed-end" fund. These funds have only a fixed number of shares available for purchase. Most mutual funds happen to be the "open-ended" type. Let's look at the reason why.

Open-ended funds can have an unlimited number of ownership shares, with the number of shares changing daily and depending upon new purchases of shares versus redemptions of existing shares bought back by the fund. Both the number of shares, and their price, changes daily. Price is determined by the *net asset value (NAV)* of each share. To determine the daily NAV, the fund managers take the total value that day for their entire portfolio of assets and then divide that by the number of shares outstanding. For example, if the Exito Mutual Fund has $10 million in total assets, liabilities of $1 million, and 100,000 shares outstanding, its NAV would be:

$$(\$10M - \$1M) = \$9M \ / \ 100K = \$90 \text{ NAV per share}$$

Closed-ended funds, on the other hand, create only a one-time, fixed number of shares. Once these shares have been sold, no more become available. Shares in closed-ended funds trade on stock exchanges, just like regular stocks. The value of these shares gets determined by the forces of supply and demand in the market just as it does for regular stocks, not by a NAV calculation.

Why Do People Buy Mutual Funds?

Mutual funds offer a unique set of features and benefits to small investors. Let's face it, most of us just love the high returns that we may get through stock ownership, but we have neither the time nor the expertise to do our own investing in the stock markets directly. That calls for carefully established investing goals, thorough research, and close attention to one's portfolio—a full-time job for people with expert knowledge. Even then, you should know that it is extremely hard to do better than average in the market day after day. If this were not limitation enough, most of us simply do not have enough money to buy enough stocks in order to receive the full benefits of a *diversified portfolio* that spreads our risks among many companies. Mutual funds, then, have become so popular for the simple reason that they were designed specifically for the needs of small, individual investors. Just look at the benefits mutual funds give us:

Professional management. Each fund gets run by professional investment managers who actively work to achieve the funds objectives for its shareholders, you and me.

Clearly defined objectives. Each fund has a clearly defined investment objective that helps us decide whether it is suitable to our particular investment needs. For example, some funds have the objective of maximizing capital appreciation through investing in under-performing companies that are likely do much better in the future. Such funds could be ideal for those of us looking to invest money long term for purposes such as college or retirement.

Diversification. A major feature of all funds, diversified portfolios mean that we gain access to the benefit of having our money spread among many companies or different types of assets, thereby reducing the impact upon us of one company or industry or asset type happening to do badly.

Convenience. Mutual funds are simply the easiest way by far to buy, own, or sell diversified portfolios of investments—for most of us, in fact, the only practical way. Each of us should spend time doing what she or he likes the most and does the best; chances are, that won't be investing in stocks and bonds. If, on the other hand, you believe that you possess these rare investing talents, perhaps you should pursue this as a career goal. Otherwise, it seems best to invest in mutual funds through our company 401(k) plans or by telephone to direct marketers such as Schwab and Vanguard, or via the Internet.

Liquidity. Most of us worry about how quickly we can get our money back in the form of cash when we invest. Most mutual funds provide for over-the-telephone redemptions of shares, check writing, and/or automatic withdrawal plans. Money access is almost instantaneous.

Cost. Mutual funds turn out to be considerably less costly than direct purchase of some of the underlying stocks. One purchase enables us to buy, in effect, hundreds or thousands of different underlying assets. Once we've bought in, most mutual fund companies allow us to transfer money among their various funds with no additional cost to us. You've often heard that "there is no free lunch," but here's a free lunch for you.

How Do You Make Money with Mutual Funds?

People new to mutual fund investing often ask this question, so let's take a look at the answer. You may make money through:

Capital gains. Whenever fund managers sell a particular stock or security for a profit, the fund makes what is called a *capital gain*. These gains must get distributed to shareholders within one year.

Income. Mutual fund portfolios may contain investments that produce a stream of income from either stock dividends or bond interest payments. You may receive your share of these incomes directly as cash, or you may have them reinvested to purchase additional shares in the fund.

Gains in NAV. If the fund managers do a great job of investing for you, the NAV of your shares goes up, due to this increase in the values of the underlying assets held in the fund's portfolio. When this happens, your shares grow more valuable, but you may have to pay a capital gains tax when you sell them.

The Tax Man Cometh!

This brings us to an unpleasant subject related to mutual funds. Wouldn't it be wonderful if we could keep all those great dividend and capital gains that we make in our mutual fund investments! But we cannot. The federal and state/local authorities will want their share of your gains. Sorry about that. When your mutual fund account receives dividend and capital gains distributions from the fund's successes, nasty things called *taxable events* get created. They automatically create tax liabilities for you. The very same activities of mutual fund managers that benefit you also create a complicated and difficult-to-calculate set of these tax liabilities.

Dividends and capital gains will be the easiest for you to understand. At the beginning of each year, your mutual fund company will send you a 1099-DIV form showing you how much income your shares made the last year. You owe taxes on this income—*even if you did not receive it* but had it automatically reinvested in the fund instead. You use the 1099-DIV information when you do your personal income taxes. Reporting capital gains and losses that come when you sell your mutual fund shares can get trickier. You may have purchased shares at different times and at different prices, so you could have a pile of fund statements to go through to determine at what prices you purchased shares. Many funds make this experience easier for you by providing you with the average price you paid for all of your shares over a period of time.

People often find themselves literally stunned by what they owe in mutual fund–produced taxes. Why? Well, mutual funds work as something called "super-compounders." Think back to Chapter Five, where I gave you the idea of a financial elevator. Some financial elevators shoot your wealth up much quicker than others—because they produce compounded rates of return that far outpace those of savings instruments such as bank CDs. This happens simply because the rates of return that they compound are simply much bigger in the first place, and the compounding happens continuously rather than quarterly or monthly.

A "super-compounding" financial elevator is a great thing to take an investment ride on; you really shoot up! Unfortunately, we sometime fail to realize that they also produce super-compounding tax events as our investment incomes and capital gains multiply the tax liabilities, too. While we will not discuss retirement plans until a later chapter in this book, you should recognize right now that you cannot *evade* these taxes, but you can *postpone* the payment of them through such retirement planning vehicles as 401(k)s and other tax-favored approaches such as Individual Retirement Annuities (IRAs).

What Kind of Fund Should I Buy?

With over 8,000 different mutual funds to choose from, Americans have very rightly become confused about which fund(s) to buy. How do I choose the right one, you may wonder.

You have already taken the first steps in selecting mutual funds! Remember, you have done an exercise to determine your level of risk tolerance (the risk questionnaire found in this book's appendix that you have completed). You have also worked hard to clarify your personal investment objectives—college for the children, personal retirement, a home purchase, or something else. Now it is time to decide upon a mutual fund that will help you reach those goals with risk that lets you sleep at night.

Did You Know?/¿Sabía Usted?

Want a sure-fire way to sleep comfortably at night by never again having to make another investment decision? Buy a fund that tracks the S&P 500 with an S&P 500 Index Fund. Remember that roughly 90 percent of all mutual funds underperform the S&P 500, so by buying a fund that tracks this index you will give yourself plenty of diversification and guarantee that your performance will beat those funds that lag the index.

Let's take a *more* detailed look at each of the three major categories of mutual fund.

Stock Funds

Stock funds fall into six basic categories:

Aggressive growth funds seek to maximize their growth in value through portfolios that emphasize smaller, newer companies that may really take off in the future but pay little or nothing for dividends now. These funds also have the highest risks attached to them.

Growth funds hold stock portfolios of well-established companies that have grown more rapidly than others in the past. These portfolios promise more moderate, stable growth than the aggressive funds, with somewhat more emphasis upon dividend income.

Growth and income funds balance off capital growth and income more evenly than do the growth funds. Their portfolios contain both growth-oriented stocks and stocks paying higher-than-average dividends, such as utilities and preferred stocks giving bond-like income returns.

Index funds. Managers of these funds buy a mix of stocks that mirror the overall stock market. As a result, these funds perform very closely to the stock market generally—no better, no worse. Average. If you doubt the ability of growth fund managers to beat the market consistently, you can buy one of these funds in the assurance that you will do at least as well as all stocks.

Global funds invest in the stocks or companies located in many parts of the world, including but not limited to the U.S. The objective is usually long-term capital growth.

International funds differ from global funds in that they do not hold any U.S. investments at all. They contain more future promise of growth than to global funds, but also higher present instability and risk.

Bond Funds

Bond funds fall into four basic categories:

Corporate bond funds invest primarily in the debt instruments of major American corporations, with the objective of attaining high current income for share holders.

The Rule of 72

Recall the Rule of 72 from Chapter 5? It is a quick way to gauge how long a rate of return will take to double your money. It works like this: Divide 72 by the percentage return you expect to get with a particular investment. For example, a 10 percent return will take 7.2 years (72 / 10 = 7.2). In the same way, an 18 percent return would take four years, and a 36 percent return would take just two.

Municipal bond funds invest in bonds issued by municipalities—cities and towns. They have the unique feature of offering completely income-tax free earnings. Of course, they have lower yields as a result. Individuals in higher income tax brackets who want current income usually find these funds attractive.

U.S. Government bond funds invest in a wide variety of Federal Government securities, thereby spreading out the risks of interest rate volatility upon share prices. Such funds attract investors who want a reasonable current income with absolutely minimal risk of capital losses—retired people for instance. They produce incomes that are federal income tax free.

Global bond funds invest in debt issued by corporations in both the U.S. and in foreign countries. Such investment portfolios offer somewhat higher yields at the cost of somewhat higher risk.

Money Market Funds

As you may remember from Chapter 9, money market funds offer you ways to increase your returns on savings. Let's look at them in more detail now.

Taxable money market funds invest in short-term, high quality securities such as CDs, Treasury Bills, and corporate obligations. They offer higher returns than traditional savings vehicles for very moderate risks. The dividends they pay are taxable income to you.

Tax-exempt money market funds invest only in securities that are exempt from federal income taxes, as well as state income taxes in some cases. They have a similar appeal to municipal bond funds.

Load, or No-Load?

Next to the sheer number of funds to choose from, this load versus no-load matter confuses people as much as anything else in mutual fund investing. At the most basic level, load versus no-load has to do with how a mutual fund pays for its costs of selling you its products. A "*load*" is just a confusing term for a sales commission. So for instance, if you buy a mutual fund investment through a sales person such as a stock broker, insurance agent, or bank representative, you will pay a fee in the form of a sales charge, or "load." If you pay this fee when you make your investment, it is called a *front-load*. You will find that this front-load will cost you between three and five percent of the total amount you invest. But the sales charge can sometimes appear as a charge that you pay when you sell your shares, or within a certain specified period of time, usually five to seven years. Then it is called a *back-load*.

Did You Know?/¿Sabía Usted?

No-load index mutual funds will make you an expert. These funds invest in a group of stocks of a particular index—such as the S&P 500 Index—and their returns mirror that index. It's an easy way to keep pace with the market. Three-quarters of all professional money managers do not regularly outperform the S&P 500 Index.

The answer to whether to buy a loaded or no-load fund turns out to be a simple one. Let's begin by looking at the reasons why you should consider buying through a financial advisor where you get charged a fee. As it turns out, the fee pays the professional you work with for his or her services to you. In return for your receiving something of value from this professional, you will pay a percentage of the amount that you invest—usually two to five percent. Whoever you deal with must do the following things for you, in order to deserve the fee that you will pay:

- Help you reach a thorough understanding of your own personal and financial situation—help you gain clarity of thought.

- Help you determine your specific financial goals and objectives.

- Determine your experience and knowledge of investments.

- Determine your feeling about risk.

- Educate you on the options available to you that will meet your own goals.

- Present you with specific ideas for meeting your objectives, and the reasons why a particular mutual fund will be an appropriate choice for you.

- Provide you with ongoing service and communication regarding your investment needs.

By now you should realize that the decision to use a fee- or commission-based sales person is a personal one that you must make for yourself, based upon your own experience, knowledge, available time to study these choices yourself, and comfort level working with an advisor versus without an advisor. If you do decide to use such an advisor, choose someone you have developed a trust relationship with, someone who you feel comfortable with and who you respect.

If you feel that you have no need to access the kinds of benefits that come from a personal relationship with a financial advisor, then by all means consider purchasing your mutual funds shares directly from a "no-load" fund company. For people who feel comfortable doing their own investing, these companies offer some people a valuable purchase source for mutual fund products, as well as advice about which of their funds to purchase.

Did You Know?/¿Sabía Usted?

Many corporations have Dividend Reinvestment Plans (DRIPs), where shareholders can automatically reinvest dividends in more shares without paying brokerage commissions. Most DRIPs allow you to buy shares commission-free. For information on DRIPSs, see the appendix, visit **www.sisepuede.com**, call the company directly, or see Standard & Poor's Dividend Reinvestment Directory.

Over the years, the no-load funds' market share has remained about the same—some 40 percent of the total industry. That tells me that a substantial number of Americans believe that the services of a financial professional are worth the two to five percent load placed upon such investments. *Remember, in any product class, a great salesperson always adds value to what you purchase by helping you clarify your own needs, and by directing you to those product that will best fill your own needs.*

Whether you buy a load or no-load fund, that fund will have expenses related to its ongoing operation. Each fund's expenses must appear in writing in its *prospectus,* the booklet that the salesperson must legally provide you prior to discussing the fund. This booklet provides you with important information about the fund's investment objectives, its management, its fees and costs, its performance over time, and your rights as a shareholder. In the fees section, you will notice a category called administrative or management fees. These are ongoing fees that pay for fund expenses. They may range from a low of about 0.5 percent for no-load index funds to 2.25 percent for loaded emerging market funds. The charges get calculated on the total assets held by the fund; you get charged your fair share.

Detailed comparative information on charges over many mutual funds appear in a number of sources, including personal finance magazines and the Internet—where Morningstar, the mutual fund research and performance-tracking organization, maintains a Web site (**morningstar.net.com**) that identifies the leading funds by category. Information includes fees and charges. When evaluating fund expenses, you should compare your fund's charges with the industry average for the particular category. If it is lower than average, then your fund manages its expenses more efficiently than most funds, for the benefit of you, the customer.

Mutual fund companies may also include additional fees used to pay for promotion and marketing costs, called 12b-1 fees. These annual charges pay the costs of the fund's ongoing sales and marketing efforts. The charges again get calculated as a percentage of total fund assets and include a portion that gets paid to brokers and advisors for servicing accounts. As do all fees, these 12b-1 charges appear listed in each fund's prospectus.

AT LAST, THE LAST THING TO KNOW!

In this chapter so far, we have taken a look at four of the minimum things you need to know about the world of fast-growth investing: what has worked in the past; why you need to focus upon growth; what the past tells you about the future; and an understanding of stocks, bonds, and mutual funds. The only thing that remains is to look into the best strategies or ways for actually maximizing the growth of your own personal wealth.

How to Use Mutual Funds

With so many funds available, which ones finally will be right for you? Which ones fit your investment objectives? Which ones should you buy? Bearing in mind that you have already identified your risk tolerance and your investing objectives, the question becomes: How should I combine my specific risk tolerance level and investment objectives with the many different kinds of funds?

I believe that the answer lies in *asset allocation*. Let me explain. Asset allocation as an investment strategy simply means dividing your money among *different classes or types of assets*—such as cash, stocks, bonds, and other forms of investments. Asset allocation strategies have been used by sophisticated, large investors for many years to achieve superior performance. This tool can now be yours; with it you can determine the optimal allocation for your money consistent with your concerns about risk.

Understanding Asset Allocation

Take a peek in your closet. You undoubtedly have a wide selection of clothes. Dressy. Casual. It took time and money to assemble your wardrobe. Now look at your financial closet. You may have a few interchangeable outfits in the form of mutual funds. Perhaps you have just one big item: cash. Maybe it's just a mess, and you're not sure what you have.

Depending on your goals and the condition of the financial markets, a formula exists for assembling a wardrobe of assets that is tailored for you. It's an organizer for financial shopping and storage problems called *asset allocation*. Your assets can consist of foreign and domestic company stocks, bonds, cash, maybe real estate or precious metals. The key is to figure out your financial goals, calculate your net worth, and divide it among a number of investments. Some may be safe, and some may be riskier but offer a speedier return. If you diversify in this way you'll largely be protected against changes in the economy and in any given market. As your goals, your age, the amounts you've accumulated, and the financial markets change, so should the percentages you keep in each asset category. Your job is to make sure those allocation percentages always stay within your current recommended range.

The biggest problem is maintaining any particular formula. For an asset allocation model to stay intact, the percentages have to be rebalanced, which is not as simple as it sounds. Let's say you have a portfolio of $100,000. You are allocated to have 70 percent, or $70,000, in stocks and 30 percent, or $30,000, in bonds. The stock market increases and your $70,000 in stocks is now worth $94,000, but your bonds didn't move and are still only worth $30,000. Your total portfolio is now up to $124,000. If you were to keep the same asset allocation percentage model, you would have to sell some stock and add about $7,000 to your bond holdings. But would you? It's difficult to sell a commodity that's making money and buy more of one that's not. And it takes

Understanding Asset Allocation (Cont.)

tremendous discipline to stay properly allocated, especially in fast-moving markets, and especially where there are tax consequences every time you buy or sell holdings. (Remember, taxes aren't a concern if you're investing in tax-deferred accounts. As a rule, feel free to rebalance nontaxable accounts and evaluate the tax consequences for taxable ones.) You also have to consider transaction costs when buying and selling within your portfolio. This can involve a lot of closet shuffling, but you should clean out your financial closet seasonally, just as you do with your clothes.

Asset allocation has been proven to be a profitable investment technique, if you can tolerate the activity and stay on top of your holdings and percentages. If you are not interested enough to do the work, a good strategy is to buy growth and income mutual funds that indirectly capture some of the benefits of asset allocation. Or buy an asset allocation series fund that maintains specified allocation targets. Remember, if you're investing in a fund outside of a retirement account, the gains within the fund will be passed to you (and taxed).

Is allocation worth it? Yes. As long as you keep track of what's in your closet.

How effective is asset allocation? The answer: It is critical. According to academic studies, asset allocation has been proven to account for *over 90 percent of the performance* of a given investment portfolio. Remember what we spoke about earlier concerning the temptation to try to time your investments to the market—to gain from a hot tip? Well, asset allocation studies have clearly shown that market timing has very little impact upon the overall performance of any portfolio.

You can access sophisticated asset allocation programs through many different sources. Any good professional advisor will have access to asset allocation software that will produce a recommended portfolio based upon your feeling toward risk and your financial situation. Mutual fund companies offer some asset allocation assistance directly, either in the form of paper-driven tools or software designed for the individual investor.

Once you have decided how to allocate your investments among funds, how should you go about actually buying shares in them? Many investors take the plunge with cash held in other accounts such as banks and money market funds. In that case, you may purchase shares in each mutual fund that you wish to allocate money to, in amounts coinciding with the asset allocations that you arrived at. For example, you may have decided to place 50 percent of your investment into an aggressive growth stock fund, 25 percent into balanced funds, 10 percent into international funds, and 15 percent into income funds. You could write a check to each fund—a check in each case made out for at least $1,000.

If you are just starting out investing and don't have such a large lump sum to invest, the mutual fund industry has come up with a process for making investing life simple for you. While most fund companies require a minimum investment of $1,000 to begin in a fund, most will reduce the initial sum to $100 if you commit to a monthly program of investing through automatic deductions from your checking account. In this way, most people can get started with mutual fund investing without having to come up with a large chunk of money to do so. And of course, it's convenient this way. As your account balance grows, you can begin to allocate your assets among different mutual funds offered by the same company. Now, you're into the growth business!

This monthly flow of dollars into your mutual funds account will also allow you to take advantage of a second strategy for investing in mutual funds, *dollar cost averaging*. This strategy means simply that you get yourself into the habit of making equal payments into an investment account at regular intervals *without regard to the price paid for each share.* Look at the benefits you receive when you begin this simple habit:

- Buying at multiple prices reduces the average price that you paid, since you do not try to time the market.

- You may end up with more shares in your account, and greater assets, because you purchased shares at lower prices.

Keeping Track of Your Wealth

Let's assume that you have now become a mutual fund shareholder. How should you track the performance of your investments? A word of caution here, if you've just recently made your first purchase, you're likely to find yourself in your excitement checking the newspapers every day to find your fund's current price. By all means have fun—but don't make a habit of this. Remember instead why you purchased the fund(s) in the first place—long-term wealth creation. You didn't (I hope) try to time the market. You instead developed a long-term wealth creation plan with mutual funds playing a clear role. You won't need the money any time soon. You used an asset allocation strategy to deploy your money into the right funds. Now sit back and relax; continue to put a little more money into your funds each pay period, and keep track of the results on a regular *annual* basis using the following tools:

- Your quarterly and annual reports from the fund company

- Annual surveys of mutual fund performance in newspapers and magazines

- The *Wall Street Journal*

- The Morningstar guide (found at libraries)

- Your professional advisor

TIP

Following stock, bond, and mutual fund prices every day will fog your long-term vision. Just look once every month or so.

SOME FINAL ACTION STEPS
FOR MAXIMIZING GROWTH

Review your own investment situation frequently, hopefully annually. Look at your company retirement plan, and at any personal retirement accounts that you may own. Ask yourself this question: To what extent have I put my money to work in equity markets?

Ask yourself how much you really know about investing and investment products. Undertake to educate yourself in order to better understand both the opportunities and potential pitfalls that surround investing. Read magazines and books, attend a course, ask your financial advisor questions, search the World Wide Web. *Take responsibility for your own knowledge about your own financial future!*

Make a conscious decision about your next step in personal wealth accumulation. What will you do next year? Do you really need to work with an advisor and pay a fee or commission? Do you feel that you now know enough to go it alone? You must decide, or events will decide for you.

Review your wealth creation goals. Ask yourself this question: How hard is my money working for me to meet these goals? Can I put my money to work harder for me?

Did You Know?/¿Sabía Usted?

Dollar cost averaging is deploying the same fixed amount of dollars every period for a regular and fixed number of equal periods of time. Suppose you have generated a cash reserve of $100,000. The market slides for three months, and you are prepared. Then things stabilize, and you think the worst is over. And you figure it may take a year to build up momentum again. Or maybe 20 months. Divide your $100,000 by 20, and spend $5,000 per month, buying whatever shares (stock or funds) that $5,000 will fetch. You will get more shares for the same money when the market is down and fewer when it is up. The net result is to bring efficiency to fluctuation and build a position at the lowest possible cost. (Unless you know the secret of exactly where all the bottoms are.) It doesn't matter whether the time periods are weeks, months, or quarters. Nor does it matter what the amount deployed each period is. It's the regularity that brings the efficiency. Nor does it matter if your estimate of duration is off. Whether that is longer or shorter, you're still in enviable position to take advantage of eventual future strength.

In sum, dollar cost average by investing the same amount every month in the same fund. You'll wind up buying more shares when prices are low, and fewer when prices are high. You can also do this for stocks. In both cases, this reduces the average price of your shares, and you don't have to try to time the market, something even the experts don't do especially well.

Determine your current risk tolerance level. You may feel more comfortable now with some risk than you did when you first began investing. Perhaps you should consult your financial advisor, or redo your risk tolerance assessment by yourself. What does this new assessment tell you about how you should be putting your money to work?

Investigate the funds that you, or your advisor, selected in the past. Read the prospectus for each, and review your objective for each. How well are they doing?

Use an asset allocation approach to investing, or reinvesting, your money among the most appropriate funds for you—given your overall objectives.

Use a dollar-cost averaging strategy to systematically make new investments each month as a low-cost way of continuing your rise toward financial independence.

Review the performance of your investment portfolio yourself, or with your advisor, at least annually. Compare the performance of your funds against the appropriate benchmarks. Consider carefully the changes that you might wish to make among funds.

Be patient...stay patient.

Investor Personality Profile Scorecard

Total Points:

8–12 = very high risk tolerance
13–18 = high risk tolerance
19 = moderate risk tolerance
over 20 = low risk tolerance

A final score of 8 to 12 marks you as an aggressive investor; a score of 13 to 18, a moderate investor; and a score of 20 to 24, a conservative investor.

Giving Back

In This Chapter

- Consider the ties that unite us as Latinos.

- Think how you can help Latino youth achieve a good education.

THE TIES THAT BIND
....

En la unión está la fuerza.

When we are really honest with ourselves, we must admit that our lives
are all that really belong to us. So, it is how we use our lives that determines what kind of people we are. It is my deepest belief that only by
giving our lives do we find life.—César Chavez

What binds us together, we Latinos? Do we hold anything in common,
we Mexicanos, Colombianos, Cubanos, Boriquas, Salvadoreños,
Peruanos, Chicanos, Dominicanos—and all of us others here in *Los
Estados Unidos?* In truth, we look, speak, eat, and dance differently—
each from the other. Some of us have been here as I write for only ten
days—or ten years, or fifty years. Some of us never came at all; the
country grew westward to reach us, the older *comunidad.*

What then unites us, diverse as we are? We grow so fast—at so many
levels of consciousness—here in America that it is a wonder we can
recognize any shared links at all. Sadly, we Latinos have never had
much difficulty finding things that separate us; all each of us has to do
is look to his or her own country of origin for comfort and power. It
then becomes easy to overlook the ties that bind us into one.

Diverse as our backgrounds may be, the truth is that we share a
common core of values and experiences that connect us directly to
one another, and indirectly to our living history. Some of these links
can be heard and felt distinctly—language, rhythm, and dance. Others
we cannot perceive quite so clearly; born in our memories, they shape
and form our beliefs that drive our everyday actions. Therefore, they are
very real, too.

We remember where the foundations of our strength and wealth
originate, that we are living beneficiaries of a long, rich history and

civilization. When the material culture of this American age threatens to overwhelm our identity, we rediscover the religious roots we spring from, the spiritual riches given us by people now long passed yet not dead to us. The central role of *la familia* still binds us to a greater existence as *hijos, hijas, hermanos, hermanas y compadres*. La familia provides the connection that we feel to *nuestra historia,* the powerful and resonant stories of our beginnings here—whether they originated ten years ago or several hundred.

We possess a living sense that the sacrifices of our parents and grandparents were not in vain, and we feel a living wonder over their accomplishments, achieved with so little materially. Could we have provided so well for our own children as they did for us, given what they struggled to overcome? Their quiet heroism inspires so many of us. We desire to do for our own children what they did for us. The desire for a good education, an appreciation for the importance of la familia, respeto, and the determination to succeed as Latinos in an Anglo world—these good things have been gifted us by our forbears. We must not let them down.

Direct, living, throbbing ligaments that bind us together as one body. The chords of memory that join us to la communidad no less persistently. Where do they finally point?

THE LIVING LIGAMENTS

¡La Música! Latin rhythms and sounds bind us like no other; they form the living ligaments that connect us together in one body and one culture. Much separates the updated Tejano sounds of Selena from the Afro-Cuban, Salsa sound of La India, but the common thread we

cannot escape: Music and dance, Latino rhythms, enliven us as vital elements of our lives, of the who-we-are. Think back for just a moment to the last non-Latino party that you went to and compare it to a recent gathering of family or close friends. Perhaps this family gathering celebrated a birthday, a graduation, a baptism, or confirmation. Almost without a doubt, music appeared as a central experience when family or friends gathered. What about that non-Latino party you attended? Probably you do not even remember what the music said to you, or even if music enlivened it at all. Whether we come from Puerto Rican, Colombian, Mexican, or Peruvian roots, our music has always been an integral part of the everyday business of life. It has always been this way; it always will be.

¡El español! Whenever we open our mouths to speak, the most powerful ligaments of all binding us together spring into action. Speech. Spanish speech. We revel in it. Notwithstanding the sometimes amusing misunderstandings that occur in conversations among us—because different Latino nationalities have given unique meanings to the same terms—we know that *el español* connects us in a way that excludes all others. Communicating in Spanish, we leap over boundaries of origin, education, and occupation. Language affords us the luxury of maintaining our rich ties to the past, while still living our fast-paced and complex modern lives today. Less obviously, *el español* connects us to a future that unfolds before our eyes. The thirty million of us here in *Los Estados Unidos* increasingly join together through language with three *hundred* million Latin American members of the greater *familia* of history and culture. *El español* becomes our language of the future. Our language grows in importance as a way to succeed in international business. It becomes important even for non-Latinos to know it. While anyone can speak it, it is still our language, the core to our feelings and to our existence as Latinos in the United States.

Pointers from the Past

Our chords of memory have so much to join us together—so much in common from the past to point us toward a rich future together. Why should we not be able to work together toward the common objectives of this future? Yet we often appear to be more fractured than whole, more quarrelsome than united. Some observers of the Latino experience in America offer up various socio-economic reasons for this, some argue for a lack of strong, national leadership. Still others argue that no such joined agenda matters, that instead, more education and assimilation into broader American culture will themselves foster Latino development. These arguments have become well known; the competing positions are staked out. Undoubtedly, you have your own position on just what the Latino agenda or common mission should be. Clearly, the priorities and needs of an ethnic community as diverse as ours will stretch across many issues, as they should. We are large. We have unlimited opportunities.

This said, what single item in a much debated overall agenda might every single one of us agree upon—the single thing that we can "give back" to the *la familia* and to the larger *comunidad?* I believe that such a single thing, compelling agreement among diverse communities of Latinos, does exist: *education.* All of our inherited passions for success, our hopes and our dreams, can focus upon this one pressing need.

The Facts Speak for Themselves

Are we too busy in our everyday lives, pressured by work and personal problems, too stressed by financial insecurities to think much about anybody else? What's in it for us, after all? Why should we care if 33 percent of all Latino high school students drop out before graduation?

What does it matter that only *one-third as many* of our young Latino adults have graduated college as have young Anglo adults? After all, they can work hard and still get ahead. And what about our younger children? Does it matter that in 1992 nearly 40 percent of Latino children under the age of eighteen were living in poverty, opposed to 13 percent of non-Latino white children? It is about time that we received a loud wake-up call!

What impact does it have that 40 percent of all Latinos in the United States have come as immigrants, with that percentage likely to grow in the future? We come here full of hopes, and poorly educated. Of what importance is the ability of Latino entrepreneurs to start, grow, and develop thriving businesses? How important is it for them to have access to information, capital, technology, and business contacts sufficient to compete in the twenty-first century?

The days may be quickly passing when an uneducated Latino immigrant could start with a used truck and build a construction empire, based upon sweat and a sixth-grade education. As a people, we understand *physical* capital all too well; we know that it takes tools and equipment to build up a successful business. Too often, we fail to understand the importance of another kind of capital—*human* capital—to the enterprises that we must start for the future. Just as factories build machines and tools, schools build knowledge, understanding, and the capacity to think through complex problems. Unless we begin to sink more of our personal *financial* capital into building up the human potential of our children and grandchildren, our great adventure in life in America may yet come to an unhappy conclusion.

Facts of life. By the year 2030, not so far away, *one in four* Americans will be of Latino heritage. No other ethnic group will have made so large an impact on American society in so short a time. What, finally, will that impact be? In order for 30 million of us today to assure that the economic pie for our children continues to get bigger, we simply must invest in our children's capacity to create new wealth in the future. We face the need for a tremendous investment in the economic and social empowerment of all young Latinos. Unless this happens, where will all the successful entrepreneurs of the future come from, the ones to employ all those new immigrants yet to come to this country?

The fact of the matter is that the continued economic success of not only we Latinos in America, but of the whole nation, will depend greatly upon how well integrated into the economic life of the nation we become. We will need to take leading roles in twenty-first century American life as the weight of our population numbers, our purchasing power, and our political influence grows. Will we be ready? Much of the answer depends upon our willingness to invest in ourselves.

I am excited by my experiences and my work within the Latino community around New York. I count myself privileged to have met Latino professionals, entrepreneurs, and community leaders who have committed themselves to giving something back, to making the kinds of personal and financial investments in our community that will assure its future success. I continue to be filled with enthusiasm for their mission. This book is a part of my contribution to building up the pace of our community's economic development. Everyday, I find my faith in the power of Latino entrepreneurship reaffirmed, but I know that much more needs to be done. We need more access to information and to capital, more contacts, business development skills, marketing ideas and knowledge, technological skills, legal knowledge, and management skills. All these are critical wealth-producing areas of life that many Latinos either do not understand or cannot yet effectively apply in their business activities.

Making Charitable Contributions Wisely

If you want to donate to a charity, never give just cash. Always write a check, even if it's just for $5 or $10. Make the check out to the organization, not the person collecting the money. It's the only way you can be sure the money gets to the charity. The charity will send you a written confirmation of your donation, which allows you to claim a deduction on your federal income taxes.

Be careful when you give. Watch out for fundraisers who implore you to send money now or else dozens of children may die. Avoid "charities" who offer to send a messenger to pick up your donation, thereby avoiding the postal service, and charges of postal fraud. They may use high-pressure tactics, which are often signs that you are dealing with a con artist.

Watch out for when someone calls on behalf of a charity and says, "I'm calling for" the charity, rather than "I'm calling from...." A subtle difference, but it can mean a telemarketing firm is collecting for a charity, which means the collection agency gets a portion of your contribution.

A caller may cite a recent tragedy or natural disaster and encourages you to provide financial information over the phone. Always ask for information in writing, and then send your check directly to the charity involved. The needy people will still appreciate your donation a week from now. There are plenty of wonderful, legitimate causes, and you don't want to waste your money on charlatans or hustlers disguised as charitable do-gooders.

Making Charitable Contributions Wisely (Cont.)

If you are contacted to donate to a charity that you are not familiar with, you may want to ask any or all of these questions:

- Are you a paid solicitor? If not, are you a paid volunteer or staff member?

- What percentage of the money will go to support the cause and what percent, to fund-raising?

- Specifically, what has the charitable organization done in the last three years to support the cause?

- Specifically, what does the charity plan to do in the next three years to support the cause?

- May I have some information in writing? (In most cases, fraudulent outfits won't have printed materials available.)

So whether we speak of our children or of ourselves, the single thing that we lack most is education. When we drop out, we simply fall farther behind. When we enter business life or when we become entrepreneurs starting our own businesses, we begin from a position behind Anglo Americans. Nothing can improve until we learn more! And yet, education, acquiring human capital, is very costly. College tuition is expensive. Even more expensive is the lost hours of work when we remain in school getting an education. Economists call this an *opportunity cost*. The real cost of a high school or college education is the earnings we give up when in school. But if we do not pay these opportunity costs, what opportunity will we have for the rest of our lives? For many young Latinos, the cost often seems just too great. That is why the rest of us must give something back to younger Latinos strug-gling with school, before they give up. This is why education must become the single thing that unites us all, behind our children especially.

LA EDUCACIÓN—¡PRIMERO!

We Latinos have to become obsessed with education.—Antonia Hernandez, Mexican-American Legal Defense Fund

Did You Know?/¿Sabía Usted?

- The proportion of Latinos with less than a fifth-grade education is 14 times that of non-Latino whites?

- The proportion of Latinos with a high school education is 53 percent versus 83 percent for non-Latino whites?

- Only 9 percent of Latinos 25 years of age or older have a college degree versus 23 percent for non-Latino whites?

- The number of Latino masters and doctoral graduates is a tiny fraction compared to non-Latino whites?

- Full-time Latino workers earn 63 percent of non-Latino whites' incomes?

- Only 7 percent of Latino males earned over $50,000 compared to 22 per-cent of non-Latino whites?

In 1992, Bill Clinton won the American Presidency on great execution and the slogan: "It's the economy, stupid!" For Latinos, we will win at wealth creation when we can focus upon and execute this national slogan: *"La Educación—¡Primero!"* Educational attainment appears as the missing link between our numbers and our social and economic success. Without this attainment, an unacceptably large percentage of our community will consign itself to the occupational dregs of life, for entire families. So is it really none of our business? In truth, our population growth and pride in our culture will come to mean little if a large segment of us becomes permanently dependent.

Unfortunately, much of the current debate about Latino education has fallen into two areas—bilingual education and affirmative action. Unfortunate, because these issues will never propel us to educational excellence; they simply take aim at the wrong targets. Our obsession with education must take on a more personal focus: What can we do for our own children and those of our neighbors to see that these children personally excel in educational attainment? Yes, we do need government to provide schools with adequate resources, but parents need to provide their own *empuje,* and an opportunity exists for those of us who have attained a measure of success—educational and/or professional—to make a contribution, however small, to the goal of attaining Latino educational excellence. We need to give back something of what we have received. We should not do so just because we think it a "good" thing to do, or because we feel a little guilty about our own success, or because somebody asks us to volunteer. We should do it because our own future and that of our children depend upon such actions. We are all a part of one community, one body.

TIP

Get your children involved in saving for college. Even a child as young as six or seven can help save for college. Many banks offer "minor savings accounts," which help encourage children to learn to save. As long as a child can sign her name, she can open a joint "passbook savings account" with a parent. There is no minimum balance, and there are no service charges. The account earns interest, and monthly statements are sent to children to show them their savings. Children love to see the interest earned.

What can I do, you may ask? Just look at the "investments" that you can make right in your own communities:

Mentor a student—especially someone in those critical pre–high school years when all the modern temptations and risks of adolescence become so visible. This is also the time when role models become most valuable, when alternative futures become pictured in a young person's mind. Make a difference!

Get involved with an English language program—to teach or reinforce English proficiency for newcomers to the United States. The quicker they become comfortable with English, the faster they will get the skills necessary to do a good job.

Join a local chamber of commerce—not just to develop your own business contacts, but to help other entrepreneurs, and those who are dreaming of becoming an entrepreneur. Remember, entrepreneurship is the very life of Latino communities.

Work to gain support for Latino scholarships—many organizations provide scholarships to deserving Latino students; the only problem is that there are too many candidates and not nearly enough funding. While fundraising is an essential activity in every community, education should be its greatest beneficiary.

Join organizations supporting Latino educational development and donate some of your time. Some well-known national organizations include:

The League of United Latin American Citizens (LULAC)
777 N. Capitol Street
Washington, D.C. 20002
202-408-0060

National Hispanic Scholarship Fund
P.O. Box 728
Novato, CA 94948
415-892-9971

The Hispanic College Fund
One Thomas Circle, N.W.
Washington, D.C. 20005
202-296-5400

Get involved with your local school board—even better if your school district contains a large Latino population. Many school districts have seen a low participation rate among Latino parents, especially immigrant parents who may simply not know about how important parental influence can be with the school authorities, how school boards really work, and how the school board election process works.

Offer to speak to student groups about your own experience. Reinforce the value and importance of a complete education to career success. Show younger people that we Latinos can succeed in many managerial and professional careers, just like anyone else.

If you belong to a professional association or society, reach out to Latino students with your own message of opportunity. Right now we have far too few Latino engineers, MBAs, scientists, economists, historians, professors, doctors, and lawyers, to name some critical occupations. Get your association to support outreach activities. Remember, young Latinos are potential future members of your own association. You never know who's life you may turn around.

Did You Know?/¿Sabía Usted?

All mothers and fathers hold in their hands the ability to endow their children with the entrepreneurial spirit. The making of an entrepreneur starts at home in the cradle, because from the day your child is born, the outside world will desperately try to squash his spirit. Schools don't teach a student how to be in business for himself, or explain the exhilaration of creating a new product or building a company. Entrepreneurship is homework in the truest sense: If you don't teach it, it won't get done. Maybe it's as simple as starting a lemonade stand for your six-year-old. Give your child the capital to buy lemons and sugar, and help provide the labor. Every month, split the profits at a formal, sit-down business meeting. When your child gives you your share, he will feel 10 feet tall. You don't need to know anything about entrepreneurship, but you do know how to give responsibility and then back your child.

Many other things remain to get done; this list is by no means complete. Ask your friends and relatives about what they are doing to help guide local education in your community. No matter how small, your community will be looking for people to join organizations and help, for people with ideas and energy to accomplish missions. You can become one of those who make a difference, rather than one of those sitting on the sidelines.

Sometimes money may be an issue, but more often than not, the real issue becomes *time*. Will you give up even one hour a week of your time to give back to your community? That one hour of time you give back will produce an *infinite rate of return* to your personal wealth creation model—because when you give precious time you give no money, but you reap the benefits of this investment for the rest of your life in your children and in others that you help. You personally can make this happen, starting right now. Think about it! *Infinite returns.*

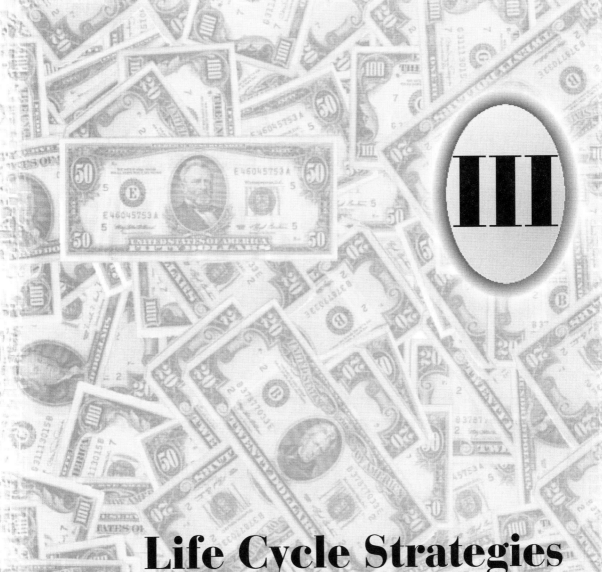

III

Life Cycle Strategies for Developing Latino Wealth

The cycles of our lives take us through changing challenges and difficult choices. Each decade that we live our lives, either we face up to those challenges, or we find that we fall more and more off the pathways that lead to achievement and success. No one can tell you what lifetime goals you must strive for; that always remains your choice. In the United States, we all possess this fundamental right to choose our life goals; we have been given a precious liberty—if we only will accept it.

Financial planning can tell you nothing about your choices in these goals. That remains your sovereign choice. Financial planning can, however, help you generate the resources to propel you toward your goals. It really is of little use if you decide to travel from New York to San Francisco but have no way to pay the airfare. Part III of *¡Sí!, Se Puede* meets you where you now live. Whatever goals you have set for yourself at this time in your overall cycle, practical wealth creation strategies can help propel you toward the success that you desire.

The life cycle approach allows us to meet together where you are now. What actual situations do you deal with? *Graduating from college and taking that first real job?* How do you deal with having to manage money on your own? *Saving for a first house or a new car? How about saving for college?* Will it really cost $200,000 to send my child to a very good college? Where am I going to find that money? *Struggling to help support elderly parents or relatives? Facing retirement in the not-too-distant future?* You've worked all of your life and panic sets in when you realize that you can no longer rely upon your earnings from work to carry you forward. What should you do to maximize your retirement income? How much do you really need to save? What is better, a regular IRA or a Roth IRA?

Many of these sorts of questions arise to trouble us, no matter what our age may be. Mostly, we fear to even ask these questions—perhaps because we so often look for the worst answers. It turns out that once we have asked the right questions, the answers are not that scary. As Latinos, we have some big advantages. Industriousness helps us overcome obstacles, no matter what age we may have attained. But we are also by and large a very young people. That means that many of us have the luxury of time on our side. We can easily succeed in the personal wealth creation process, if only we ask the right questions today, rather than fritter away our tomorrows in delay. We must seize upon the time that has been given us, while it is today. Remember, tomorrow is only written in the calendar of fools. *¡Adelante!*

13

Creating Wealth in Your Twenties

In This Chapter

- Learn how to get control of your financial life.
- Take the initial steps to creating your first million dollars.

NO GUARANTEES

· ·

El tiempo perdido no se recupera jamás.

Things somehow seemed much more certain for my generation—the forty-somethings—when we lived out our twenties. Probably we saw less opportunity but also fewer threats to our future well-being. Today, when I meet people in their twenties, the overriding sense that you communicate to me gets captured in just one two-word phrase: No guarantees.

What has changed so much over the past twenty to thirty years? Partly I think it is our *aspirations.* As younger Latinos today, you have so many more options to make a big difference in your own lives, and in the lives of those you love. To a much greater degree, challenges, *los desafíos,* surround you with all of their potential rewards. On the other hand, so much more gets expected of you—and there are no guarantees for a good outcome. Good English matters more than ever, even while knowing Spanish, too, has its big rewards. An excellent education matters more than ever. More and more of you move into the ranks of the college-educated. This becomes more essential every year; a college education gives you the surest beginning on a pathway that leads to personal achievement and wealth creation. If you do not have a college education, you begin to worry about how that might hurt you. In any case, you need to begin adult life.

This means finding the right career track and the right first job on that career pathway. It means doing all that is expected of you, and more. You should continue to learn, go back to school, or get a master's degree; add new skills, make new contacts, develop relationships with people who will mentor and guide you along your way. No, it is not a simple road to travel. In the super-competitive world that we live in, each step of the way can seem fraught with peril. No guarantees. Of course, this must be true when we get asked to take charge of our own lives, not have someone else run them for us. It is the price of human liberty. When you encounter it for the first time, it can be awfully scary.

This is not a career planning book. You may wish to look at *Latino Success* by Augusto Failde or *Just Because I'm Latin Doesn't Mean I Mambo* by Juan Job if you have career concerns. Once you have set out on a career pathway and have your first real job, what then? What's next? Suddenly, you find yourself overwhelmed with choices. You now earn a regular paycheck—perhaps more money that you've ever earned in your life. A miracle! You rejoice, until the bills start coming in—which are also bigger than anything you've ever imagined in your life! Unfortunately for you, Personal Finance 101 was not offered at your college or high school, or you did not bother to take such a course. You suddenly have what seem like a million financial decisions to make, small and large, all hitting you just when you have to get your personal life in order. These include:

- Rent to pay

- Car buying decisions to make

- Paying phone, electrical, and cable bills—things you did not know existed

- Paying off school loans, perhaps

- Paying off credit card bills you ran up so easily

- Buying clothes for work, shell-shocked at the cost; up goes the credit card balance

- Paying for transportation to work

- Buying food and a million little incidentals

- Paying taxes; when you made much less, you didn't worry about this one

- Paying for insurance; before, you had nothing to insure and didn't worry about this one

- Going out—*gozando*

- Saving some money for a rainy day or ????

When you get that first paycheck, it seems as if you hit the jackpot, and then all these bills come pouring in. Reality strikes like a bolt of lightning: You're only a temporary holding account for money—holding it until you begin writing checks for all of these things. If you live in this place, then this part of *¡Sí!, Se Puede* has been designed for you. How can you get your financial life in order, under control, so that you can put your efforts where you need to—into family, education, career, and community?

PUTTING YOUR FUTURE FIRST— PAYING YOURSELF FIRST

First things first. Why do you always seem to pay bills in a way that rewards you last? As you have doubtless discovered by now, the person who gets paid last usually does not get paid at all. The money runs out. So why not start to pay yourself first? That means starting to save something for your future—priming the pump of your own personal wealth creation engine. Otherwise, you will watch the years go by, while you still pay others first. Your earnings go up each year, but so do the bills you pay to others. You just continue to break even—or worse, those credit card statements pile up.

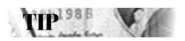
TIP

> Credit card companies want you to just pay the minimum on your monthly balance. Don't do it. Just paying the minimum on your credit card will keep you in debt forever. Add something extra every month, even if it's only $10.

Of course, no one forces you to take advantage of your greatest asset; you have freedom of choice—at least until the credit straitjacket starts to pinch. What is your greatest asset? Your own ability to start paying yourself first and then watch your assets grow. Can't I wait until I am older, you ask? Can't I wait until I have family responsibilities—spouse, children, a mortgage? Yes, you can. And then, you will simply find that you have to pay even more people, before you can pay yourself. So that's not a very good solution. The only responsible solution to the problem of whom to pay is to pay yourself first—today! Let me show you the difference.

Suppose at age 22 you take your savings to date from work and gifts, $2,000 that you have squirreled away in a passbook savings account, and you consciously invest it at a rate of return of 10 percent per year. (That's not a great return, but only a little less that the stock market has averaged over the past fifty years.) What happens when you pay yourself first this way, rather than spend it on something you could live life without? Well, in eight years, by the time you reach 30, you'll have slightly over $4,000—enough to help pay for a wedding, first home, first child. Or you may keep this money invested. By the time you reach your mid-forties and you have a child near college age, you now have nearly $15,000 toward a college education—not enough, but a beginning. But if you have earmarked that first $2,000 for retirement, at age 65 you now have $120,000! If you decided early on to be a bit more aggressive in your investments, and you averaged 14 percent on your money, you would have some $35,000 for a child's college education, or some $410,000 by retirement! A relatively small, one-time investment *made early enough* can cover what may otherwise become a hopelessly high future obstacle.

Now let's take that first $2,000 investment and make a commitment to paying yourself first every year—matching that first $2,000 with another $2,000 each year (about 8 percent of a $25,000 starting salary). What happens now? Again, let's assume that your investments give you an annual yield of 10 percent. By age 65, you now have $1.3 million. Invest for a return of 14 percent, and you have over $3 million.

Now, let's assume that your salary increases over time by a modest 2 percent per year, and therefore, you can invest a little more each year. At a 10 percent rate of return, by the time you retire, you will have more than $2 million. Of course, you must pay taxes along the way, and you may choose to use some of this money for a house and college education. But the fundamental point is this: *If you start saving 8 percent of your earnings early enough in life, you will always have the money for every good thing that you desire for yourself and your family!*

Remember, no guarantees. We do not know today just how much money Social Security will pay when you reach retirement. That means that we all need to start planning for the distant future much earlier than we thought we had to just a few years ago. Third Millennium, a New York–based advocacy group made up of people in their twenties and thirties, has expressed great concern about the future adequacy of federal programs such as Social Security and Medicare. Remember, when these programs finish paying for all the graying "Baby Boomers," the federal government may hand your generation the bill for providing your own benefits. Not fair, but it may happen.

Let's forget about retirement for a moment. That seems so far away. How about a bigger home by the time you reach middle age? College for your children? These things seem more real, and more immediate. How will you pay for them? Again, the answer is to start now when you are still young, not later, when it may be too late. That means paying yourself first, then pinching to pay other people next. It will amaze you how well this simple formula can work. If you're not sure how to go about this, look to Chapters Six and Seven as a guide.

Let's look at this matter of paying yourself first from another perspective. How does the prospect of *becoming a millionaire* appeal to you? Does it excite you? How about the prospect of achieving financial independence—where you choose what you want to do when? If these possibilities appeal to you, you can reach them. It takes a plan, and some strict discipline so that you keep to it. How can I begin this journey, you may wonder?

Determine what your current situation is. This is where it all begins. What is your cash inflow, and outflow, right now? Perhaps you earn $20,000 a year, or $25,000, or even $30,000. That's gross. What's left after taxes? Depends upon where you live—in a high-tax state such as New York or California, or a low-tax one such as Florida or Texas. You'll pay federal income tax of about 28 percent, maybe a state income tax of 5 to 7 percent, and even a municipal income tax if you live in a city such as New York. Then add in payroll taxes (FICA) at 6.5 percent and the 1.65 percent Medicare tax. Now who do you think you work for—yourself, or the government? In truth, that wonderful $25,000 starting salary comes out to only about $1,200–$1,400 each month in take-home pay.

TIP

When you buy a house, look at the school district. Resale values are better in the higher-rated school districts.

Now, what's your outflow? Here's where the spending plan from Chapter Seven comes in handy, for without it, you may find it impossible to identify all your destinations for your cash outflows. Let's say it looks something like this:

Rent	$350
Utilities	75
Food	300
Transportation	100
Student loans	150
VISA payments	75
Auto insurance	100
Going out	200

We've already got some $1,350 in monthly expenses, and we haven't included such things as health insurance premiums (if your employer doesn't pay them), car payments if you buy a car, vacations, clothes, more courses, and minor things in life such as laundry, dry cleaning, and dentist visits. Saving money? Well, that seems like a distant dream.

Other than by living like a hermit, or not eating, or sleeping in a park, what answer is there? Let's take a look.

As you have already learned in Chapter Six, where we went through the creation of a spending plan, *the benefit of knowing where your money goes is having the freedom to make choices about how you spend your money*— and to come up with alternative methods of meeting your daily needs. For example, look at the costs of housing to you. In our example, I used $350 per month for rent. If you live in San Antonio or Tucson, that may buy you a decent one-bedroom apartment; in New York, it won't even come close. Individual spending plans, then, get affected by the general cost of living in your area. If you live in an area where $350 gets you a decent place, one way to reduce your cash outflows is to share an apartment with someone else. This not only saves rent money, it can also save money on utilities, food, and transportation (if you can carpool).

Do you know where money most easily slips through our fingers? Food—especially if you eat out in restaurants. When you set up a spending plan, however, you can determine just how much of your income you want to spend on food—before you spend it. Perhaps you may not be able to go out six or seven nights a week—and still do the other things that you want—so you face reality and cut back to three or four nights. The key to managing these things comes in the form of *knowing exactly what you are spending today*—so that you gain the freedom to make decisions on what you will spend in the future. An investment in a couple of good cookbooks, some kitchen supplies, and some time will allow you to spend more money somewhere else in your life— maybe even on a saving plan for all of your bright tomorrows.

Now that you're on your own, credit card payments, car payments, and school loans probably eat up more of your income than you thought they would. You can refer back to Chapter Eight on how to eliminate debt. Some key points that you should remember:

If you have many different school loans, your lending institution may offer you a special consolidation loan program to reduce your monthly payments.

If you have a high-interest (19 percent plus) credit card, look into lower-rate interest offers by shopping around. You can shop on the Web at **www.bankrate.com** for a listing of some of the best (lowest) credit card rate offerings nationwide. Credit unions and alumni associations can be good sources as well.

TIP

> If you ever need to locate an out-of-town business, try calling the "800" directory first (800-555-1212); or log onto **www.555-1212.com**; **www.bigbook.com**; **www.bigfoot.com**; **www.whowhere.com**; or **www.switchboard.com**.

Cut back on impulse spending through the discipline of a spending plan. Do you really *need* that sweater, CD, or pair of shoes? Remember to ask yourself the golden questions: *Do I really need this, or want that? Can I wait to get it later?*

Once you get your spending under control, you can begin to create *future wealth* for yourself. Here's how you can begin.

Did You Know?/¿Sabía Usted?

Slow and steady—and early—wins the race to retirement. A national survey of 1,200 working people found that nearly half of them had saved less than $10,000 for retirement. That included 30 percent of people closest to retirement, ages 51 to 61, and 40 percent of baby boomers, those in the 33 to 50 age group. When asked why they hadn't saved more, 68 percent of all respondents said they could have if they tried harder.

Saving doesn't come naturally to Americans, and retirement isn't our only financial concern. We have day-to-day living expenses, home mortgages, and college tuition to think about. That's why it's important to start saving early for your retirement and other life goals. Starting early and staying with a regular savings plan can make a big difference in the value of your investment over time.

Step One

Remember, you can find many ways to save and invest money. Your first steps will be determined in a large part by your own particular situation. Does your employer offer a retirement plan? If so, you simply must participate in it, as soon as you become eligible. Or does your employer offer a 401(k) plan or a Simplified Employee Pension (SEP)? Then you will be eligible to contribute 15 percent of your pay up to $10,000 *before taxes* into these plans (see Chapter 15 for more details). Your contributions are made by a payroll deduction, so you do not even see the money in your paycheck—and you avoid the temptation to cheat on yourself.

In addition to offering such plans, your employer may also match your contributions to encourage employees to save for retirement. Your employer may match the first 2, 3, 4, or 5 percent of your contribution, up to a maximum level. *Employer matching is found money to you!* You should always contribute at least the minimum necessary to qualify for the largest payment your employer will make. For example, if your salary is $28,000 and your employer offers a 401(k) plan, you can contribute up to 15 percent of $28,000, or $4,200 each year. If your employer provides a match of the first 4 percent, the company then pays $1,120 per year into your account. That makes a total of $5,220 each year. Even if you cannot swing the maximum, you should at least pay in enough to qualify for your employer's maximum—you pay at least 4 percent in this example; remember, your employer's matching payment is found money to you. Even if you only pay the minimum to get your employer's maximum matching funds, you will have total contributions of $2,240 each year.

If this does not sound like very much to you, remember how the compounding financial elevators of life work: Your $2,240 each year, earning 10 percent compounded, will exceed $1.2 million by age 65. Your contribution works out to $15.50 per week after taxes. Can you afford to invest $15 per week in order to become a millionaire? The more relevant question is this: *Can you afford not to? The first step in your lifetime wealth creation plan is the pay yourself first—$15.50 per week!*

Do you know how much a week after taxes it costs you to become a millionaire by retirement? $15.50 per week after taxes!

Step Two

The new generation! Now in your twenties, you have become the new generation of Latinos—the generation facing a totally different set of lifetime issues, obstacles, and opportunities. No previous generation of our people have faced all of these choices. An incredible number of new opportunities await us; the challenges of living life in the twenty-first century also appear very real. Step two involves making yourself ready to take advantage of those opportunities as they appear.

The careers of today have become less stable; those of the future will become even less stable. Rapid changes in technology and communications have created a tremendous growth in new jobs, career opportunities, and entrepreneurial venturing. We Latinos must continue to develop skills, knowledge, and experience to match these fast-moving changes. This means continuing to invest in personal development—in "human capital" as the economists put it. How much human capital do you possess? Have you invested enough in yourself? A bachelor's degree is a fine *first step!* It is only a beginning. Possibly your particular career interest will not require something more—but do not bank on it. To stay current in your knowledge with all these incredible changes going on is merely a minimum. Ideally, we should each get a step ahead. Here are some ideas for stepping out ahead of the pack:

- Get a master's degree.

- Become computer literate.

- Build new communications skills.

- Build up public speaking skills and confidence in your ability to speak in public.

- Volunteer for charitable work to build up new experience and create new contacts.

- Learn a *third* language.

- Read books and magazines in your area of professional interest.

- Join professional organizations and associations.

- Find a mentor—an older, experienced person in your profession—to guide you.

Did You Know?/¿Sabía Usted?

HispanData, a subsidiary of Hispanic Business, Inc., is a national résumé database that links major corporations, such as IBM, Amoco, GTE, Nike, Time Inc, Kraft, and Miller Brewing, with Hispanic professionals and others with expertise in the Hispanic market. The service matches employers with employees. To learn more about becoming a member, call 805-682-5843, ext. 800, or see their Web site: **www.hispandata.com**.

Remember, a long road lies ahead of you—unlimited opportunities await you, if you can see them and be ready to seize them. You may get only one chance to prove yourself and stand apart from the crowd. Be ready. Don't stop learning; instead think of learning as a *lifelong* process. Continual personal development will become the basic requirement for successful life in the new millennium. Read on!

The Possible
Dream: College

In This Chapter

- Learn how to save an enormous amount by taking a value approach to selecting a college.

- Learn how your child's education, or your own, can be paid for.

- Learn the most cost-effective ways to borrow money for college.

- Learn where *not* to go for money.

- Learn how to find special Latino scholarship money.

IMPOSSIBLE DREAM—BIG LIE!

Al hombre que sabe hacia dónde va, el camino se abre para dejarlo pasar.

To achieve economic success, we must face the truth about college, about advanced levels of education and the resulting knowledge that we gain: *College is not the impossible dream.* College is the readily attainable goal for every normal young Latino person, female as well as male. Never allow yourself to accept the *Big Lie*—that you or your children are not good enough or rich enough to earn a college degree. Remember, the truth is that you not only can do this, you must do this for your own and your family's sake.

It has not always been this way. Many readers of this book have already become the first college graduates in your families. You achieved something not readily available to your parents. You remember your parents struggling to pay college bills; working one, or even two jobs, while attending school; struggling to find some financial aid. It was not easy; the good things in life never are.

TIP

Teach kids the value of investing for the future. Open up a custo-dial mututal fund account and you can both watch the accounts grow in value over time.

Others will not have graduated from college; I am sure that you are determined that your own children will receive the opportunity to better their conditions in life. Some older readers of this book will wonder if it is not too late for them. Fortunately, it is not. Did you know that today in America, over half of all educational services go to adults beyond traditional college age? Nobody who can still work is too old to gain a college education. It used to be that gray-haired teachers taught children and adolescents. That still happens of course, but today in America, many young teachers teach gray-haired men and women! No matter what your age may be, you can still do it. *¡Sí!, se puede.*

We've dealt with the Big Lie. Now to the Big Hurdle.

LEAPING OVER THE BIG HURDLE

From professional dealings with my Latino clients, I have seen so many strong feelings related to the challenge of paying for college. People are brought to tears over how to pay for their children's college education. Next to retirement planning, college financing has become the biggest money challenge in life for so many Latinos. I think that we have reached the point as a people where the problem has ceased to be the Big Lie—that we somehow are not good enough to go to college. The problem has become the Big Hurdle—that we cannot afford college, that it is only for people richer than us. So let's tackle the Big Hurdle.

I believe that too many of us live in fear of the financial services industry. We think such things as, we won't measure up to what they will tell us. They won't give Latinos loans. Our children can't go to college because we cannot save enough, or we did not start saving soon enough. All of these *emotional* fears cloud our understanding. And the financial services industry has not helped: These firms have tradition- ally ignored us, and they typically market their products based upon appeals to fear and guilt. This is all too bad. Why? A financial services firm can be a big help in achieving our college goals. Let's see how.

TIP

> Go to college with your kids. Parents enrolled for six credits in a college degree program may be considered full-time students. The more full-time students a family has, the more likely someone in the family will be granted financial aid.

First, how do the experts look at the challenge of financing college costs?

Almost all of the marketing approaches used by financial services firms get based in fear and guilt, and paint an unrealistic picture of how college actually is financed.

A well-thought-out plan coming from some patience and research can eliminate the confusion and fear associated with paying for college.

Be realistic! The average middle-class family will not be able to save enough to pay for all college expenses, especially if more than one person will go to college. Some use of loan money and current income will have to be made as well, and there is nothing wrong with this.

A quality college education that will prepare Latinos for the twenty-first century can be paid for—but only through a realistic understanding of the concept of "value" and the use of multiple financing sources.

So much for the overall approach. Now let's start at the very beginning. Financing college should not begin where most people believe that it does—with a big tuition bill to pay. Financing college instead should properly begin with *value determination* and with evaluation of choices. What do I mean? Let's look at an old adage from the stock market: You make money when you buy, not when you sell. What this old adage means is that if you buy any asset—stocks, bonds, real estate, college education—you only make money on it if you buy it at a reasonable price in the first place. If you pay too much when you buy, how can you hope to make money when you sell? You see, if you pay too much, you do not receive enough *value* for the money you paid—so nobody will want to pay you that much when you wish to sell.

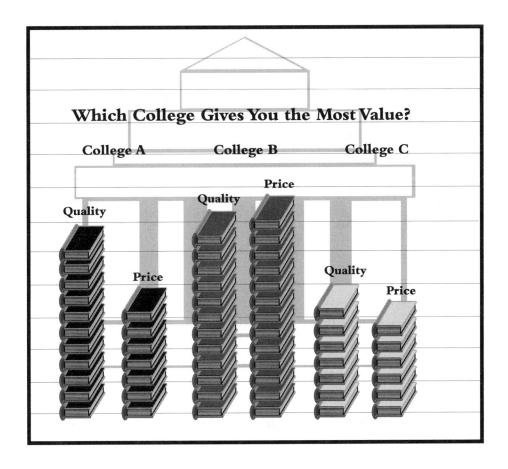

Value is defined as the excellence or quality of a thing compared to its price. When we say that we have gotten a great value when we buy something, that means that its excellence or quality compared to its price is high—compared to the other things that we could have purchased. To help understand this, we can think of every product as having both a quality column and a price column—and the taller the quality column compared to the price column, the better the value. In the graph shown on the previous page, which college offers you the best value? Wouldn't you say that College A does? Its quality is not quite that of the exclusive college B, but its price is much lower. Similarly, College C does offer low price, but it also offers low quality. Value matters.

I believe that we all intuitively understand this idea of value—that it is *relative* to the quality and price of each choice that we look at when we buy. Value is *value to me*. In the supermarket, we ask ourselves the question: Does the greater value, and higher price, of a name brand item give us more for our money than the store brand product? Most of us tend to think so, and we buy the name brand product. There is a danger in the name brand strategy, of course: It can trap us into thinking that high price necessarily means high quality. But sometimes, high price may not mean *added value to me*. When we look at purchasing a college education, this can get us into a misty confusion, and we seem to lose our good sense. Let me explain.

Choosing a college has become one of the most complicated and emotion-laden decisions that any of us face. Obviously, we take into consideration location, size, resources, reputation, course offerings, majors, sports, teachers, and activities. Then we run around looking at schools—perhaps a dozen or so. We have been told that a thing exists called a *perfect match*. A perfect match is supposedly the school that perfectly fits every requirement that an individual college student feels she or he has. And when finding the perfect match becomes our college selection strategy, then it is inevitably the case that *prestige* enters in. After all, shouldn't the perfect match include a great name?

But just think about this for a moment. If you need a new pickup truck, will you try to go out and buy a Porsche sports coupe at nearly $80,000? Of course not! Even if you could afford it, it's a terrible value for you: Too much money and running expense, and it won't even haul anything. Why is it, then, that we tend to throw good sense out the window and try to buy Porsche *colleges*? They cost too much, and probably won't even haul anything.

I believe that the problem starts with the strategy that the so-called "experts" on college choice give out: the strategy of the perfect fit. Throw that away. There is no such thing, not in the real world. Shop for a college just like you shop for anything else. Remember, reputation and high cost do not equal value; they may equal a bad buy. In truth, the "reputation plus high cost equals value" equation all too often merely creates totally unnecessary financial pressure and emotional burdens upon college students and parents alike. Get rid of the *myth* of the perfect college. Shop for *value*.

The first step in today's college financial plan for you, then, is to *make money when you buy*—by shopping for value in a college. Otherwise, those student loans that you take out will seemingly go on forever, eating up the future earnings gains that you thought a college education would bring you. Remember, you have great choices among colleges in America; choice is your sovereign right—and responsibility, if you wish to maintain your family's financial health. Choice means that we can search for alternative outcomes—some product of higher value to us than others. Let's look at choices among value strategies for selecting a college:

Consider the very best public universities that offer the programs you are looking for. Even an out-of-state public university with a national reputation will have fees less than average private colleges. And some states have reduced fee arrangements with the public universities in neighboring states. Check it out. Value.

Consider attending a local community college for the first two years and then transferring to a very good four-year college after the sophomore year. Community colleges often do a good job with introductory courses, allow living at home, and have the lowest fees around. What you save the first two years pays for the additional costs of the last two years. Value.

Consider a less-well-known private college with lower tuition prices, if its programs meet your needs. An above-average student can sometimes qualify for merit-based scholarship aid at such schools as well. Value.

Consider a low-cost public university for a bachelor's degree if you plan on getting a master's degree; that way, the combined cost of both degrees can be kept moderate. Value.

TIP

Encourage your kids to take college courses while in high school. Each course they take will save about $600 off tuition.

Here's the basic lesson so far: When you have identified a value strategy for college selection *before you even begin to shop*, you can begin to make money when you buy. This, in turn, means that you also have to finance less when you buy.

Compare this approach to the more common method of financing a college education. The common approach looks first at the likely or average costs of public and private colleges and universities, assumes that these numbers must be the real costs, and then asks the question: How can I pay for these costs? The table below should open your eyes—and also make a point. Hidden in these projected *average* costs for all college tuitions will be many, many great buys costing much less than average—if only you search them out. You do not have to finance these huge sums, if you shop to make money when you buy.

Projected Four-Year Costs for American College Education

Year Entering College	Private College Cost	Public College Cost
2000	$123,777	$49,511
2001	132,813	53,125
2002	142,509	57,003
2003	152,912	61,165
2004	164,074	65,630
2005	176,052	70,421
2006	188,903	75,561
2007	202,693	81,077
2008	217,490	86,966
2009	233,367	93,347
2010	250,403	100,161

Source: The College Board. Estimates based upon an annual college tuition inflation rate of 6.8 percent.

The financial services industry loves for you to focus upon numbers such as the ones I have just showed you. Why? They want you to invest as much money as you possibly can in their products. So show-ing you these average figures enables them to sell you the greatest amount of investments—if you do not die from shock first. Sadly, it also leaves many parents convinced that they will never be able to send their children to college. But as we have already said, that is the Big Hurdle. It can be jumped. Let's look at how to do it.

As you've already learned, the first step is to shop for value. If you can cut your actual college costs by two-thirds, or even half, of what the averages show you, look how much you have saved up front—before you ever save or spend a dime! Next, look at the various sources for college tuition dollars that you will need in the future:

Investments and savings
Retirement plans
Life insurance
Home equity
Current income
Financial aid
Scholarships
Loans
Student earnings

As you can see, saving hundreds or even thousands of dollars out of your income each month—dollars that you may not even have—is not the only way to pay for college. While it would be nice to save enough to pay for all our childrens' tuition costs as well as for securing our own retirement, we do also need to live day to day and enjoy our lives. After all, on an income of say $60,000 with a $120,000 home mort-gage, how much can you realistically save? The college money answer should lie in a strategy of mixing the preceding tuition dollar sources, rather than checking into the poor house. Let's begin considering these sources by looking at how much needs-based financial aid your children can expect to receive.

To begin with, American colleges have figured out all of this as well—that there is an upper limit to what parents can pay toward college. Colleges call this upper limit to what you can afford the *parental contribution*. College administrators know that they must find a way to make college affordable to you, or they will not have students. In both private and public colleges and universities, they use this upper limit to calculate various sorts of dollar aid amounts that will help your children pay for college.

Both your current income and the assets that you own enter into a parental contribution calculation. Fortunately, the federally mandated calculations used to determine your qualification for public college and university aid do not include the value of your home and retirement assets. Parental contribution calculations are based upon these basic items:

- Family income and assets

- A federally determined minimum standard for your everyday living expenses

The difference between your income and living expenses determines the amount you should have available to pay for college expenses, your parental contribution. After making this basic calculation, you can subtract the amount that your child will be expected to pay out of his or her own assets and income. The balance will be your child's eligibility for financial aid. A college that accepts your child as a student will next try to develop a package of money from various sources sufficient to cover the expenses that it will charge—less your parental contribution of course. The package will typically include grants, loans, and student employment offers.

While this may all sound easy to understand and fair, the minimum family budget imposed within the calculation results in an unrealistic determination of your actual family expenses—and a higher-than-reasonable parental contribution. For instance, mortgage payments and real estate taxes do not enter into the minimum family budget and therefore do not offset your expected parental contribution. The College Scholarship Service of the College Board estimates that a middle-class family with 1996 annual income of $60,000 and net assets of $80,000 (not including home equity, retirement plan assets, and life insurance equity) should be able to make a parental contribution of $9,200 per year toward a child's college expenses. Wow!

The expected parental contribution declines if you have more than one child at home, if you have another child in college, and if you happen to be older than forty-five. Nevertheless, access to official financial aid will be tightly limited for most middle-class families. To get a better idea of how much aid you might qualify for, you can use a free calculator on the College Board's Web site at **www.college-board.org**. You can also get a copy of a free booklet describing how your expected family contribution (EFC) is calculated by writing:

Federal Student Aid Information Center
P.O. Box 84
Washington, D.C. 20044

Now that you know how to shop for colleges and how to calculate your expected parental contribution, the big question still remains: Where do I come up with all the additional money? As you will remember, just a moment ago we outlined all of the various sources for college money. Let's take a look at each one in detail.

Savings and Investments

In Chapter Eleven, we looked at how you can maximize the growth potential in your wealth creation plan by utilizing investment products such as mutual funds, stocks, and bonds. We have also seen how starting early to save and invest for college expenses provides more time for the compound earnings elevators in these products to work for you. Starting to invest for college when your child is thirteen or fourteen will limit the amount that you will have available at age eighteen, because there is simply not as much time for the miracle of compounding to do its work. If you can start saving early for college expenses, do it. Remember, the least expensive source of money for college costs will always be your own invested savings. But you cannot relive yesterday. Even if you did not start saving early, you do not have to panic. You still have time to prepare a plan that pays for college costs. Let's go on.

Retirement Plans

Your personal retirement plan money can be used to pay for college. It does not represent the best choice—which is a long-term college savings and investment plan—because taking money from qualified retirement plans will have a cost attached. Most retirement plans provide for personal loans, up to certain limits. You can borrow up to 50 percent of your account balance—up to a maximum of $50,000. If you borrow more than that, the additional amounts will be treated as a taxable withdrawal, subject to penalties as well as taxes. And your loan will cost you one to twp percent more than the current prime interest rate. The main drawbacks to such retirement plan loans are these.

Repayment terms are not easy or flexible. You must pay back the loan over a five-year period, payable monthly or quarterly. If for any reason you cannot make these payments, the loan goes into default, causing an early distribution from your retirement assets—an event that has taxes and penalties attached.

Paying interest on a payroll-deducted retirement plan loan will probably limit or eliminate your contributions to the retirement plan itself, slowing the growth of the plan's assets for your retirement.

Neither the interest you pay nor the repayments to the plan will be tax deductible. Your money now gets taxed twice, once when you earn it to make the loan payment and again when you receive the money in retirement.

These drawbacks do not necessarily mean that modest retirement plan loans should not become a part of your overall college cost payment plan. They simply mean that these loans have higher costs to you than the ideal payment form.

Home Equity

While I can find no statistics on this, my own personal experience and that of many of my clients indicates that much home equity loan financing gets used to pay college expenses. If you have a home and have built up some equity in it—both through paying down your mortgage and through property appreciation—you can tap that equity to help pay college costs. Home equity loans have great usefulness because:

- They give you inexpensive loan money because they are secured by the value of your home. Secured loans always give you lower interest rates than unsecured loans.

- Payments will usually be tax deductible for you, reducing your income taxes.

- Equity loan programs have great flexibility, allowing for either lump-sum or credit-line borrowing. Credit lines can be accessed via checks that you write, so you only use loan money when you need it.

- Payment terms can be extended to as many as fifteen years, greatly reducing your required monthly payments.

Clearly, home equity loans when used for college tuition purposes can serve you very well indeed.

TIP

Colleges do not consider home equity a family asset when allocating financial aid. After financial aid is awarded, take out a home equity loan to pay remaining costs. The interest will be tax deductible.

Life Insurance

If you have purchased some form of *permanent* life insurance in the past, you can use the cash values that the policy has accumulated to help pay college costs. Permanent life insurance, as you may remember from Chapter Ten, comes in two basic types—whole and universal. One of the advantages of these products is that they do build up equity for you that you can use later in life as a loan source. These cash values are readily accessible, inexpensive, and quite flexible. Withdrawals or loans from life insurance are certainly superior to retirement plan loans— because they do not come with fixed repayment terms (they do not even have to be repaid), involve no tax penalties, and do not divert money going toward retirement wealth creation.

Current Income

Developing your own personal spending plan for your children's college years can free up money from current income to use for college costs. Remember from Chapter Six that a spending plan gives you the information to make decisions about where your money is going. It frees you to make choices about spending priorities—making it an excellent tool for helping pay for college costs. Postponing vacations, some retirement contributions, new auto purchases, and many other similar expenditures for just a few years can maximize your current income devoted to paying current college expenses. Remember, ask yourself the magic questions: *Do I really need this, or want that? Can I wait to get it later?* In the case of college costs, waiting to get it later can become the smartest move you ever made. Why? The least expensive source of money for you to pay college costs will always be your own current income. Of course, what you are doing through a spending plan is maximizing your actual *parental contribution*.

Financial Aid

Earlier we looked at how the standard parental contribution is determined, which in turn determines eligibility for student financial aid. All colleges require that you fill out specific forms to qualify for such aid. All schools require that you complete a Free Application for Federal Student Aid (FAFSA). These forms require extensive personal and financial data on both student and parents. Tax return information is also required, so you may wish to get your return done early in that year. You will be asked to name the schools that you want to receive your report for the purpose of determining aid decisions. The sooner you complete the FAFSA paperwork, the sooner you will learn what your expected family contribution (EFC) will be. The expected family contribution is the balancing amount that you must come up with each college year. It's the gap that you must fill through all of your own other sources. (Notice that if you use your spending plan effectively, you have a much better chance of meeting the EFC.)

How can you improve your chances of receiving financial aid?

Save money in your own name instead of your child's name. All of your child's assets will count in the financial aid calculation, while many of your own assets will not.

TIP

If you think your child may qualify for financial aid, don't put money into a "Uniform Gift to Minor" account. Thirty-five percent of a student's own money is counted toward his expected contribution to tuition, and the larger his account, the smaller his financial aid need.

Reduce reportable assets such as savings accounts, CDs, and money market funds by making deposits into life insurance, retirement plans, or annuities.

Apply to colleges that want students like your child. This may improve your chances of getting financial aid, because your child has some of the right characteristics—academics, extracurricular, sports, ethnicity, and religious background, to name a few. A word here about being *Latino*. Notwithstanding the national argument about affirmative action and race preferences, many schools see the obvious advantage in having

a diverse student body. Qualified Latino students who market themselves to the right colleges can increase their chances, not only for
admission, but also for generous financial aid awards.

Don't Put All Your Children's College Savings in Their Names

Parents often wonder whether they should be saving in their name or their child's.
There is an argument for either, but generally you should not put all your college savings in your child's name. When you open an account in your kid's name through a
custodial account, such as the Uniform Gift to Minors Act (UGMA) or the Uniform
Transfers to Minors Act, the savings belong to your child. When your child reaches 18
or 21 years of age, depending on the age of majority in your state, he or she can take
the money. If the age of majority where you live is twenty-one, your child will presumably have used most of the money for her education. However, at age eighteen,
your child could just take the money and blow it—on a trip to Tibet, a car, or whatever. While you may be certain now that you will have instilled the right values in your
child, there are no guarantees, and you will not be able to prevent your teenager
from squandering the money.

Having sizable assets in your children's names can hinder their chances for financial
aid. Colleges generally expect that entering students will contribute 35 percent of
their savings, but parents are expected to contribute only about 6 percent of their savings. So if your child has $20,000 in savings, a college would expect $7,000 to go for
paying college bills. On the other hand, if you as a parent have $20,000, the college
would expect you to use only $1,200.

Don't Put All Your Children's College Savings in Their Names (Cont.)

There is one clear advantage to saving in your child's name, especially when your child is young. If your child is under 14, he or she will not pay any tax on the first $650 of investment income. The next $650 is taxed at the child's rate of 15 percent, which is much lower than yours. For children over the age of 14, any investment income is taxed at 15 percent. If you're fairly certain that you won't qualify for any aid because you're in a high tax bracket, then you may want to keep the savings in your child's name.

Grants

Grants differ from loans, in that they are outright gifts of money for students, usually undergraduates. Most grants are given by the federal government to support lower-income families. The biggest grant program is called the Federal Pell grant. Pell grants range from a few hundred dollars per year for families earning more than $35,000 up to $3,000 per year for low-income families. You automatically apply for a Pell grant when you complete and submit the FAFSA paperwork. Other grant opportunities include:

- Federal Work Study Program money administered by your college's financial aid office

- State grants

- Tuition discounts offered by colleges

- Volunteering for Americorps

- Joining the Armed Forces

- Federal Supplemental Educational Opportunity Grants

You can also achieve some *grant-like effects* when you do such things as the following:

- Take advanced placement courses or tests that allow the early completion of a college degree, reducing tuition and other expenses.

- Attend a junior college for the first two years, making sure that your credits will transfer to a four-year school.

Scholarships

The most frequently asked question about education that I asked with my Latino clients is this: Will a scholarship be available for my child? Let's face it, we'd all like to get as much free money as we can. *Do scholarships exist? Yes! Are they easy to find? No!*

Trying to find scholarship money requires a well-thought-out plan, persistence, and some creativity. You do not need to pay some scholarship search service several hundred dollars to do a computerized search for you, although such services do exist. These search services will come up with information that is commonly known and available— moneys that are tied to specific colleges or in such small amounts as to be practically worthless. Better to spend the money yourself on telephone calls, faxes, Internet searches, and letters.

Your scholarship money search should concentrate upon two areas: state and national organizations offering Latino scholarship aid and academic or occupation-specific awards granted by corporations, not-for-profit groups, associations, and colleges themselves. You can begin your research easily by getting a copy of the *VISTA Scholarship Guide for Latinos*, sponsored by Chrysler Corporation and *VISTA Magazine*. Call Chrysler at 800-521-0953 to get your free copy. In addition, you

Did You Know?/¿Sabía Usted?

Billions of dollars are available in federal, state, and privately funded aid if you know where to look. Start with guidance counselors and financial aid offices. Libraries and bookstores have sections on college planning. The Internet is also a good source of information.

Check out these sites:

www.collegeboard.org (with access to College Scholarship Service)
www.fastweb.com
www.college-prep.com
www.collegeview.com

You can also contact the College Board at 45 Columbus Avenue, New York, NY 10023-6992, 212-713-8000.

can turn to the two national Latino organizations that provide scholarships for Latino students on an application basis:

The National Hispanic College Fund
P.O. Box 728
Novato, California 94948
415-892-9971/415-445-9930
www.nhsf.org

Hispanic College Fund
One Thomas Circle N.W.
Washington, D.C. 20005
202-296-5400
www.hispanicfund.org

Other organizations that can help you with scholarship searches are:

Hispanic Association of Colleges and Universities
Student Support Groups
4204 Gardendale Street #216
San Antonio, Texas 78229
210-692-3805

League of United Latin American Citizens (LULAC)
National Educational Services
777 N. Capitol Street SE #395
Washington, D.C. 20002
202-408-0060

Mexican-American Women's National Association (MANA)
Raquel Marquez Frankel Scholarship
1101 17th Street NW #803
Washington, D.C. 20036
202-833-0050

Finally, you may search out the numerous Latino professional associations that represent thousands of Latino engineers, physicians, accountants, lawyers, and others. These organizations can be a useful source of potential financial support via their own members. Your success with any of them will depend upon your child's interest in their academic or professional areas of specialty. You might wish to start with this list:

American Association of Hispanic CPAs
19726 E. Colima Road, Suite 270
Rowland Heights, CA 91748
626-965-0643

Society of Hispanic Professional Engineers
5400 East Olympic Blvd., Suite 210
Los Angeles, CA 90022
213-725-3970

National Association of Hispanic Investment Bankers
4037 Tulane Ave., Suite 100
New Orleans, LA 70119

InterAmerican College of Physicians and Surgeons
1721 I Street NW, Suite 200
Washington, D.C. 20006
202-467-4756

National Association of Hispanic Nurses
1501 16th Street NW
Washington, D.C. 20036
202-387-2477

Hispanic National Bar Association
P.O. Box 66105
Washington, D.C. 20035
202-293-1507

Hispanic Organization of Professionals and Executives
1700 17th Street NW, Suite 405
Washington, D.C. 20009
202-234-2351

Hispanic Public Relations Association
735 S. Figueroa, Suite 818
Los Angeles, CA 90017
818-345-3425

National Hispanic Corporate Council
2323 N. Third Street, Suite 101
Phoenix, AZ 85004
602-495-1988

National Association of Hispanic Journalists
1193 National Press Building
Washington, D.C. 20045
202-662-7145

Let's go on to the next item on the list.

Loans

Both you and your child may qualify for loans, from a variety of sources. The least expensive of these sources is the Federal Government–supported student loan program. Other loans may be obtained through your state, through private lenders, and through colleges and universities themselves. Let's look at these options:

Federal Stafford Loan Program. This program provides both subsidized loans for qualifying students via their FAFSA paperwork and unsubsidized loans for all other students. In a subsidized Stafford Loan, the federal government pays the interest while your child remains in school; in the unsubsidized program, your child becomes responsible for interest costs immediately, although interest payments can be deferred until after graduation or leaving school. Both loan programs provide a lower interest rate (3.1 percent over the 91-day Treasury Bill rate, with a 8.25 percent cap). Repayments do not have to begin until six months after graduation or leaving school. Stafford loans are available for amounts up to $2,650 for freshmen, $3,500 for sophomores, and $5,500 for juniors, seniors, and fifth year students—for a maximum total of $23,000 per student. Graduate students are also eligible and can qualify for up to $18,500 each year. Stafford Loans can be obtained either directly through colleges as direct loans or through various banks, S&Ls, and credit unions.

Federal Perkins Loans. This program has been designed for students from low-income families and is part of a total financial aid package that a college might offer to an incoming student. Eligibility comes through the FAFSA paperwork. Undergraduate students can receive a low-interest loan of 5 percent, up to $3,000 per year.

PLUS Loans. These are parent loans for undergraduate students. Parents can borrow the full amount of their child's education at a reduced interest rate of 3.1 percent over the one-year Treasury Bill rate, capped at 9 percent. A credit check will be necessary, although the credit evaluation is very liberal. Interest and principal can be deferred until six months after your child's graduation—with repayments stretched out over five to ten years.

Professional Loan Programs. These are special loan programs for students training to become teachers, doctors, nurses, dentists, or other health professionals.

Extended Payment Plans offered by some colleges give you the option of stretching your tuition and board payments out over ten or twelve months rather than two lump-sum payments, making it easier for parents to self-finance these big amounts at least partly out of current income.

Commercial tuition plans are offered parents by many colleges. These plans gain you access to long-term (10–15 year) tuition payment plan money. Key Educational Resources of Boston, MA (800-539-5363) is a leading provider of these loans.

In addition to all of these, some additional sources for college funding that you might look into include:

A government publication entitled *The Student Guide: Financial Aid from the U.S. Department of Education,* **www.ed.gov**

Peterson's College Money Handbook (800-338-3282)

The College Board's *College Costs and Financial Aid Handbook* (800-323-7155)

VISTA Scholarship Guide for Hispanics (800-521-0953)

SOME FINAL THINKING ABOUT THE BIG HURDLE

Let's pull all of this together into some final principles for overcoming the big financial hurdle facing your college-aged children.

Principle One. Paying for college these days almost always requires a long-term, multiple-sources-of-funds strategy. Realize this.

Principle Two. The earlier you start to put money away for this purpose, the more likely that you will have an adequate amount when you need it. Starting early, even with small monthly savings payments into high-yielding, growth investments, will always be the cheapest way to pay for college. In this way, the powerful, compound financial elevators all work in your favor. Start early.

Principle Three. If you do not save and invest ahead of time for college, instead of receiving compound interest to help you, you or your child will *pay* compound interest after college on all those loans. Too bad, but often this cannot be helped.

Principle Four. Taking out loans and paying them off after college *is not a bad thing!* Remember, a large part of the reason for getting a college degree is to increase your child's future lifetime stream of earnings. So long as this happens, all you are doing when you borrow college money is capitalizing ahead of time a small part of that increased stream of earnings in the form of loans. The future earning stream should, however, become so much larger that it easily makes up for the loans plus interest. This is no different than taking out a car loan so that you can get to a better job; you pay for the use of the car that enables you to make more money. Borrowing money for college is a much better choice than not going to college at all!

Principle Five. Never forget the old rule that you make money when you buy. Do everything that you can do minimize the costs of college itself, first; then your money needs will be much smaller in the first place. Always look for value!

Principle Six. Never, never forget that in America excellence matters and does get rewarded eventually. Always encourage your children to study hard in school, right from the earliest grades. Then they will form successful habits for college and adult life. They may get college scholarships they otherwise would not. They almost certainly will earn more in their adult lives. Putting hard work into doing well becomes the easiest and cheapest lifetime success strategy that you can ever teach to your child. More precious than gold!

ACTION STEPS FOR MAKING COLLEGE A REALITY

Sit down and start developing your college payment plan—right now! What kind of college, how much will it likely cost, how much aid will you likely qualify for, how much time do you have to save and invest? These are the basic elements to any good college payment plan.

Start investing right now in stock mutual funds to grow your money as much as possible. Do not worry about how much you can start with; you can always add more later. The important thing is to start with something each month right now, so that the powerful, compound interest elevators will go to work for you.

Start investigating sources for scholarship money via national, state, and professional sources.

Make sure that you have enough life and disability insurance to protect your family fully for the difficult years prior to and during college. Remember, life insurance cash values can be a very good sources for college money.

Apply for all the financial aid you can get. Fill out FAFSA forms as soon as you can, and get them in early. Too much aid never hurt anybody!

Search for ways to reduce both parental assets and children's assets through smart asset switching.

Shop for value in colleges by checking out state schools and less-well-known private schools.

Search for colleges with merit scholarships available, scholarships that do not get needs-tested. Here's one of the areas where doing well in school can pay rewards.

Persevere! Never, never give up.

15

The Sustaining Wealth of Your Later Years: How Will Retirement Find You?

In This Chapter

- Learn the five *myths* of retirement planning and how they affect Latino wealth creation.

- Learn the sources of money that we Latinos have available to us to fund retirement.

- Learn all about 401(k) plans: what they are, how they work, what their benefits are, and what *dis*advantages they offer you as well.

- See first-hand the power available to you in tax-deferred compound investing.

- Learn why life insurance is your ultimate wealth creation tool.

OH, THE TIMES THEY ARE A-CHANGIN'

Hoy fuiste, mañana serás.

How will retirement find you? No, this is not a mixed-up sentence. I know that the usual, clichéd sentence is: How will you find retirement? But your answer will depend upon this first question. How so? First, let's define retirement: Retirement is the time when we no longer want to, are able to, or need to work—whichever comes first! If retirement for you comes when you no longer need to work, blessed are you. But what if it comes when you can no longer work? Will retirement then find you with enough sources of *unearned* income to still live a good life? Or will retirement come suddenly upon you, like a thief in the night, stealing away your earning power and leaving you with nothing, or very little, in return? How *will* retirement find you—prepared, or unprepared?

We can get a better perspective on this issue by reviewing some facts. In November 1997, at a meeting sponsored by *Third Millennium,* a New York–based non-partisan "generation X" advocacy group, Latino community and civic leaders from around the country got invited to address the coming crisis in Social Security and other federal entitlement programs. Conference attendees stressed the fact that for many Latinos, Social Security still remains the biggest, if not the only, source of retirement income. Latinos need to find a way to take control of their own financial destinies. Here are some of the sad facts that we Latinos have to face:

Only 32 percent of the 12.3 million Latinos in the American work force participate in pension plans, compared to 44 percent of other minority groups and 51 percent of Anglo workers. Our false sense of self-sufficiency hurts us.

Only 9 percent of Latino workers are college graduates, compared to 27 percent of Anglos, giving us lower-paid jobs, lower expected lifetime earnings, and *reduced retirement benefits.*

Only 32 percent of Latinos age fifty-five or older receive a pension, compared to 40 percent of African Americans and 52 percent of Anglos.

A Rand Corporation study found that the top 10 percent of Latino senior households held liquid assets of only $14,000 in 1995, compared to $172,000 for the top 10 percent of Anglo retirees.

By any measure, we Latinos face a looming catastrophe in later life—unless we change our thinking about our later life right now.

We do not face this major threat alone. Every American today faces the challenge of how to prepare for a dignified and enjoyable retirement—*without relying solely upon the government.* As the old Bob Dylan song goes, "The times, they are a-changin'." The only thing that separates us from other Americans is this: We are even more poorly prepared than most Americans for this new reality. Fortunately, we also possess one priceless asset in this battle against time—we have more of it. As a people, we are young right now; we have the time to prepare for these changes, if we only have the heart to change our own habits.

What has to change, you may wonder? Well, at the *Third Millennium* conference, all the experts were saying that government intervention in this problem will not provide a solution. The only solution is the combination of increased education and personal attention to the challenge of living comfortably without job-related earnings at some point in our lives.

The Generation Gap and Social Security

Young, baby boomer, and retired Americans have very different and conflicting views on retirement, aging, and Social Security. A survey of nearly 2,900 Americans found that while only half of those aged 18 to 40 expect to benefit from Social Security when they reach retirement, 85 percent of Americans in the preretirement ages of 50 to 64 either already receive benefits or expect to receive them. These findings are important because they illustrate the different concerns that will need to be addressed in Social Security reform.

Throughout this book, I have stressed the importance of long-term thinking and taking calculated risks in order to accelerate Latino wealth creation. Investing in stocks and mutual funds must become a critical and essential part of every Latino's wealth creation plan. The rest of this final chapter will tell you in more detail how to do this for your own retirement's sake.

KNOWLEDGE WILL NEVER HURT YOU

To do better, we have to learn more. It's just that simple. Let's begin with a basic test of what we should know about our retirement futures. When you have completed this test, you'll have a much better idea of your general knowledge level about this important subject.

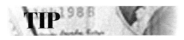

TIP

Do your own research. Go online. Read annual and quarterly reports, brokerage firm research reports, newsletters, and business magazines. For a start, see the appendix at the end of *¡Sí!, Se Puede.*

A Little Knowledge Test

See how many of the following simple questions about retirement planning you can get right.

1   When it comes to investing for retirement, do you believe you should take more or less risk than you do with other investments?

a) more b) less c) the same

2   IRA contributions are no longer tax deductible for income tax purposes.

a) true b) false c) don't know

3   Over long periods of time, bonds have frequently outperformed stocks.

a) true b) false c) don't know

4   Women and men receive the same Social Security retirement benefits.

a) true b) false c) don't know

5   Over the last thirty years, which one of the following investments has gone up the most?

a) stocks b) corporate bonds c) government bonds d) treasury bills e) CDs

6 People turning sixty-five this year can expect to live to what age?

a) 77 b) 80 c) 84 d) 87 e) 89 f) 91

7 What percentage of your preretirement income (last five working years) do experts say you will need to live comfortably once you retire?

a) 40–50 percent b) 50–60 percent c) 60–70 percent d) 70 percent or more

8 A sixty-five year old retiring this year with a preretirement income of $50,000 can expect what Social Security monthly income benefit?

a) $500 b) $1,270 c) $3,380 d) $6,000

9 In addition to making a maximum annual contribution of $2,000 to a traditional or a Roth IRA, a $500 annual contribution can also be made to an education IRA.

a) true b) false

10 What will it cost to maintain a $30,000 per year standard of living with three percent inflation in ten years?

a) $30,000 b) $35,000 c) $40,317 d) $54,183

Answers:

1. a) more	4. b) false	7. d) 70 percent+	10. c) $40, 317
2. b) false	5. a) stocks	8. b) $1,270	
3. b) false	6. b) 80	9. a) true	

Evaluating your score: If you got 8–10 correct, you score ahead of most people in you understanding of critical financial issues affecting retirement. Keep updated and monitor your retirement plan.

If you got 6–7 correct, you have done better than most people but need to update your knowledge on key issues and their impact on your investment program. Review your portfolio on the basis of your expanded knowledge.

If you got 5 or less correct, you probably have not considered many of the issues affecting retirement security. Get educated to move on.

Next, let's expose a number of myths about retirement reality so that we can begin to respond to the challenge facing us:

Myth One. Social Security and Medicare will cover most of my needs. Many Latinos assume that Social Security will become the cornerstone of their retirement security. The reality is that assuming a current income of $60,000, Social Security will replace only 23 percent of your preretirement income! And this estimate is based upon *current* assumptions that may be too high. Who knows what reductions in benefits we will face in the future in order to make the numbers balance?

Myth Two. My money only has to last a certain number of years. Back in 1938, when Social Security became a reality, the average life span for Americans was sixty-two years. Most people did not live long enough to collect! The expected life span for members of the baby boom generation is 80–85 years. Medical technology is pushing the limits of human life out to 110 or even greater. If you are thirty today, you may spend more of your life retired than working!

Myth Three. I only need a relatively small amount of savings to live. This myth has been pretty much destroyed but resulted from the assumptions behind the previous myth. Inflation is the real threat to a dignified retirement. This stealthy tax erodes our purchasing power and thereby our standard of living, by eating away our wealth a dollar at a time. For example, to earn $10,000 in yearly annual retirement income for twenty-five years without inflation you would need only $115,000 earning eight percent. With inflation running at four percent, you now need $165,000. Big difference.

Myth Four. I can keep my money in safe investments. This is a critical issue directly related to the myth just above. What is "safe" and what is "risky" when inflation exists? Is it riskier to take the chance of losing some money, or to definitely lose purchasing power to inflation? Compare these average annual pre- and postinflation rates of return between 1926 and 1997 for some well-known investment vehicles:

	Money Market	**Bond Market**	**Stock Market**
Average Annual return	3.8%	5.2%	11.0%
Inflation	3.1%	3.1%	3.1%
"Real" return	0.7%	2.1%	7.9%

How "secure" is a low-return investment, after inflation?

Myth Five. I do not have to worry because by employer is taking care of me. Sadly, this has never been the case for Latinos, and it is less so now than ever. Many companies no longer provide company-paid pension plans. Most Latinos work for small firms or are self-employed, so the great majority of us receive no free coverage at all.

All Right! How Much Money Will I Need?

I hear this question so often after I tell my clients the real facts of life about retirement planning: All right! How much money will I need?

Whenever I hear this question, I resist the urge to smile. I do not wish to be impolite, but it's simply the wrong question. If you ask the wrong question, how can you hope to get a right answer? The question of *need* is one that I believe shortchanges nearly every American, Latino or not. Whether it is for retirement or for life insurance for that matter, need has very little to do with the calculation. The correct question to ask: How much money do I *want?* After all, we do not *need* to do anything in retirement; we can just sit back in a rocker and do nothing! What matters is what we want to do in retirement. Unless we become physically unable to do the things we want to, the only thing to stop us is money—or rather the lack of it.

Now obviously, each person will want to do different things in retirement. Some people may want to simplify their lives, scale back and enjoy the quiet things in life. Others will want to do all those things that they put off doing while they worked full time: buy a nice car, do world travel, undertake new hobbies, fulfill the lifelong dream of golfing in Scotland, or sail around the world. The conventional wisdom among financial planners is that the average person will need 70–80 percent of their average last 3–5 years' preretirement earnings as a postretirement income. Other planners have argued that it's possible to make it on 60 percent, 50 percent, or even 40 percent of preretirement income. But who is this average person, and what will that person's income be during the last 3–5 years of working life? Who knows?

I am now forty-three years old, and I have no idea what my average income will be during my last 3–5 working years. So how can I determine what 70 percent of a question mark will work out to be? I cannot even assume that my current income will increase by a steady 3–4 percent per year. I certainly have bigger plans than that for myself, but who knows whether they will all work out, and for how much? *The future is uncertain,* as an old business professor of mine used to put it. Trying to run out the numbers on this calculation becomes even more futile when you are thirty-five, thirty, or twenty-five. We live in the most dynamic period in history, and somehow we are led to believe that we can preprogram our retirement planning to percentage points of an unknown income some twenty-five years or more in the future.

What if we just try to create as much wealth as we can? How can we do this? More important, how can we do this without denying ourselves and our families the kind of life we would like to live while we are working, raising our children, and participating fully in our communities? This is really a question about where retirement money comes from, when we want to balance our working and retirement lives. Read on.

WHERE DOES THE RETIREMENT MONEY COME FROM?

According to a recent study by the U.S. Treasury Department, the average U.S. household gets less than 45 percent of its retirement income from the combination of Social Security and pension funds. Of the rest, 24 percent comes from earned retirement income—we still keep working after so-called "retirement," partly to keep busy but mostly to make ends meet—and 32 percent comes from savings and investments. This percentage of non–Social Security and –pension fund retirement income will only keep growing in the future as government and businesses both shrink their contributions. Sadly, most

Latino senior citizens have nothing like this income distribution; they rely mostly upon Social Security, so you can see how rough retirement can be for many of us.

Let's summarize what we've learned. Money for retirement comes from three basic sources:

- Social Security

- Private pensions

- Personal savings and investments

I believe that there is a fourth source—permanent life insurance. More on that later. Remember, we need to plan to generate at least twenty years' retirement income, if not twenty-five to thirty years. Let's look more closely at what each of these three basic sources can do for us.

Social Security

Notwithstanding all the debate and argument in Washington about Social Security, there are 60 million reasons why the program will survive in one form or another—60 million baby boomers who will demand that they get "theirs" just as their parents did. After all, the baby boomers pay the highest taxes and will see to it that something comes their way. The big question remains: How much? You can be sure of just one thing, that it will never be as big a proportion of our contributions as our parents received. Increasingly, our wealth and security will depend upon our ability to earn and invest our own way into financial independence.

TIP

Compare your W-2 withholding with the Social Security Administration's printout. Errors occur, and an uncorrected mistake can cut your lifetime benefits.

Pensions

Do you know what pensions are rapidly becoming? *The dinosaurs of the retirement universe.* Why? Fewer and fewer companies offer them. Most new jobs being created today come from smaller companies that do not usually offer pension plans because of their cost. Remember also that less than one-third of all Latino even have pension plans, compared to over 50 percent of all Anglos. Latinos will clearly be less likely to receive this source of retirement funding *than any other group in the United States.*

This said, if you happen to be fortunate enough to work for a company that provides a pension plan, you should know that these plans come in two distinct forms:

Defined-benefit plans. These plans are the traditional ones that most Americans over fifty remember or have. The company guarantees to its covered employees a certain retirement income (the defined benefit) for the future. That monthly benefit is set, or defined, by the number of years worked and the ending salary. Covered employees are eligible to receive a certain proportion of their ending salary as a benefit. Usually, the employee does not pay into the plan directly. Great deal, no? Well, that's the problem. It's so great a deal that even the largest companies are cutting back on this benefit because of the huge future liabilities it creates for them. Companies have been transitioning to plans that place more of the future burden upon the employees, or to plans that do not lock the company into a specific future benefit. So if you are fortunate enough to have a defined-benefit plan, keep the following in mind:

Each plan has a vesting schedule for employees. This means that the longer you work for the company, the higher the benefit you qualify for. There may be severe penalties if you leave before a specific cutoff date. Read your annual benefit statement carefully and talk to the human resources people to get a handle on your specific plan, its vesting schedule, and how you can maximize your retirement benefit.

If you want to maximize your retirement benefits, don't change jobs. That's a tall order these days. Understand that if you do leave, you may lose valuable pension benefits that may not be available at your new company. If you are considering a move, find out how much of a benefit you are vested for, what you will be giving up, and whether the new job is worth it. Your future pension benefits become an important consideration for you in making your decision. The older you are, the more critical the decision to stay or leave becomes, because you can be potentially giving up hundreds of thousands of dollars of guaranteed pension income!

TIP

Your pension benefits grow most during the last few years of work. Make sure any early retirement package is enough to cover benefits lost by leaving before you're 60 or 65.

Stay on top of your accrued benefit. Read your statements each year.

If you do leave, don't forget about these vested benefits. Even if you only worked for the company for five years, you may have a vested benefit of several hundred dollars a month at retirement. That makes it worth keeping an eye on.

TIP

When you switch jobs, ask your old employer to deposit your retirement savings into a rollover account, or your new company's plan. If the distribution is made to you, your former employer must deduct 20 percent for taxes.

Defined-contribution plans. As companies have cut back upon Cadillac-style defined-benefit plans, they have greatly expanded their use of defined-contribution plans. What's the difference? The Cadillac plan guarantees a retirement payout to you, whereas the newer plans guarantee some amount of contribution by the company. These newer defined-contribution plans include money purchase plans, profit-sharing plans, Simplified Employee Pensions (SEPs), and 401(k) plans. These plans have exploded in corporate popularity recently for one simple reason—they let the company off the hook for guaranteed benefit payouts. Your final benefit amount gets determined by how well the plan's investments perform in the market. In these plans, the company can contribute either a certain percentage of your salary (called money purchase) or a percentage of its profits (profit sharing). Your company's plan may also include a provision under which you can make voluntary contributions that the firm will then match. SEPs get used by small business firms, usually with under twenty employees. Their popularity comes from their being inexpensive to set up and administer, an important consideration for any small business. In essence, SEPs work like company-paid Individual Retirement Accounts (IRAs). In all these defined-contribution plans, the employer usually decides how much money gets invested. Money can get invested in stocks, bonds, cash, mutual funds, company stock if the company is publicly owned, and other types of investments as well. The company becomes the trustee for the plan and manages the money (or hires an investment manager to do so) to maximize the potential benefit to its employees. If you contribute to the plan out of your own income, you may or may not have any control over where your money gets invested. Check it out.

As something to watch out for, these plans can get used by companies to support their stock prices, by using a large proportion of the contributions to buy their own stock. This tends, of course, to keep the price up. If you happen to work for a Coca-Cola or Microsoft, then this may not be a bad thing. However, most firms' shares do not perform like these two! Tying too much of your future retirement money up in a poorly performing company stock exposes you to far more risk than is necessary. Check out your pension plan where appropriate. While you probably can do nothing about a pension plan that invests 50 percent or more of your money in company stock, at least you know where you stand and can make adjustments in other areas of your saving and investments plan to offset the risks in your pension plan.

401(k) Plans—How Great Are They?

Twenty years ago, almost nobody knew about 401(k) plans. Today, they have become the subject of cocktail party conversations, employee cafeteria seminars, magazine articles by the hundreds, and books by the dozens. Millions of people now possess these accounts, and many of them consider them to be magical money-making engines—for some good reasons:

- You get an immediate tax reduction and can increase your take-home pay.

- You may get a company "match" that adds to the size of your own contributions.

- You maximize growth via a tax-deferral advantage.

- You get the convenience of an automatic payroll deduction for your contributions.

- You can get a decent offering or investment options.

- Your account is *portable*—you take your account with you if you leave your job. Pretty important in today's job market.

- In an emergency, you have access to your investment money.

- Most plans offer high-quality customer services—and you're the customer.

Let's go on. If you want to create maximum wealth, the experts say, what could be better than not paying taxes on the wonderful gains you make investing in the stock market? It certainly is not crazy to join the 401(k) movement, because of all the obvious benefits. In fact, by now you probably are asking me how to get into a 401(k) plan if you have not done so already. Or if you're already in the game, how can you maximize your benefits from playing? Let's see.

The 401(k) plan works very simply. You as an employee agree to put aside a percentage of your salary each year toward your own retirement. The law specifies that your contribution is exempt from current federal income taxes, although not from Social Security (FICA) taxes. The earnings, or interest, on your investments grow tax-deferred, meaning that you do not have to pay taxes on any growth in your account—until retirement—when all assets get sold and you pay the deferred tax. If you're just starting out in a 401(k) plan and its earnings growth comes to only $200 a year, that may not seem like so great a benefit. But look how it adds up.

Investing in a Tax-Deferred Account versus a Taxable Account ($2,000 per Year for 25 Years)

Tax Bracket	Tax-Deferred Account	Taxable Account
15%	$134,223	$111,591
28%	113,694	80,785
31%	108, 957	74,695
36%	101,062	65,291
39.6%	95,377	59,377

This table assumes an eight percent annual rate of return on each account and no withdrawals from the tax-deferred account until retirement, when all assets are sold and taxed.

How much can you contribute to such a plan? You can put away a certain percentage of your salary—up to a maximum of $10,000 per year. You can also make after-tax contributions to a savings plan if your employer offers such a plan. Total contributions to all company-sponsored savings plans gets capped at $30,000 per year. Now remember, one of the benefits of a 401(k) plan is the company match. This is on top of any contribution you make. So for instance, suppose that you earn a $50,000 salary and decide to contribute ten percent of it, or $5,000, to your 401(k) plan. Your company agrees to match the first three percent of your contribution, or $3,000. The total contribution made in your name is now $8,000.

How does your money get invested? Here comes the biggest challenge and opportunity for employees. Remember that companies have moved away from those rich defined-benefit pension plans to get off the payout hook. You're on the hook now. Your retirement account performance will depend upon the type and performance of the investments *you* choose to include in your plan. One of the reasons I chose to write this book came out of my experiences with clients who put the bulk of their 401(k) assets into so-called "safe" investments such as money market accounts and government bond accounts. I watched my clients badly short-change themselves. A 401(k) plan is a long-term investment. Remember our discussion in Chapter Eleven on long-term growth: over the long term and after inflation, nothing can be "safer" than stocks.

Did You Know?/¿Sabía Usted?

If you participate in a 401(k) plan, the following information must be provided to you:

Employee enrollment form. To be filled out by you, this indicates the percentage amount you can contribute to the plan, and how you want the contributions allocated among the available investment options.

Summary plan description. This is an abbreviated listing of plan provisions, including vesting rules for employer contributions, distribution rules, and grievance procedures.

Information on investment options (upon enrollment in a plan, and in periodic reports). Regulatory definitions are sketchy, and the amount of information varies from company to company. Firms using mutual funds usually provide prospectuses and periodic reports.

Periodic financial statements. These reflect your account, including contributions, any outstanding loans, income earned, and capital gains and losses, plus the beginning and ending balance.

If you participate in a 401(k) plan, your company will offer you a range of investment options, usually mutual funds, to fund your own retirement investments. These mutual fund offerings will probably range from money market to international growth fund. You should determine your risk tolerance level, what your retirement goals are, what portfolio of funds will likely reach your goals, and how much of each type of fund you should have to help you get where you want to go. Take advantage of company education seminars that provide you with additional information. Remember, it really is not all that difficult; you are in for the long haul. Invest in a portfolio of high-quality mutual funds, and keep putting money in. Remember, too, how much your company's matching funds can be worth to you.

To see just how much this last matter can benefit you, let's look at a simple example of a powerful compounding financial elevator at work along with a match. To do so, let's visit Jesús once more. He earns $60,000 per year in a managerial position and decides to contribute ten percent of his salary to his 401(k). In addition, his employer agrees to match his contributions up to the first three percent. So, we have Jesús's contribution of $6,000 plus the company contribution of $1,800—for a total of $7,800. Let's also say that Jesús invests the total $7,800 in a portfolio of growth funds offered in his plan. Let's also assume that Jesús continues to work until age sixty-five. To make things simple, we can make the highly unrealistic assumption that his salary remains the same, as does his contribution level. Of course, in reality they will both likely go up considerably. Even in this conservative example, what will he have at age sixty-five?

- If his investments average a 10 percent growth rate, he'll have some $1,400,000!

- If his investments average a 12 percent growth rate, he'll have $2,100,000!

- If he does even better and receives a 14 percent average return, he will have $3,172,000!

Are There Any Downsides?

This all sounds so good. Who would not want to have a chance at accumulating $3 million by retirement? However, let's take a closer look at the 401(k) and review some of its characteristics. Remember: *Every financial decision has its own set of costs.* What costs come along with a 401(k)?

You have limited access to your own money, until you retire. While 401(k) plans allow you to withdraw money early should you need to, withdrawals in reality are severely limited. To get an early withdrawal, you have to prove that you have a financial hardship that is immediate and pressing, and that you cannot get money anywhere else. Even if you qualify, strict limits define how much you can get, set restrictions upon when you can participate again, and present you with tax and penalty payments.

Avoid taking out money from a retirement plan before you're 59½. You will pay a 10 percent penalty plus tax. The exception is if you're taking it in equal installments from an IRA.

Loans are available, but again, they are very restricted. You can usually borrow up to 50 percent of your account balance—to a limit of $50,000. However, the repayment time period is limited to five years.

Paying back the principle and paying the loan interest cannot be done with nontaxable money and may lessen your ability to make new contributions in the future, slowing down your long-term asset accumulation even more. Finally, if you are terminated or jump to another firm prior to age fifty-five, any outstanding loan balance can be counted as an early distribution of benefits, making it taxable as current income. Once more, you become liable for taxes and penalties.

Contributions to your 401(k), or any other investment program for that matter, will be subject to the twin risks of premature death, or, more likely, long-term disability. Remember, a 401(k) places the burden of your retirement planning upon you. Your current income drives the whole accumulation elevator. Without an income, payroll contributions cease; your 401(k) does not contain a disability provision. Even if you have 60 percent of your (taxable) pay covered by a company long-term disability plan, you will barely have enough net income to live on, let alone continue your 401(k) contributions.

401(k) plans only postpone taxes; they do not eliminate them. The biggest misconception about 401(k) plans surround the issue of taxes in retirement. Tax-deferral strategies are based on the assumption that your tax rate will be lower in retirement than it is while you are working. This may not always hold true.

To see just what is involved here, let's return once more to Jesús and Marta. We already know his earnings and 401(k) plan contributions. They plan to defer taxes until they retire, when their tax bracket should be lower—perhaps even lower than the lowest current rate of 15 percent. Now, what happens at retirement? We have already seen that Jesús would have a 401(k) plan account balance of somewhere between $1.4 and $3.2 million, depending upon his average rate of return over time. That is probably more money that he and Marta ever dreamed of having. And of course, this total does not include any other savings and investments that they may have. If we use a round number for their 401(k) gains of $2 million, what rate would Jesús and Marta pay taxes at? Remember, their assumption was that they would have lower incomes and therefore would pay lower taxes in retirement. But all this financial success poses some questions that they did not consider thirty years ago:

- How much income will they *want* to have in retirement if they have $2 million in retirement funds? *How about you?*

- What will it cost to live for them thirty years from now—after all that could easily be how long they do live after retirement. What kinds of things will they wish to do with their money?

- Do they wish to leave any money for their children, grandchildren, or to a favorite charity?

- What has happened to estate and inheritance taxes in the meantime? Is this an issue that should concern them?

Tax rates today happen to be at one of the lowest levels since the federal income tax began in 1913. Think about it. It was not too long ago that the highest rate on incomes over $100,000 was over 80 percent! Does it make sense to assume that tax rates in the future will be lower than they are today? Does it make sense to assume that we will *not* be financially successful? I realize that these questions may be unfamiliar to you and even make you uncomfortable. Yet they do have to be faced if we will pursue our goal of increasing Latino family wealth creation.

Now, 401(k) plans are great; don't get me wrong. But could there be a better way, a *fourth way*, of creating more wealth, enjoying it more while we live, and passing more of it on to our loved ones when we're gone? *Yes!*

Did You Know?/¿Sabía Usted?

According to Robert Walsh, Assistant Professor of Accounting at Marist College, it is true today that withdrawals from the Roth IRA will be tax-free under certain conditions, but this may not be true in the future. Congress has the power to change the laws at will—and in the past has changed many tax laws. About 20 to 30 years from now the Social Security system may be going bankrupt. If that's the case, a revenue-starved Congress may see a vast accumulation of wealth in the Roth IRAs and enact a tax anyway.

Nonetheless, if you are young and in a low-tax bracket, a nondeductible Roth IRA may be the thing for you. For example, from ages 25 to 34 you invest $2,000 a year in a Roth earning 10 percent annually. You never deposit another cent—just let it grow. At age 59½, you would have $362,000 tax free. Now consider how much you would have saved in taxes if you'd opted for a deductible IRA. In a 15-percent bracket, your tax saving would be around $300 a year, or $3,000 (plus yield). No sense paying taxes on $342,000 later in life (when you may be in a higher bracket) just to save $3,000 now. If your bracket changes, you can switch anytime to a regular IRA.

LIFE INSURANCE—THE FOURTH WAY TO WEALTH CREATION

Now, I realize that you may think that I'm either crazy or a pawn of the life insurance industry for saying this, but life insurance can be the great fourth way to wealth creation. How can this be? Let me summarize my findings, based upon my experience with clients very much like you, who focus completely upon maximizing wealth creation. This is what I have found.

Permanent life insurance perfectly *complements* the wealth-creating potential of retirement plans such as 401(k)s, IRAs, and SEPs.

Permanent life insurance provides necessary protection for your retirement plan through a disability waiver benefit and death benefit.

Permanent life insurance provides a very low-cost source of loan funds in preretirement years should you need it, thereby preserving the wealth-creating power of your 401(k) or other retirement plan.

Permanent life insurance creates a tax-favored buildup of cash values that you can access at retirement to offset the future erosion of your wealth caused by adverse tax rule changes.

Permanent life insurance creates a "permission" slip for you to do things with your money that you might not do without it—for example, spending down your assets more quickly in retirement to produce greater income for you, taking the highest retirement benefit from your pension plan because you know your spouse is protected, taking a reverse mortgage on your home late in life knowing that the home will remain in the family, and using charitable trusts to produce income and tax benefits at the same time.

Permanent life insurance is *not* a replacement for your 401(k) or similar plan, or for your personal mutual fund holdings. Instead, life insurance works as the fourth way to assure an enjoyable retirement when it is used properly. If you are single and will stay single with no dependents, then its value is less than for someone who is married and has children. In this situation, permanent life insurance becomes a wealth-creation tool without equal. Its power comes from owning as much of it as you can. It has importance to your retirement plan because it fills in the gaps in your wealth-creation plan. Together with other retirement sources, it will help you maximize your total retirement wealth shelter.

The biggest objections having to do with life insurance, as we have already described, come from seeing its purchase in terms of two issues: How little can I get away with buying (how much do I need), and how little can I get away with paying? This is zero sum thinking—certainly not wealth-maximization thinking.

PULLING IT ALL TOGETHER

Remember when we described a new architecture for Latino wealth creation early in this book? I then described to you a system that focuses upon enhancing the coordination and integration of all aspects of a total personal financial system—of thinking holistically about wealth creation. Permanent life insurance is simply the last block put into place in this edifice. When we looked over savings products and identified the need to enhance yields on our savings, I suggested that it might be possible to gear up the performance of these guaranteed savings products to produce greater returns within your total financial system. If you own CDs, passbook savings accounts, or money market accounts, review their performance. How much are they actually *costing you* in taxes and lost growth? What are they really doing for you? If the money is merely there because you do not know what to do with it, and you have no money invested in mutual funds, get your money working harder, *now!* Consider buying some guaranteed protection via a permanent life insurance policy, and put the rest of your money to working hard in stock market mutual funds.

We Latinos are now emerging into the spotlight of America. A growing awareness exists for the size of our community, for our entrepreneurial spirit and successes, for our desire to create our own American dreams.

We face many challenges in making our mark upon the twenty-first century in America. We find ourselves behind in every wealth category known—including education, experience, income, and accumulated assets. We must accelerate our wealth creation efforts, until we reach Anglo levels of wealth attainment. New approaches, risk-taking, and an understanding of how the powerful compound financial elevators of life work are critical to our individual and community success. Why should we not have wealth commensurate with our time of existence in this country? If we are to be 20 percent of America's people, what is the reason for us not to have 20 percent of the wealth? *¡Adelante! ¡Sí!, se puede.*

Resources

In This Chapter

- Resources for the Small and Home-Based Business
- Consumer Protection
- Computer and Online Resources
- Investing Online
- Insurance Information
- Buying and Selling a House
- Taxes
- How to Pay for College
- Retirement and Elder Care

This appendix will direct you to information that will make you better informed about several of the key topics discussed in *¡Sí!, Se Puede*. It is by no means comprehensive, since each topic in its own right could be a full-length book. However, it is a good start. Also, be sure to see the *¡Sí!, Se Puede* Web site at **www.sisepuede.com**.

The appendix contains several resources that will make you smarter, help you build a business, make you a better consumer, help you through the maze of computers and the Internet, manage your money, handle your insurance, help with retirement and elder care, buy or sell real estate, handle your taxes, and pay for college. The appendix could be much longer, but the objective is to make your life easier and to save you time, so it is distilled down to the necessary information.

The Internet—and its electronic opportunities—is the defining technological innovation of our lifetime. If you do not yet have a computer, and are not yet "surfing" the "Net," you will be. Soon. Prices for computers are now under $1,000, and Internet access is simple. The challenge is in knowing where to go for information, and how to access the right information without wasting a lot of time. That's why there are so many Internet Web sites referenced both here and in the book.

RESOURCES FOR THE SMALL AND HOME-BASED BUSINESS

This section covers government and private sources of financing and other resources for small businesses.

Government Resources and Loan Programs

The Roadmap Program provides answers, contacts, government reports, and additional sources of information. Contact: Office of Business Liaison, U.S. Dept. of Commerce, 14th and Constitution Ave., N.W., Washington, DC 20230, 202-482-2000.

If you have a question about a federal program but don't know which agency to contact, call your local Federal Information Center (800-346-3346). They will locate an expert who can answer your question, and they are set up to help citizens find out and take of federal programs and services.

The Service Corps of Retired Executives (SCORE), consists of over 12,000 volunteers who are active or retired business people. They offer basic business advice; will check business plans, strategic marketing plans, and financial plans; and give advice on obtaining loans. There is no charge, and each user is matched with an experienced volunteer. Contact SCORE, Small Business Administration, 1441 L Street, N.W., Washington, DC 20416, 202-653-6768.

The Small Business Administration (800-827-5722, Answer Desk) administers loan, grant, and direct payment programs for small businesses. There are over 100 SBA offices, and since SBA loans are approved at the local level, you should contact your local SBA office early in your loan application process. Here are some of the largest SBA programs:

- Small Business Loans (Regular Business Loans—7 (A) Loans) For businesses demonstrating an ability to repay a loan but that have been unable to obtain private credit financing. This is a guaranteed loan program, the largest SBA offering, but is not open to not-for-profit organizations, or companies in real estate or investment, or businesses involved in the creation or distribution of ideas (such as magazines).

- Certified Development Loans (504 Loans)
  This is to finance fixed assets, such as land, buildings, and equipment. Loans are long term (10–20 years).

- Small Business Investment Companies
  Establishes investment companies, who in turn provide management and financial assistance on a continuing basis to eligible small business concerns. Financial assistance is provided by making long-term loans and/or by the purchase of debt or equity type securities in the business.

- 8 (A) Program Loans
  This program provides direct and guaranteed loans to small businesses owned by socially and economically disadvantaged people. The loans are used for capital improvements and working capital.

Small Business Development Centers (SBDCs) provide a variety of services, including low-cost seminars and workshops, management consulting, technical assistance, research studies, and other specialized help. The over 650 sites are generally located at colleges and universities. SBDCs provide management training to small businesses, because the SBA estimates that "managerial deficiencies cause nine of ten business failures." Small business owners or managers are eligible. Fees are low. Contact the SBA Answer Desk (800-827-5722) or the SBA (202-653-6768).

The Small Business Administration's Fa$trak program is available if you need ready capital to expand your business. It offers low-documentation loans of up to $100,000 through 18 participating banks. You can qualify quickly—in as little as 10 minutes—through the SBA's Internet site (**www.sba.gov/business_finances/fastrak/index.html**).

Should You Start Your Own Business?

Evaluate your commitment on a scale from 1 (low) to 10 (high):

_____ I will make this work. No matter what. Nothing will tear me away, not family, not a personal crisis, nothing.

_____ I love my work. I feel alive when I'm working. I would rather work at this job than do anything else.

_____ This is what I've always wanted to do. My dream is to do this.

Evaluate your business on a scale of 1 (no) to 10 (yes):

_____ Do people need what I have to offer?

_____ When I explain what I'm doing, do people want it?

_____ Does it create excitement?

_____ Do I understand my product or service?

_____ Can I explain it clearly and simply?

_____ Do I know how to reach customers?

_____ Can I market myself?

_____ Does it fit my personality? Do I feel good doing this?

_____ Am I good at this? Does it utilize my skills?

_____ Will I be able to make enough to make it worthwhile?

_____ Will I feel better about myself doing this?

Financing Your Venture and Getting It Started

Private investors can be more flexible than traditional lenders with terms. Sometimes you can't avoid taking a bank loan and need other options to access low-cost money. If you know individuals who are looking for a good investment, approach them. If you don't, ask a local stock broker, lawyer, or accountant. Or advertise in a trade journal, newspaper, or magazine aimed at entrepreneurs or investors.

Private foundations are another, underutilized, source of funding. A foundation will often provide outright grants, low-cost loans, letters of credit, or consulting services to small businesses that are engaged in activities that further the foundation's charitable goals. Sometimes they make this assistance available directly, especially if they are involved with socially beneficial activities or are owned by minorities in economically depressed areas.

Business "incubators" provide facilities and services to assist fledgling businesses to start and grow. Incubators are a combined effort of federal, state, and local governments and the private sector, and they provide businesses with free management, technical, and financing consulting, plus rent-abated facilities and use of business equipment. Not every business is eligible, however, and the application process is lengthy and involved. Contact the Office of Private Sector Initiatives (OPSI) at 202-331-9800.

For information on who is providing what business development programs at the state and local level, contact The National Governor's Association, Hall of States, Suite 267, 444 North Capitol Street, N.W., Washington, DC 20001. There is no charge except for the call (202-624-5300).

For information on who's providing business development programs at the state and local level, assistance in accessing programs, and help in obtaining loans and consulting advice, look to your state's Office of Economic Development. This agency will know of the programs available to help you and will put you in touch with local sources. Programs are usually restricted to residents of the state or business located in the state, at no cost.

Minority Business Development Centers (MBDCs), with about 100 sites run through state and local economic development offices, have programs aimed at Hispanics, minorities, and women. These centers, run by the U.S. Department of Commerce, provide business development services for a minimal fee to minority firms and individuals interested in entering, expanding, or improving their efforts in the marketplace. Services range from initial consultation to the identification and resolution of specific business problems. Advice includes: preparing financial packages, business counseling, business information and management, accounting, marketing, business/industrial site analysis, production, engineering, construction assistance, procurement, and identification of potential business opportunities.

Existing minority-owned businesses and minorities interested in starting a business are eligible. The cost is low, sometimes free, and you should apply to a local MBDC. To find out if you qualify, contact the MBDC office nearest you for more information:

Atlanta	404-586-0973 (Regional)
Boston	617-723-4216 (District)
Chicago	312-567-6061 (Regional)
Dallas	214-767-8001 (Regional)
Kansas City	816-471-1520 (District)
Miami	306-591-7355 (District)
New York	212-264-4743 (Regional)
Philadelphia	215-597-9236 (District)
Washington, DC	202-785-2886 (Regional)
Washington, DC	202-482-1936 (National)

The Office of Women's Business Ownership provides information, seminars, counseling on a variety of topics, including getting financing and doing business with the U.S. government, and mentoring programs (all geared for the special needs women have when it comes to starting and managing a business). The fees are free, or nominal. The Women's Entrepreneurial Lunch program is run in almost every city, and a mentoring program pairs experienced women business owners with novices. Call 202-205-6673.

The National Association for the Self Employed (NASE) offers products and services catered to solo businesspeople. First among its 100 benefits is health insurance designed for small businesses and the self-employed. NASE members are protected from being singled out for cancellation or rate increases. Call 800-232-NASE or click on **www.nase.org**.

Bank Rate Monitor (800-327-7717, **www.bankrate.com**) will help you find a small-business loan, the best online banking services, or the lowest credit care interest rate, This 1,600 page site features comprehensive listings, step-by-step money management guides, is updated daily, and is backed by 15 years of industry experience. It also includes a Spanish language link.

Consider finding an "angel" when you are trying to grow a business and have exhausted your finances as well as family and friends, but lack the means to attract venture capital or conventional bank financing, In 1996, over 250,000 angels invested over $20 billion in 30,000 companies. Frequently, self-made entrepreneurs who are looking for companies to nurture will take a chance with an unproven venture. To find an angel, consult the following sources:

Private Capital Clearing House (**www.pricap.com**). For $500, you get the eye and ear of a select pool of member investors, each accredited by the SEC.

ACE-NET (**www.sba.gov**). The SBA sponsors this forum, intended for businesses needing investments of $250,000 to $5 million.

American Venture Capital Exchange (800-292-1993). You pay a fee for a one-page listing that connects you to investors.

Angel Financing (**www.azeta.com**). A free worldwide matching service that also allows entrepreneurs to hold direct public offerings.

The Capital Network, Inc. (512-794-9398). Introduces investors to growth ventures, offers education on financing issues, and links emerging companies with business-service professionals.

National Venture Capital Association (**www.nvca.org**, 703-524-2549) publishes a list of investors.

Austin Technology Incubator (**www.utexas.edu**, 512-305-0000)

National Association of State Venture Funds (**www.nasvf.org,** or 405-848-8570)

¡Sí!, Se Puede has exposed you to many Internet resources and Web-related sites. As you begin "surfing" and discovering all of the wonderful things cyberspace has to offer, be mindful of protecting yourself. Cyberangels Internet Safety Organization has a Web site (**www.cyberangels.org**) with information on personal and business security. Topics include Internet fraud, computer security, e-mail abuse, and e-mail etiquette and safety.

TIP

HispanData, a subsidiary of Hispanic Business Inc., is a national résumé database that links major corporations, such as IBM, Amoco, GTE, Nike, Time Inc, Kraft, and Miller Brewing, with Hispanic professionals and others with expertise in the Hispanic market. The service matches employers with employees. To learn more about becoming a member, call 805-682-5843, ext. 800, or see their Web site: **www.hispandata.com**.

The U.S. Chamber of Commerce can give you information on local and regional programs, small-business initiatives, and nonprofit activities as well as the usual organization information. You can reach them at **www.cais.com/chamber**. You can reach the U.S. Hispanic Chamber of Commerce at **www.hispandata.com** or **www.ushcc.com**.

CONSUMER PROTECTION

If you think you have been wronged by a salesperson or repair technician, take action. Complaining to a manager is the first step, but if you aren't satisfied, try these resources:

The Better Business Bureau (**www.bbb.org**) is the leading consumer advocacy group in the United States. Use its Web page to post online complaints.

National Fraud Information Center (**www.fraud.org**) specializes in Internet and phone fraud.

National Consumers League (**www.naticonsumersleague.org**) is a nonprofit consumer agency that provides tips on dealing with fraud.

The Federal Trade Commission (**www.ftc.gov**) alerts consumers on scam trends, and provides an online resource guidebook.

You have rights, and there are shelves of books telling you about how to get what you deserve. Following are some key contacts you can reach out to when you run into consumer problems with a particular product or service.

Council of Better Business Bureaus, Inc.
4200 Wilson Blvd.
Arlington, VA 22203
703-276-0100

This is the national office of the nonprofit Better Business Bureaus. You can contact the headquarters to get free consumer bulletins, but if you are having problems resolving a complaint against a particular company, you should contact your local BBB.

National Foundation for Consumer Credit
8701 Georgia Avenue, Suite 507
Silver Spring, MD 20910
301-589-5600

This nonprofit group runs local debt counseling services that can help you work out repayment plans with your creditors.

Call for Action
3400 Idaho Avenue NW Suite 1101
Washington, DC 20016
202-686-8225

This consumer group has been alerting consumers to fraud for over thirty years. If you need help, write and explain the problem and include copies of receipts and documents.

National Fraud Information Center
800-876-7060

Run by the National Consumers League, this group passes along consumer complaints to government agencies and helps to resolve problems.

Automotive Consumer Action Program
8400 Westpark Drive
McLean, VA 22102

For new car problems that dealers won't resolve.

TIP

Car salesmen are trying to meet quotas monthly, and you may be able to get a better deal toward the end of the month.

Booklets on avoiding scams and traveling safely are available from the ASTA. You can get lists of agents in your community, or make a complaint if you feel you've been treated unfairly by a travel agent.

American Society of Travel Agents (ASTA)
1101 King Street Alexandria, VA 22314
703-739-2782

If you would like to have your name removed from mailing lists, contact this organization, which oversees direct mail, telemarketing, newspapers, and such.

Mail Preference Service Direct Marketing Association (DMA)
P. O. Box 9008
Farmingdale, NY 11735

COMPUTER AND ONLINE RESOURCES

Want to buy a computer? Better know the "lingo."

Bit: A tiny switch inside the computer that forms the nuts and bolts of all information storage.

Boot: To turn on the machine. To reboot is to reset.

Byte: Eight bits clumped together to form a single nugget of information (a character) inside the computer.

CD-ROM: Compact disc—read only memory. An optical storage disk containing millions of bytes of information.

CPU: Central processing unit. A term for the computer's microprocessor (brain).

DOS: Disk Operating System. The program that controls the machine, the programs that run on it.

Hard disk: A long-term storage file inside the computer. They are faster and hold more than floppy disks.

Megabyte: One million bytes. *War and Peace* could easily fit into a megabyte.

Modem: Stands for modulator-demodulator, a device that translates electronic information in the computer into sounds that can be transmitted over phone lines.

If understanding your computer's specs is making your head spin, you can look up the definitions and descriptions at **www.techweb.com/encyclopedia**.

A computer buying tip: Don't buy a new model computer, or any consumer electronic product for that matter, until the third generation of the product has been introduced. Most electronics are improved or updated twice a year, so wait about one and a half to two years after a new product is introduced.

You can buy a computer and peripherals online at: PriceScan (**www.pricescan.com**), Computer ESP (**www.uvision.com**), NetBuyer (**www.netbuyer.com**), BuyDirect.com (**www.buy-direct.com**), Technology Net (**www.technologynet.com**), or Cyberian Outpost (**www.cybout.com**). If you are looking for a secondhand PC, visit the Used Computer Mall (**www.used-computer.com**) or the Boston Computer Exchange (800-262-6399).

Internet bidding exchanges are flourishing. Some you may want to visit:

Aucnet (**www.aucnet.com**) has a ratings system that helps buyers judge the quality of cars.

Eworldauction (**www.eworldauction.com**) holds auctions of books and maps.

Netmarket (**www.netmarket.com**) is a subscription service that lets you shop for a variety of products ranging from cars to music.

IntelliChoice (**www.intellichoice.com**) provides dealer prices and ownership costs on many car makes and models.

Priceline (**www.priceline.com**) lets you name your price, and they will try to match it.

Narrowline.com (**www.narrowline.com**) brings together media buyers with Web sites looking to sell ad space.

E/town (**www.e-town.com**) provides reviews of home electronics products.

INVESTING ONLINE

You can manage your money at your desk, and buy and sell stocks within seconds, for a fraction of even a discount broker's fee by using an online brokerage. Internet brokerage companies charge less than a traditional broker because they exist in "virtual offices" and have not invested in bricks and mortar, like traditional stock brokerages. You save because of the low cost of doing business. For instance, you can buy a hundred shares of PepsiCo online for $9.95, or you can buy them through Smith Barney for $107.25. The difference—$97.30—is found money: enough to buy two more shares of PepsiCo (plus a nice lunch), in effect for free.

This fee gap results in a measurable difference in portfolio performance on the same stocks. If the 102 PepsiCo shares you bought online gained 10 percent in value every year, after thirty years you would wind up with $1,413 more than if you'd bought 100 shares through a full-service broker. That's nearly a two percent performance gap, and it grows wider as more money is invested.

Individual investors have never been so empowered. There could be 14 million online accounts by 2002, and fueling this surge are low transaction costs.

To Trade Stocks Online

DLJ Direct (**www.dljdirect.com**)

Web Street Securities (**www.webstreetsecurities.com**)

Lindner Funds (**www.linderfunds.com**)

National Discount Brokers (**www.ndb.com**)

Quick & Reilly (**www.quick-reilly.com**)

E★Trade (**www.etrade.com**)

Waterhouse (**www.waterhouse.com**)

Schwab (**www.wschwab.com**)

Discover Brokerage (**www.discoverbrokerage.com**)

Wall Street Electronica (**www.wallstreet.com**)

Datek Online (**www.datek.com**)

Never before have individual investors been so empowered, and never before has managing money been so easy. There could be 14 million online accounts by 2002. Fueling the surge in online trading are lower transaction costs. In 1997, the average commission charged by the top 10 online brokers fell by more than 50 percent, from $34.65 at the start of the year to $15.95 at year end.

Virtually any topic can be found on the Internet, and there are several hundred investment-related sites. These sites are worth a visit by you and can be accessed without a fee.

Sites Offering Market Updates, Research, and Tips

Morningstar, Inc. (**www.morningstar.net**)

The Motley Fool (**www.motleyfool.com**)

The Street.com (**www.thestreet.com**)

IBC Financial Data (**www.ibcdata.com**)

American Association of Individual Investor (**www.aaii.com**)

Nest Egg (**www.nestegg.com**)

Zacks Investment Research (**www.zacks.com**)

Sites Offering Research that Mimics the Professionals

Yahoo!Finance (**www.yahoo.com**)

Microsoft Investor (**www.investor.msn.com**)

Market Guide Inc. (**www.marketguide.com**)

Standard & Poor's Personal Wealth (**www.personalwealth.com**)

Invest-O-Rama (**www.investorama.com**)

S&P'S Personal Wealth (**www.personalwealth.com**)

Wall Street City (**www.wallstreetcity.com**)

Financial Web Sites, General

EDGAR (**www.sec.gov/edgarhp.htm**)

IRS forms and publications page (**www.irs.ustreas.gov/prod/ forms_pubs/index.html**)

American Stock Exchange (**www.amex.com**)

The Web Financial Network (**www.webfn.com**)

The Silicon Investor (**www.techstocks.com**)

Wall Street Journal's Interactive Edition (**update.wsj.com/ welcome.html**)

The MIT Artificial Intelligence Laboratory's StockMaster
(**www.ai.mit.edu/stocks**)

Stockwhiz.com

Sites with Mutual Fund Information

NETworth (**networth.galt.com**)

Mutual Funds Magazine Online (**www.mfmag.com**)

Other Financial Sites:

Informanage International Inc. (**www.infomanage.com
/investment/default.html**)

Department of Finance—Ohio State University—The Financial Data
Finder (**www.cob.ohio-state.edu/dept/fin/osudata.html**)

Investment Brokerages Guide (**www.cs.cmu.edu/~jdg/
invest_brokers/index.html**)

Essential Links to Taxes (**www.el.com/ToTheWeb/Taxes**)

Microsoft Money Insider (**moneyinsider.msn.com**)

Deloitte & Touche (**www.dtonline.com**)

Fidelity Investments (**www.fidelity.com**)

FinancCenter/Smartcalc (**www.financenter.com**)

Intuit (**www.intuit.com**)

Quicken (**www.quicken.com**)

Gomez Advisor's (**www.gomezadvisors.com**) has a scorecard
ranking more than 50 Internet brokers on areas such as ease of use, on-
site resources, and overall cost. Gomez scores firms according to their

appropriateness for four kinds of investors: Life Goal Planner, Serious Investor, Hyperactive Trader, and One-Stop Shopper.

How to Follow Stocks by Reading Stock Quotations

Stock prices change daily, and there are no guaranteed values in common stock investment. Stock prices reflect information available to the market, and the market's interpretation of the information. The risk to the investor is the variability in stock prices and dividends. Some of the information available to investors is the current stock price quotation. Common stocks may be listed on the New York Stock Exchange, the American Stock Exchange, Nasdaq, or regional exchanges. For a company to be listed, it must meet listing requirements that specify a minimum number of share-holders, the number of shares outstanding, minimum assets and net worth, and other such variables.

Information about companies, industries, and the economy is readily available, and this information changes stock prices and moves markets. Without a framework for evaluating this information toward the goal of valuing a common stock, an investor will find it difficult to make an intelligent judgment.

The NYSE, Amex, and Nasdaq publish information daily (examples of these stock quotations are shown on the next page). The NYSE, Amex, and Nasdaq quotations present the same information in similar formats. The definitions of the major information points found in the stock quotations are shown below:

52 Weeks Hi, Lo: The highest and lowest prices of the stock for the prior year

Stock: The abbreviated name of the company (may also be further abbreviated with its symbol, under the column SYM)

Sym: The exchange symbol of the company

Div: Annual cash dividend per share, given in dollars and cents

Yld%: Dividend yield; cash dividend divided by market price of the stock. For example, if the cash dividend is $6 and the stock price is $100, then the dividend yield is 6% ($6 / $100).

PE: The market price per share divided by the most recent annual earnings per share. For example, if the earnings per share figure for a stock is $8 and the stock price is $100, then the P-E Ratio is 12/5 ($100 / $8).

Sales 100s: Number of round lots (100 shares each) traded for the day. If 50 round lots are traded, a total of 5,000 (50 × 100) shares were traded.

Hi: The daily high

Lo: The daily low

Last: Price at the close of the day's trading activity

Net Chg: The price change from the prior day's close

52 Weeks Hi	**Lo**	**Stock**	**Div**	**Yld %**	**PE**	**Vol 100's**	**Hi**	**Lo**	**Last**	**Net Chg**
18½	11⅜	PepsiGem	.15	1.2	...	173	12⅜	12	12¼	+¼
44½	33⅜	PepsiCo	.52	1.2	33	33542	43¾	41⅜	43¼	+1½
86½	55	Perk El	.68	1.1	59	1519	64¼	62	62⅛	-1¾
5⅛	4¼	Prmian	.17	1.1	19	29	4⅜	4½	4 ⅞	+¼
24	14⅜	PersGp	.09	...	23	1386	20	19	⅛	19½
28⅜	17⅛	Petersen	...	1.4	51	33	25¼	25	⅛	25¼

Announcements of a company's earnings and dividends may have an impact on the stock price, especially when the new figures were not what analysts and investors were expecting (see the table on the next page). A company's earnings are its profits, reported four times per year. This is considered the most important factor influencing stock prices. Earnings are the scorecard by which companies are judged to be successful or not. Earnings increases make dividend increases possible and make the stock more attractive. Read the column from left to right as follows.

The **name** of company is listed, followed by a code for where the stock is traded, for example, Humana Inc. trades on the NYSE. Comparisons are made between the current quarter and that of a year ago. Gross income is listed as **revenues** for service companies and as sales for manufacturing companies. **Net income** is the profit made for the time quarter. **Share earns: Net Income** is defined as the net income divided by number of shares. If this is not the first quarter, the same information for the year-to-date is given.

Humana Inc. (N)		
Quar May 31:	1998	1997
Revenues...	$891,143,000	$744,471,000
Net income...	63,820,000	52,274,000
Shr earns:		
Net income	.64	.53
Revenues...	2,531,068,000	2,169,228,000
Income...	168,828,000	135,371,000
Extrd chg...	16,133,000	14,354,000
Acctg adj...	12,639,000	...
Net income...	168,909.000	135,371,000
Shr earns:		
Income...	1.71	1.38
Net income	1.71	1.38

INSURANCE INFORMATION

For general questions or help resolving insurer problems, call the Insurance Information Helpline. They can also send you *Nine Ways to Lower Your Auto Insurance Costs, Taking Inventory, Home Security Basics*, and other free brochures.

> Insurance Information Institute
> 110 William Street
> New York, NY 10038
> 800-942-4242

> Mutual Fund Educational Alliance
> 1900 Erie Street, Suite 120
> Kansas City, MO 64116

The *Investor's Guide to Low-Cost Mutual Funds* lists almost 1,000 mutual funds you can buy directly from the fund company (send $7).

The American Homeowners Foundation will send you, for free, their *Mini Guide to Home Ownership,* a booklet with tips to help you decide whether or not you really want to own a home. Contact them at:

> 6776 Little Falls Road
> Arlington, VA 22213-1213
> 800-489-7776

To get quotes for term and whole life insurance:

> **www.quotesmith.com**
> **www.quickquote.com**

www.insweb.com
www.insuremarket.com

To get quotes in Spanish:

Boston Mutual, 800-669-2668 (**www.Bostonmutual.com**)

Mutual Funds Directories and Performance

CDA/Wiesenberger Mutual Fund Report: CDA/ Wiesenberger, Inc., 1355 Piccard Dr., Suite 220, Rockville, MD 20850; 800-232-2285. This statistical service presents risk-adjusted return figures on all mutual funds listed in the financial media.

Directory of Mutual Funds: Investment Company Institute, 1401 H St., N.W., 12th Floor, Washington, DC 20005-2148; 202-326-5800; provides a list of names and addresses of over 5,000 load and no-load mutual funds.

The *Individual Investor's Guide to Low-Load Mutual Fund:* American Association of Individual Investors, 625 N. Michigan Avenue, Suite 1900, Chicago, IL 60611; 800-428-2244; a detailed analysis of over 750 low-load mutual funds, including 10 years of historical performance, a statistical summary, fund objectives and services, the name of the portfolio manager, fund addresses and telephone numbers, and strategies for effective mutual fund investing.

Morningstar Mutual Fund and Mutual Fund 500; Morningstar Inc., 225 W. Wacker Dr., Chicago, IL 60606; 800-735-0700; full-page reports on individual mutual funds similar to the Value Line stock reports.

Mutual Fund Fact Book: Investment Company Institute, 1401H Street, N.W., 12th Floor, Washington, DC 20005-2148; 202-326-5800; ten-year statistical data on over 5,000 funds.

Dividend Reinvestment Plans

Common Stock DRP Report: S.A.M. Designs, Box 7969, Tyler, TX 75711; 903-592-5465; 800-377-9235

Directory Of Companies Offering Dividend Reinvestment Plans: Evergreen Enterprises, P.O. Box 763, Laurel, MD 2072-0763; 301-549-3939

The Individual Investor's Guide to Dividend Reinvestment Plans: American Association of Individual Investors, 625 N. Michigan Ave., Suite 1900, Chicago, IL 60611; 800-428-2244

The Moneypaper Guide to Dividend Reinvestment Plans: 1010 Mamaroneck Ave., Mamaroneck, NY 10543; 914-381-5400, **www.moneypaper.com**

Moody's Dividend Record: 99 Church Street, New York, N.Y. 10007; 800-342-5647, ext. 0547. Information concerning dividend payments.

Standard & Poors Directory of Dividend Reinvestment Plans: 65 Broadway, New York, N.Y. 10006; 800-221-5277. Companies with dividend reinvestment plans, giving contact information and dividend history. Detailed plan options of each, including if company allows direct investment.

Variable Annuities

Morningstar Variable Annuity Performance Report: 225 West Wacker Drive, Chicago, IL 60606; 800-876-5005. Performance data on over 3,700 variable annuity and variable life subaccounts.

Variable Annuity Research & Data Service (VARDS) Report: Financial Planning Resources Inc., P.O. Box 1927, Roswell, GA 30077-1927; 770-998-5186. Contains contract profiles, five years of performance data, risk statistics, and general information about variable annuities.

BUYING AND SELLING A HOUSE
....

Next to the investment you make in your career, your home is likely to be the largest. You can save by buying and selling it yourself, and you don't need a real estate license.

Buying a House

What can you afford? Go to several lenders—banks, mortgage banks, savings and loan associations, credit unions—to see how much of a mortgage you qualify for.

Shop rates. Mortgage rates change about every day. Check with as many lenders as you can, as frequently as you can.

Look into "first time buyer" assistance. As long as you have not owned any real estate in the past three years, you'll qualify.

Plan your financing. Take no points—or as few as possible—if you'll be in a house less than ten years, and take a higher interest rate. If you plan to stay longer, take the points and pay a lower rate.

In the short term, it's better to rent. You won't make up all your costs if you're only going to keep a house for three or four years.

Get help. You need help to buy a house: a buyer/broker to find suitable properties, an attorney to review the contract, an engineer to assess the house, and an accountant to show you how the purchase will affect your tax situation.

Protect your deposit. When you put money down, make sure the money is totally refundable if the deal fails.

Be careful of the legalese. Savvy sellers often draw up their own "official" contracts. While this is not illegal, signing a personalized contract is not likely to be in your favor. Have a real estate lawyer explain each clause and make necessary changes.

Watch for quitclaim deeds. Do a title search and consult a real estate attorney before buying a property with a quitclaim deed.

Don't accept oral promises. They're worthless. Put it in writing.

Be specific, down to the light fixtures, washer and dryer, and so on.

Watch the details. To ensure the work gets done, the contract should stipulate that the seller set up an escrow account at the time of closing to cover work not completed. If he's doing the work himself, set aside a reasonable amount and agree to return it when the job is done.

Get a "good faith" estimate of closing costs. Closing a house deal can cost thousands in taxes and professional fee; get an estimate.

Set limits on an adjustable rate mortgage (ARM). To minimize the risks of an ARM—a loan with a fluctuating interest rate—make sure the papers state the following information: the maximum rate you are willing to pay over the life of the loan, the maximum annual increase allowed each year, and the maximum monthly payment increase.

Find ARMs with the least risk. Lenders use financial indexes to base rates. Indexes that cover a longer span of events change more gradually than other indexes and can keep your rates fairly stable.

Look at hybrid ARMs. These carry a fixed interest rate for seven to ten years and then switch to a variable rate; they are good if you plan to sell your house after a few years. You'll typically get a lower rate than with a fixed-rate loan, but you'll be out before the variable rate kicks in.

Selling Your House

Hold an auction. Most sellers list the highest price they think they can get and work down from there. But that strategy often turns prospective buyers away. Instead, list the lowest you'd accept and then hold an auction, with your minimum price as the starting bid.

Run a good ad. Include a brief description of the highlights, a low price indicating you're willing to bargain, and an open house date; create a sense of urgency. Your ad should run in major newspapers from Wednesday to Sunday. Here's a blueprint:

> WEST SIDE BY OWNER
> 4BR House on cul-de-sac Deck Patio
> Den w/fpl Din Rm Liv Rm 2½ Baths
> $299,500 or Best Offer
> Open Sat.- Sun. 10-4:30
> Home will be sold Sunday Night to
> Highest Bidder
> 914-555-1234

If you don't get 25 calls by Friday, your price is too high. Pull the ad and relist it at a lower price next week. This system assumes you will get a total of 100 calls and at least 40 will show up to look.

Price it below a "magic number." If you list your house at a round figure like $200,000 or $250,000, buyers may think you won't budge. Instead, set it just below the "magic number," at $149,500, for example. People may think you'll go as low as $140,000.

Skip the appraisal. The market determines the price, not an outsider.

Skip the broker. He has a conflict of interest: He wants your house at a price that assures his commission, not at a price that assures you of the best price.

Be honest. Show buyers the home inspection report. Tell them everything that is wrong, and that they are bidding on an "as is" basis.

Wage a price war. During the open house, place a bidding sheet on the table near the entrance so people can write their name, phone number, and bid. On Sunday night—between 5 and 8 P.M., after the open house is over—have a round-robin bid over the telephone. First call the highest bidder. Tell him he has made the top offer and ask him if he'd like to up it before you call the others. Then call the next highest bidder to see if he can beat the top bid. Go through as many rounds as necessary until there's only one bidder left.

Explain the bidding process. Give buyers a rundown when they call for directions to the open house and post a clear description next to the bidding sheet.

Use an attorney. Each state has its own laws governing sales and auctions, so contact an attorney before you list your ad. Once the sale is made, have the attorney qualify the buyer and handle the close.

Don't wait until spring. The sooner you sell your house, the better, even if you expect the market to take a bit of an upswing in a year. Every day you hold onto it, you have to pay mortgage interest, taxes, and repair bills. The only bad times to try to sell a house are over holidays and three-day weekends.

Refinancing Your House

Should you refinance?

If you have a variable-rate mortgage, should you lock in a lower rate on a fixed-term loan? Do you have a conventional 30-year mortgage—even one that you refinanced just a year ago? Whatever your situation, as long as interest rates remain low, you should explore refinancing your mortgage.

This worksheet can help determine whether refinancing is right for you. First, note your current monthly mortgage expenses. Then, use the interest-rate table that follows to estimate what your monthly payments would be with a new loan at a lower rate.

For example, if you can get a rate of 7.25 percent on a $125,000 loan, you'd pay $852.50 per month ($6.82 from the table multiplied by 125 for the number of thousands of dollars you are financing equals $852.50). Subtract this figure from your current payment to determine what your gross monthly savings would be.

Add the transaction costs you will incur—points, appraisal, attorneys' fees, and so on. Divide the total by the monthly savings. This shows how many months it will take to recoup your costs. It probably pays to refinance if you plan to stay in your current home longer than this period.

Computing your monthly payment on a 30-year loan

Rate %	Payment $
7.00	6.65
7.25	6.82
7.50	6.99
7.75	7.16
8.00	7.34
8.25	7.51
8.50	7.69

Computing your monthly payment on a 30-year loan (Cont.)

Rate %	Payment $
8.75	7.87
9.00	8.05
9.25	8.23
9.50	8.41
9.75	8.59
10.0	8.78

Worksheet:

1   Your current monthly mortgage payment
(excluding insurance and taxes) $_____

2   Monthly payment for your new loan
(use chart above to compute) $_____

3   closing costs: (points, fees for application,
title search, attorneys, and appraisal) $_____

4   Monthly savings
(subtract line 2 from line 1) $_____

     Number of months you'll need to stay
in new home to recoup cost of refinancing:
(Divide line 3 by line 4) $_____

There are numerous new ways to refinance your house. Besides adjustable-rate mortgages, there are 10- and 15-year fixed-rate loans; "reset" loans, on which the rate is adjusted after a number of years; and "no-cost" loans, which hike your rate a bit so that you spend next to no cash up front. A variant is the "negative-point" mortgage, where a lender gives you a rebate on some closing costs—in return for a rate that's higher.

What's right for you depends on several factors. Among them are how long you intend to keep the loan, how high your tax rate is, and what you might be able to earn by investing what you would have to spend on closing costs and points. A point is a fee the lender collects, one percent of the loan amount.

Some places to go for help on the Web:

Smartcalc (**www.smartcalc.com**) has an interactive calculator to help you decide when to refinance.

Quicken Mortgage (**mortgage-quicken.com**) has daily average mortgage rates by state.

Federal Home Loan Mortgage (**www.freddiemac.com**) provides national and regional averages for mortgage rates and fees.

HSH Associates (**www.hsh.com**) will give you a guidebook to refinancing and the going rates for closing costs.

Guide to Online Mortgages

The following sites are helpful with real estate financing:

HSH Associates (**www.hsh.com**) provides literature, a guide to refinancing, and a list of average interest rates from town to town.

Most major banks and mortgage-lending institutions have their own Web sites, such as Norwest Corp. (**www.norwest.com**), Country-wide Credit Industries Inc. (**www.countrywide.com**), and Chase Manhattan Corp. (**www.chase.com**).

E-Loan (**www.eloan.com**) creates bar graphs and other visuals that let you compare different loans at once, and it e-mails you when the rate and term package you're looking for becomes available.

Computer Loan Network (**www.clnet.com**). The company posts application forms on a bulletin board for participating lenders to peruse. Lenders then telephone the applicants within 48 hours.

Quicken Mortgage (**mortgage.quicken.com**)

Homeshark (**www.homeshark.com**) offers a streamlined mortgage comparison system that doesn't estimate monthly payments and makes you compute the total closing costs.

FinanCenter (**www.financenter.com**) has an online calculator.

GetSmart (**www.getsmart.com**) tells prospective borrowers how much they will have to pay each month and up front, and allows applicants to pick lenders based on geographic proximity or compatibility with their frequent flier programs.

TAXES

Usenet newsgroups (**home1.get.net/brcpa/mtmfaq.htm**; see **misc.taxes.moderated** in the FAQ) can answer specific tax questions.

The IRS site (**www.irs.ustreas.gov**), 800-829-1040, lists Frequently Asked Tax Questions, part of the section on the agency's site called Taxpayer Help and Education (**www.irs.ustreas.gov/prod/tax_edu/index.html**). The tax FAQ is divided into such categories as IRS Procedures, Alternative Filing Methods, General Information, Types of Income, Adjustments to Income, Itemized Deductions, Tax Credits and Filing Requirements, Filing Status, and Exemptions.

SecureTax (**www.securetax.com**) will let you prepare a return online and file it electronically.

TaxAttack (**www.taxattack.com**) will give you a questionnaire to fill out; a CPA will call within 24 hours to review your return and offer advice.

The U.S. House of Representatives (**law.house.gov./usc.htm**) will answer your questions in the Internal Revenue Code. The site offers a powerful search engine and is quite complex.

Several directories can guide you to more online tax information:

Essential Links to Taxes (**www.el.com/ToTheWeb/Taxes**)is a table of links covering multiple categories.

NetTaxes (**www.ypn.com/taxes/index.html**) provides information on sites available on consumer services such as AOL and CompuServe, plus categories for Easing the Pain, Filing, Getting Help, and Preparing Your Taxes.

Tax Related Sites (**www.abanet.org/tax/sires.html**) gives links to federal, state, judicial, and foreign tax information.

Tax Resources (**www.biz.uiowa.edu/misc/links/acct_tax.html**) has more than a dozen categories, including Tax Pages of CPA Firms.

TaxSites (**www.best.com/~ftmexpat/html/taxsites.html**) has annotated links arranged by category, designed primarily for accountants, but much of the information may be useful to nonprofessionals, too.

How to Pay Less in Taxes

Realize you can pay less. Tax planning isn't only for the wealthy. Most people pay too much tax because they don't take advantage of simple tax planning strategies.

Max out your IRA. Most Americans can deduct their contributions to individual retirement accounts. Whether you work for someone else or are self-employed, putting $2,000 a year—the maximum—into an IRA is the best tax break available. If you're in the 28 percent tax bracket, a $2,000 deductible automatically saves you $560 in taxes, and the money grows tax-deferred until you withdraw it.

Take every deduction. Not taking a deduction you deserve for fear of being audited is the equivalent of paying protection to the IRS.

Monitor your investments. Many overpay the tax on their stocks and mutual funds because they don't keep accurate records. The biggest mistake is paying tax twice on reinvested dividends. Here's an example: Say you buy $1,000 worth of stock. Then you reinvest $100 of the dividends to buy more shares before selling the whole lot a year later for $1,200. Your reported gain should be only $100, not $200. You paid tax on the dividend the year it was paid to you; if you count it as part of your gain, you'll pay tax on it again when you sell.

Do it yourself. If you have a fairly simple financial situation, you're better off filing your return on your own or using a computerized tax preparation kit than paying an accountant to do the job. But use an accountant if you have a number of investments, run a side business, bought or sold a home, or inherited a significant amount of property.

Know when to itemize. For most people, taking the standard deduction is usually better than itemizing. But if you add up the three major deductible expenses: home mortgage interest, state income taxes, and charitable contributions, and if the total falls within $200 of your standard deduction, itemize—it will probably save you money.

Use an employer reimbursement account for medical and child-care expenses. If your company offers them, these accounts are one of the best tax breaks around. If they are offered, designate the amount of pretax money you want transferred directly from your paycheck to the account. After you pay a child-care or medical bill, submit it to your employer for reimbursement from the account. You are paying health and child-care bills with tax-exempt money. However, leftover money is not refunded to you or carried over to the next year. But it's such a big tax break, you can forfeit one-third of the money and still come out ahead. Use any excess funds for a new pair of glasses or a checkup.

Deduct your points. In the past, only buyers could deduct the points they paid to get a mortgage on their principal residence. But if you as the buyer convinced the seller to pay all or part of the points for you, no one got the deduction. In almost all cases, the buyer deducts the points, even if paid by the seller. Remember that each point represents one percent of the mortgage amount.

Invest in tax-free bonds. They may be more lucrative, even though they have lower yields than most corporate bonds. If you're in the 31 percent tax bracket and are choosing between a tax-free bond with a 7 percent yield and a taxable bond with a 10.14 percent yield, use this formula to see how they compare: Subtract your tax bracket from 1 (1 − 0.31 = 0.69). Divide the tax-free yield by that number (0.07 / 0.69 = .1014). If you multiply your answer by 100, you'll get the percentage yield you'd need on a taxable bond to match the tax-free yield (0.1014 × 100 = 10.14 percent) In this case, you get the same return on the tax-free bond as the taxable bond. And if the tax-free bond also escapes state income tax, you'll come out ahead.

Educate your kids on tax-free savings bonds. Typically thought of as lousy investments, if you use them to put your kids through college, they can be free of state and federal income tax.

Don't overpay inheritance tax. There's a tax break that forgives the levy on any profit that has built up in stocks, real estate, or other assets when the owner dies. Say, for example, you inherit stock your father bought for $1,000 and was worth $10,000 when he died. When you sell the stock, your base for figuring taxable gain or loss is that $10,000 date-of-death value. So if you sell the stock for $9,000, you actually have a $1,000 tax-deductible loss —even though you've got $9,000 in your pocket.

Know the rules—even if you use an accountant. Your accountant is only as good as the information you give him. Most community colleges offer basic tax courses, and many tax preparation offices give low-cost seminars to help you brush up. Or you can get an up-to-date tax preparation book at your local bookstore.

Cut your withholding. If your typical tax refund is more that $1,000, you're letting the IRS use money that could be earning you interest. To keep the government from taking more out of your check than it has a right to, ask your employer to add more allowances to your W-4 form. For each withholding allowance you add $50 to $60 extra in your monthly paycheck. For a rough estimate of how many allowances to add, divide your refund by $700 (if you're in the 28 to 31 percent tax bracket) and round to the nearest whole number.

Filing Your Return

The IRS offers an interactive map of the U.S. (**www.irs.ustreas.gov /prod/where_file/index.html**) that will be helpful in filing your return. Click on your state to find out the correct address.

If you're interested in electronic filing options, visit the IRS Electronic Services section (**www.irs.ustreas.gov/ prod/elec_svs/index.html**).

You can find details about several programs, including On-Line Filing for Individuals, Federal/State Electronic Filing, the 1040-PC return, and TeleFile, which lets some 1040EZ users file their returns over the phone.

If you can't make the April 15 deadline, visit the IRS section that explains extensions (**www.irs.ustreas.gov/ ptod/forms_pubs/ extensions.html**). Download Form 4868, Application for Automatic Extension of Time to File U.S. Individual Income Tax Return, and Form 2688, Application for Additional Extension, in PDF, PCL, or PostScript format.

To find information on extensions for state taxes, visit TaxWeb (**www.taxweb.com/index.html**). See the section called Filing Extensions, where you can find general information, a list of states that honor federal extensions, and contact information for the appropriate state agencies.

HOW TO PAY FOR COLLEGE
....

The average annual cost at a four-year public college is now over $10,000, and at a private school over $21,000. What to do? First read Chapter 14, then construct a college savings plan and complete this worksheet to estimate the cost of your children's higher education:

1	Child's current age	_____
2	Years until college (18 minus line 1)	_____
3	Annual college costs	_____
4	Public school:	$10,069★
5	Private school:	$21,424★

6 Rising cost factor
(obtain factor from chart that follows) _____

7 Future annual college cost
(multiply line 3 by line 4) _____

8 Total cost of college (multiply line 5
by number of college years planned) _____

★ estimated annual cost for 1997–98 by the College Board

Years to college	Rising cost factor
1	1.08
2	1.17
3	1.26
4	1.36
5	1.47
6	1.59
7	1.71
8	1.85
9	2.00
10	2.16
11	2.33
12	2.52
13	2.72
14	2.94
15	3.17
16	3.43
17	3.70
18	4.00

Next, refer to the charts that follow to see the number of years you have before your child enters college. By seeing where that line intersects with the amount from line 6, you can gauge how much you would have to save in a lump sum now, or monthly to reach the full cost (these figures assume an eight percent yield compounded annually).

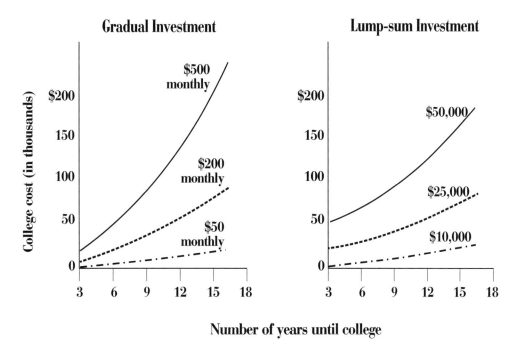

These figures assume an 8% yield compounded annually.
Source: Mutual Fund Education Alliance

Here are some resources to help you plan as you start saving for college:

Calculators: The National Association of Student Financial Aid Administrators (**www.finaid.org**) and Student Loan Corporation (**www.salliemae.com**) project what college will cost.

Prepaid tuition: Fourteen states offer plans that allow you to pay tuition at today's level, guaranteeing that the money will cover tuition when your children are ready. More states are joining in. Check out The College Savings Bank (**www.collegesavings.org**), or call 800-888-2723.

Read The College Board's *Meeting College Costs: What You Need to Know Before Your Child and Money Leave Home,* available for $13.95 at 800-239-5888. Sallie Mae's "Paying for College" is free at 800-891-4599.

Strategies for College (802-773-4291 **www.Swiftsite.com/ Fothergill/McGrath**) can tell you more about selecting and paying for college.

RETIREMENT AND ELDER CARE

If you have retirement or elder care concerns, consult these sources:

Consumer Information Center
Pueblo, CO 81009
What you should know about pension law.

American Association of Retired Persons (AARP)
Worker Equity 601 E Street NW
Washington, DC 20049
A guide to understanding your pension plan.

National Center for Women & Retirement Research Group
800-426-7386
Booklets, worksheets, and videos are available.

National Academy of Elder Law Attorneys
602-881-4405
Information available on finding an elder law attorney.

Eldercare Locator
800-677-1116
Provides help in finding local services to assist you or an elderly relative.

Consumer Information Center
Department 40
Pueblo, CO 81009
Many useful brochures are available.

How Much Life Insurance Do You Need?

What You Need	Your Needs	Totals
Immediate Expenses		
Federal estate taxes		
State inheritance taxes	_____	
Probate costs	_____	
Funeral costs	_____	
Uninsured medical costs	_____	
Total final expenses		_____
Future Expenses		
Family expense fund	_____	
Emergency fund	_____	
Child-care expenses	_____	
Education fund	_____	
Repayment of debts	_____	
Total future expenses		_____
Total needs		_____

What You Have Now   Your Assets

Cash and savings   _____

Equity in real estate   _____

Securities   _____

IRA and Keogh plans   _____

Employer savings plans   _____

Lump-sum employer pension
benefits   _____

Current life insurance   _____

Other assets   _____

   Total assets

_____

_____

Extra Insurance Needed

Total needs minus total assets

   Total needs   _____

   Total assets   _____

   Additional insurance needed   _____

How to Have a Million by 65

In saving for retirement (or anything), time and return are key. In the chart that follows, find your age and notice the difference a few points in annual return can make to your bottom line. The chart shows how much you need to save every month, starting *now,* to have a million dollars by age 65. It also shows that the earlier you start, the richer you'll be.

Amount You Have to Save per Month

Starting Age	8% return	10% return	15% return
25	$310	$180	$45
30	470	300	90

Amount You Have to Save per Month (Cont.)

Starting Age	8% return	10% return	15% return
35	710	490	180
40	1,100	810	370
45	1,760	1,390	760
50	2,960	2,500	1,640
55	5,550	5,000	3,850
60	13,700	13,050	11,600

Know Your Net Worth

Knowing your net worth is an important first step in charting your financial future. Net worth is the value of what you own (your assets), minus what you owe (your liabilities). You may own a home, cars, jewelry, a retirement plan, an IRA, and perhaps some stocks and bonds. These are all assets. From this you subtract your liabilities, such as mortgage payments, outstanding loans, and credit card charges.

If you've never calculated your net worth or haven't done so in the last few years, here's your chance. Set aside some time. Get your check-book, bills, financial statements, and calculator; pick a date; and complete the accompanying worksheets as follows:

1   Add up the value of everything you own (your assets).

2   Add up the value of everything you owe (your liabilities).

3   Subtract your liabilities from your assets. The difference is your net worth.

1. Assets as of _____ (date)
Cash on hand
   Checking accounts   _____
   Savings accounts   _____
   Money market accounts   _____
   Life insurance cash value   _____

Retirement funds
   Annuities   _____
   IRA or Keogh   _____
   Retirement savings plan, vested portion _____
   Pension plan, vested portion   _____
   U.S. Savings Bonds   _____

Investments
   Market value of stocks   _____
   Bonds   _____
   Mutual funds   _____
   Other   _____

Real Estate, market value
   Residence and vacation home   _____

Personal assets
   Car(s)   _____
   Boat(s)   _____
   Furnishings   _____
   Jewelry and other luxury items   _____
   Collections, hobby equipment   _____
   Other   _____

   Total Assets   _____

2. Liabilities as of _____ (date)

Unpaid bills

Charge accounts, credit card charges _____

Rent or monthly mortgage payments _____

Installment loan payments _____

Car payments _____

Taxes due _____

Balance due on:

Mortgage on residence and vacation home _____

Car loans _____

Installment loans _____

Life insurance policy loans _____

Other loans _____

Total Liabilities _____

3. Net Worth

Total Assets _____

Minus Total Liabilities _____

Net Worth _____

Glossary

American Stock Exchange (AMEX)   A trading house in New York where stocks are auctioned. Small to medium-sized companies as well as oil and gas companies are traded here.

annual report   A publication put out by management that summarizes the performance of a company or mutual fund over one calendar (or fiscal) year and discusses future prospects. It's also a public relations tool to attract new investors.

asset allocation   The process of investing among several different investment types (such as stock, bond, and stable value) to help lower the risks associated with investing in only one investment type.

back-end load   A deferred commission fee or sales charge that is paid when a mutual fund is sold.

balanced fund   A mutual fund that invests in both stocks and bonds—usually with a ratio of 60 percent to 40 percent.

bear market   When stock prices fall. Since World War I, there have been ten major bear markets. Bear markets are typically brought on by concerns of declining economic activity.

beta   A way of evaluating volatility (risk) for a mutual fund or stock, relative to the market. A fund with a beta of 1 has the same risk as the market. A beta 2 fund is twice as risky, so an investor is likely to double their profits—or losses—compared to the market. A beta of less than one means the mutual fund or stock moves less than the market.

blue chip stock   Like the blue chip in poker, these are the most valuable, with a long history of profits and dividends. Typically established companies like IBM or PepsiCo. The 30 Dow Jones Industrial Average stocks are all blue chips.

bond   A certificate from a corporation, the U.S. Treasury or local governments to pay back a debt—with interest—at maturity. Unlike stockholders, bondholders do not own a share of a corporation, only the debt.

bond fund   A mutual fund that invests only in corporate, U.S. Treasury, or local government bonds. They provide lower returns and emphasize income over rapid gains or losses.

bond rating   A grade given to bonds that indicates the investment quality. The more A's the better, and ratings range from AAA (very unlikely to default) to D (in default). Moody's Investment Services and Standard & Poor's are the two major bond raters.

broker   A certified individual who acts as the intermediary between the buyer and seller of securities, such as stock. Brokers typically charge a commission for their service.

bull market   When the overall price of stocks rise. Historically, stock prices tend to rise over the long term.

capital   Money.

capital appreciation   The increase in value of a security, such as a stock. Suppose you buy a share of stock for $10 and it increases in value to $15, the capital appreciation is $5.

capital gain/loss   The amount of profit gained—or lost—after selling an investment. A stock bought for $10 and sold for $15 has produced a $5 capital gain. However, that same stock sold for $5 results in a $5 capital loss. Capital gains are taxable.

certificate of deposit (CD)   Like a savings account, but pays a higher interest rate because the length and amount are locked in—typically from 30 days to several years. The most frequently used type of money market instrument. CDs redeemed before maturity are subject to heavy penalties.

closed-end fund   A mutual fund with a limited number of shares that is bought and sold on the stock exchange or over the counter (OTC). Unlike an open-end fund (where the share price is based on the value of the fund's assets), the price of a closed-end fund is determined by supply and demand, like a stock.

commercial paper   Short-term certificates that range from 2 to 270 days and are typically sold by corporations to raise capital.

commission   A fee paid by the investor to a broker or dealer for a transaction or advice. Commissions are charged when a security is bought or sold.

common stock   A security that shows ownership in a corporation. Stockholders share profits or losses through dividends and changes in the stock's market value. Common stocks are the most typical.

compounding   The process of an investment building upon itself, which results in increased gains over time.

Consumer Price Index (CPI)   Followed by the Bureau of Labor Statistics in Washington, this is the rate of inflation as shown by the change in price of a set group of consumer goods and services.

convertible bonds   Certificates that can be exchanged for a corporation's common stock. Unlike regular bonds that fluctuate in value based upon interest rate, these bonds tend to fluctuate in price based on the stock's price.

corporation   A business organization with limited liability. The owners, including shareholders, can lose only the amount they invest.

current return   How much your original investment grows over one year.

cyclical stock   When the economy falters, a manufacturer of expensive durable goods such as automobiles may see sales drop, while a company that produces staples—such as food—isn't bothered as much. In lean times, a thrifty household will focus on food, not new cars. A durable manufacturing company is said to be cyclical because its performance is tied to the cycles of the economy.

defensive stocks   The opposite of cyclical stocks because they are not affected by business cycles. Utilities are defensive because even in lean times consumers will still need electricity and heat.

defined-contribution plan   A retirement plan such as a 401(k) with set employer/employee contributions, usually a percentage of salary. The amount of income that an individual is able to withdraw is based upon contributions, length of service, and earnings.

discount broker   The opposite of a full-service broker, and one who provides basic trading services at a low cost, including online trading services. They do not dispense advice or make recommendations.

diversification   A way to reduce risk by investing in more than one type of device. Mutual funds provide diversification by investing in many different companies.

dividend   Cash profits that are distributed—usually quarterly—to shareholders from the net profits of a corporation or mutual fund.

Dividend Reinvestment Plan (DRIP)   A commission-free arrangement where corporate dividends are automatically used to purchase more shares of that firm's stock. DRIPs provide a low-cost way to increase the portfolio value of a particular stock.

dollar-cost averaging   A strategy in which an investor buys the same dollar amount of a stock at regular intervals, regardless of the price. Since shares are bought at both high and low prices, the costs average out over the long run.

Dow Jones Industrial Average (DJIA)   The average cost of 30 of the largest NYSE-listed stocks. The most widely quoted indicator of the market, but because it's so narrow—there are about 3000 stocks on the New York Stock Exchange—it doesn't accurately reflect broad market activity.

earnings   Profits. The money a company clears after paying all expenses.

Federal Deposit Insurance Corporation (FDIC)   A public corporation that insures accounts in participating banks up to $100,000.

financial risk   The chance a company will not pay back its investors.

fixed income   A guaranteed rate of interest. Bonds that pay specific amounts of money over time are an example of a fixed-income security.

401(k)   Employer-sponsored retirement plans that permit employees to defer taxes on a portion of their salaries by contributing to a company investment account.

403(b)   Similar to 401(k)s, but for employees of universities, public schools, and nonprofits.

front-end load   An up-front commission investors pay when they buy shares in a fund. Calculated as a percentage of the amount an individual invests into a mutual fund. The commission on a $1000 investment with a 2 percent load is $20.

full-service broker   A dealer who provides a full range of investment advice that includes research, investment planning, and trading.

growth stock   Shares of, typically, small companies with potentially bright futures and fast growth potential that are expected to achieve better-than-average appreciation due to higher profits and expansion. They are riskier investments than blue chip stocks.

income   Dividends or interest paid by stocks or bonds.

income stock   Utility firms, like telephone or electric companies with consistent cash flows, and stocks with a history of paying high dividends but lacking fast growth. Utility companies, such as gas and electric firms, with a constant customer base and income flow are some of the best-known income stocks.

index   A way to measure market performance based on a set of stocks, such as the Dow Jones Industrial Average or the Standard and Poor's 500.

index fund   A mutual fund that strictly invests in shares of a particular stock index, such as the Standard and Poor's 500 or Russell 2000.

Individual Retirement Account (IRA)   An account that allows individuals to contribute money for retirement without paying taxes on either the money that is added or the interest that is generated. In general, money from IRAs cannot be removed until age 59½ without paying a 10 percent penalty.

inflation   The declining value of money due to rising prices.

inflation-indexed bonds   U.S. Treasury certificates pegged to the inflation rate. The value of the bond increases at the same pace as inflation.

initial public offering (IPO)   When a private company goes "public" by selling shares for the first time.

interest   The price paid for the use of money. A lender earns interest; a borrower pays interest.

investing   Putting money into securities such as stocks, bonds, or mutual funds.

investment   Putting your money into a vehicle—such as stocks, bonds, mutual funds, real estate—with the expectation it will increase in value.

investment grade   Of bonds with moderate to low risk, usually with a BBB rating or above.

investment objective   The goals of a mutual fund or other investment. Usually, portfolios seek income (blue chips), capital appreciation (growth stocks), safety (bonds), or a combination of the three.

investment risk   The risk that an investment will be worth less at any given point in the future than at the time the investment was made.

junk bonds   Certificates from companies that have high debt and are therefore likely not to pay the certificate back. They offer high interest rates and high risk.

Keogh Plan   A tax-deferred retirement plan for small businesses and the self-employed.

liquidity   The ease with which an investment can be converted to cash. All savings and investment options are less liquid than cash, which is 100 percent liquid.

load   A mutual funds sales charge shareholders pay when buying or selling. In general, low-load funds charge 1 to 3 percent; medium-loads, 3 to 6 percent; and full-loads, 6 to 8.5 percent, while no-load funds charge no load.

market capitalization   The amount of stock a corporation is permitted to issue.

market risk   Fluctuations in prices for the market, either in whole or specific sectors, brought on by outside forces. For example, the price of orange juice increases when there is a late-season freeze in Florida.

maturity date   The day when a bond or certificate of deposit must be repaid to the lender.

minimum distribution   The amount an investor's retirement plan must pay when he reaches 70 years of age.

money market account   An account at a financial institution where the funds are invested in safe, short-term debt instruments, such as CDs and U.S. Treasury bills. Ordinarily pay a higher return than regular savings accounts.

money market fund   A mutual fund that invests in relatively safe, short term debt instruments. The price for one share is usually $1.

municipal bond   Certificates sold by state and local governments to investors. Usually, the interest earned is tax exempt.

mutual fund   A professionally managed pool of money that individuals invest in stocks, bonds, and other securities. This offers shareholders the benefits of portfolio diversification by owning a broad swath of shares and so spreading risk.

NASDAQ   National Association of Securities Dealers Automated Quotations. It's a computerized system for brokers and dealers to trade shares in companies in the over-the-counter market. No actual trading floor exists as all price quotes and stocks are exchanged electronically. Smaller and newer companies are typically traded on NASDAQ, as are many technology stocks, such as Microsoft and Intel.

net asset value (NAV)   The price of one share of a mutual fund, calculated by adding the total investments in a fund, subtracting costs, and dividing by the total number of shares. A key indication of your investment and usually given in newspaper listings of mutual fund performance.

new issue   The first public sale of an investment instrument by a company.

New York Stock Exchange (NYSE)   Located on Wall Street in Manhattan. Known as the "Big Board," it's the world's largest and oldest trading house and typically trades older, established companies.

no-load mutual fund   A mutual fund that does not impose a load (sales charge) when bought or sold by an investor.

noncyclical stock   A firm whose stock price weathers the ups and downs of the economy.

odd lot   When you buy or sell fewer than 100 shares of a company's stock at one time, your broker may charge an additional commission.

open-end fund   A mutual fund designed to sell more shares, and also buy back shares, to meet demand and increase the amount of money available to invest. Most mutual funds are open-end funds.

penny stock   Although not literally traded for pennies a share, these are very low-priced, high-risk, speculative shares in unproven companies with little history that have the potential for huge returns or losses for their investors. Many technology companies are considered penny stocks.

portfolio   The assortment of investments—such as mutual funds, stocks, bonds, and money market accounts—owned by an individual.

preferred stock   A stock that gets the first shot at dividends and money— before common stock—if the corporation goes under. These stocks do not fluctuate as greatly in price as would common stocks in the same firm.

price/earnings (P/E) ratio   The share price of stock divided by the last 12 months of its profits. This ratio reflects how much investors are willing to pay for a share's earning power. The P/E ratio is calculated by taking the price a share of stock is trading at and dividing by the earnings per share of that firm (that's the total profits of the company divided by the number of shares it has outstanding). It's used as a gauge to find out how high or low a stock is trading compared to its real earning potential.

principal   The amount of money originally invested.

prospectus   A document that describes a mutual fund's investment objectives, policies, and fees. You should read the prospectus for a mutual fund or investment prior to investing. If you don't understand it, find someone who does.

proxy   Authorization giving someone else your right to vote at a shareholders' meeting. Often used by shareholders who are unable to, or do not wish to, attend a shareholders' meeting.

rate of return   How much money you get back for your investment. For stocks, it's the annual dividends divided by the purchase price. For bonds, it's the actual amount of interest earned.

real estate   Property consisting of land and all permanently attached structures and buildings.

risk   Uncertainty whether or not an investment choice will meet expectations—in other words, the odds an investment will make or lose money.

risk/reward   The pressure between preserving your investment and maximizing your profit. The higher the promised return, the more likely you are to lose your initial investment. Conversely, a lower risk usually results in less profit.

risk tolerance   The degree to which an investor is willing to take risk for a certain level of reward.

rollover   Shifting retirement savings from one qualified fund to another without having to pay a tax penalty.

securities   The term for stocks, bonds, and money market investments.

Securities and Exchange Commission (SEC)   The Federal regulatory board that oversees stock and bond trading to help protect investors. The SEC was founded after the Great Crash in 1929 to help guard against another crash.

share   A unit that represents a measure of ownership ("equity") in a corporation or mutual fund.

Social Security   A government program that provides income and health benefits to retirees and others. Benefits paid are based on the contribution an individual makes during his or her lifetime.

Standard & Poor's Rating   A grade assigned to a bond that represents the chance the debt will be repaid. Ratings of BBB to AAA are called "investment grade" because they are low-risk investments.

stock   A security representing partial ownership in a corporation. The value of a stock reflects the financial performance of a company.

stock certificate   The legal document giving ownership of a specific number of shares in a corporation.

stock fund   A fund whose value generally increases during periods when stock markets rise and decreases when they fall.

stockholder   An individual investor in a corporation.

stock split   Dividing the total stock of a company into proportionately more shares in order to bring the price down. This makes the stock more marketable. For instance, if a stock splits two-for-one, an investor owning 50 shares would get 100, but the price per share would drop by half to maintain the same portfolio value.

stop order   A way to protect yourself by directing your broker to sell a security if it drops or climbs to a predetermined price. For example, if you buy a stock at $40 per share, and it moves up to $55, guarantee yourself a profit by putting a stop order to sell the stock if it falls to $50, or if it rises to $65.

street name   When investments are held in the name of a broker rather than the name of the investor.

taxable income   The amount of money you earn that you have to pay Federal and state taxes on.

tax deferred   Affording the opportunity to put off paying federal taxes on your investments.

total return   The percentage of total profits earned on an investment.

Treasury Bills (T-Bills)   Low-risk, low-income debt—usually sold in $10,000 blocks—of one year or less issued by the U.S. Treasury Department to cover costs. No interest is paid, but the debt is sold at less than face value and repaid for full value when it comes due.

Treasury Bonds   Similar to Treasury Bills, but the debt is sold in $1,000 denominations and repaid between seven and thirty years, with fixed interest on the debt paid every six months.

Treasury Notes   Similar to Treasury Bonds but with maturities of one to seven years.

12b-1 Fee Different and often in addition to loads, this is an annual mutual fund sales charge levied on investments for promotion and marketing costs in the fund. It's named for the Securities and Exchange Commission rule that allows funds to charge the fee.

U.S. Savings Bonds Registered, nontransferable certificates sold by the federal government with a variety of interest and maturity dates specified by the series of debt (type). These are the types of bonds you received as a gift back as a youngster.

venture capital Money invested in a start–up company. The hope is to make big profits, such as when the company goes public.

vesting When an employee becomes eligible for retirement benefits from her employer, whether or not she remains with the company. Cliff vesting is when you can keep 100 percent of the employer contributed money at the end of a predetermined length of service, such as five years. Graded vesting is when you gradually become vested between a certain number of years. For instance, you may become vested 20 percent each year between your second and seventh years until you eventually reach 100 percent.

yield The amount of money you get from your investment, stated as a percentage of the original investment.

zero coupon bond A certificate that sells for less than its stated value. Though no interest is paid, the debt gradually increases in value until it is paid back at full value.

Index